I0091633

Tangled Goods

Tangled Goods

The Practical Life of Pro Bono Advertising

Iddo Tavory
Sonia Prelat
Shelly Ronen

The University of Chicago Press   CHICAGO AND LONDON

The University of Chicago Press, Chicago 60637
The University of Chicago Press, Ltd., London
© 2022 by The University of Chicago
All rights reserved. No part of this book may be used or reproduced in any
manner whatsoever without written permission, except in the case of brief
quotations in critical articles and reviews. For more information, contact
the University of Chicago Press, 1427 E. 60th St., Chicago, IL 60637.
Published 2022
Printed in the United States of America

31 30 29 28 27 26 25 24 23 22   1 2 3 4 5

ISBN-13: 978-0-226-82016-3 (cloth)
ISBN-13: 978-0-226-82018-7 (paper)
ISBN-13: 978-0-226-82017-0 (ebook)
DOI: https://doi.org/10.7208/chicago/9780226820170.001.0001

Library of Congress Cataloging-in-Publication Data

Names: Tavory, Iddo, 1977– author. | Prelat, Sonia, author. | Ronen, Shelly, author.
Title: Tangled goods : the practical life of pro bono advertising / Iddo Tavory, Sonia Prelat,
    and Shelly Ronen.
Description: Chicago : University of Chicago Press, 2022. | Includes bibliographical
    references and index.
Identifiers: LCCN 2021057022 | ISBN 9780226820163 (cloth) | ISBN 9780226820187
    (paperback) | ISBN 9780226820170 (ebook)
Subjects: LCSH: Advertising—Psychological aspects. | Altruism.
Classification: LCC HF5822 .T38 2022 | DDC 659.101/9—dc23/eng/20220103
LC record available at https://lccn.loc.gov/2021057022

To our daughters:

Eliana and Amalya Tavory
Elena Sofía Prelat
Thisbe Gilbert Ronen-Backer

Contents

1. Advertising for Good

Against the background of a squalid hut, looking straight at the camera, a Haitian man smiles as he speaks: "I hate it when my house is so big I need two wireless routers." The frame shifts to another scene. On the stairs of an unfinished house, a teenager with a shirt that may have once been white: "I hate it when I have to write my maid a check and forget her last name." This goes on. Haitian men and women, a child with his goat, all deliver Twitter messages written by affluent Americans who posted them online and tagged them as #FirstWorldProblems. The video montage ends with the simple text "#FirstWorldProblems Are Not Problems"—and then, an image of a child drinking from a faucet and a plea to donate to a nonprofit called Water Is Life, which provides clean drinking water in developing countries. When the video was released in 2012, it went "viral," the digital dream of web advertising, garnering almost seven million views. Stories about the campaign ran in the *Guardian* and on CNN and other major news outlets; both *Ad Age* and *Adweek*, the two main publication outlets of the advertising industry, ran admiring stories; donations to Water Is Life went through the roof.

The campaign was developed free of charge, pro bono. The two advertising professionals who dreamed up the campaign were Sam and Frank, a copywriter and an art director team at DDB, one of New York's largest and most successful advertising agencies. They were the ones who decided to focus on the provision of clean water in developing countries, the ones who identified the nonprofit and then pitched it their work. When Sam and Frank took a skeleton crew to Haiti to shoot the video, they did so on their own dime, taking a loan that they only hoped their agency would reimburse them for later. They had to become their own production team—Sam learned how to record sound; a creative director, Menno, who believed in the project and quickly became as engaged as they were, held the light reflector on the shoot.

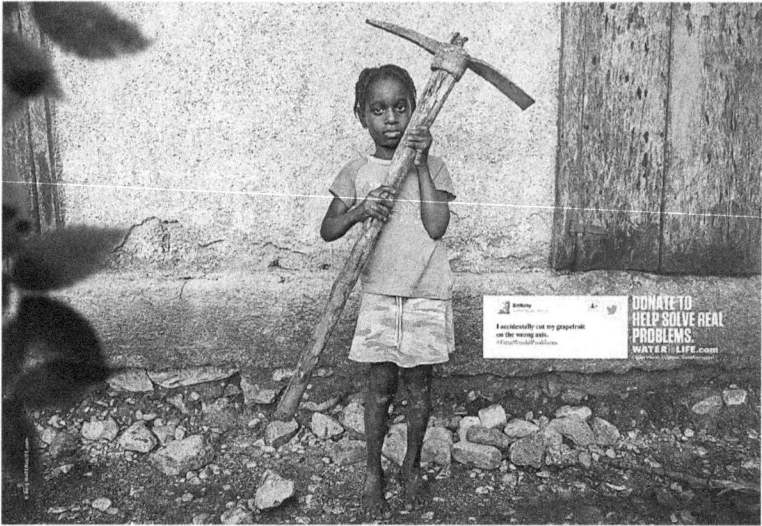

FIGURE 1. The First World Problems campaign for Water Is Life by DDB included images of Haitians posed to contrast real tweets that were tagged with the hashtag #FirstWorldProblems. A tweet below a young girl holding a large rusted and splintering pick reads: "I accidentally cut my grapefruit on the wrong axis."

The First World Problems campaign was no aberration. As part of their portfolios, the advertising equivalent of a résumé, almost all professionals at major advertising agencies in New York do some work for nonprofits, either completely pro bono or at reduced price, asking the nonprofit only to cover some of the campaign's operation costs. Much as in law, advertising is a world in which pro bono work is a common and even expected part of the job, sometimes (though by no means always) an exhilarating part of it. But why advertising? Why is an industry known for biting cynicism and cutthroat competition also an industry in which people dedicate time and effort to "doing good"? How has "the handmaiden of capitalism" ended up doing this work?[1]

What this book shows, primarily through interviews with advertising professionals in New York City—from some of the industry's top chief executives to the strategists and creatives who work the projects—is what it is that makes such work compelling for those who work on it and the kinds of challenges and tensions they navigate.[2] At the end, we show both a structural and an existential fit between pro bono work and the advertising environment, and how such work plays a role in alleviating some of the frustrations professionals often feel in their everyday work. As such, we uncover and characterize an otherwise-unseen arrangement of professional, organizational, moral, and economic dynamics that enable the advertising world to interact so successfully with the world of nonprofits. As we have come to appreciate, it is through overlapping modes of reasoning, and the corresponding pursuits of what is deemed worthy, that pro bono makes sense on the ground.

This book is not a simple morality tale of people who want to do good. Of course, many projects we trace did have their beginnings with an impassioned individual: the father of a child with autism worked his nights on Autism Speaks, a man whose father has Parkinson's threw himself into the Michael J. Fox Foundation for Parkinson's Research, a gay executive leveraged his ad agency position to advocate for queer teenagers coming out. Many of the people we talked with grew animated as they described this type of work as the reason they could live with themselves while they put their creativity in the service of big pharma or corporate banks. There was, as we show, a palpable sense that some advertising professionals were using their work for nonprofits as a way to sweeten the Faustian bargain they struck between art and commerce.

Yet while dedication to a cause is one route into pro bono work, just as many campaigns start quite differently: a CEO sat on a board of trustees and another trustee roped her into his favorite cause; a bored creative was looking to mix things up, hungry for more interesting work; the Advertisement Council of America solicited proposals for curated causes.

Take Sam and Frank. Although they went into advertising imagining that they would quickly find themselves working on TV, making inspirational ad campaigns, they were both stuck doing banners: writing the texts and the visuals of the ads we see running on our screens as we surf the web. This was not what they hoped for. As Frank observed, "Nobody's mom shows their friends banners at the parties." They needed to find a way to make more interesting work on the side. And in today's advertising world, that often means finding a nonprofit.

Without a strong commitment to a specific cause, they looked for what was "hot"—where nonprofits were booming, which causes people seemed to care about. Their search led them to water. It was, as Frank put it, "a little bit calculated." There were a lot of water charities out there, so even if one wouldn't like the work they proposed, they could "just go on to the next one." They also came up with an idea—putting cup dispensers next to leaking water pipes in New York, juxtaposing the abundance of clean water in the city to the deprivation of the developing world by inviting New Yorkers to drink their dirtiest. Next, they needed an organization they could work for. They Googled different nonprofits and went down the list: "We started cold calling different water charities. I met with, I think I talked with three or four different ones. . . . We made a little pitch talk. I told them about the idea and said, 'Hey this is what we are doing and this is what we plan to do,' and I think the last call I took was for Water Is Life."

But if Sam and Frank weren't in it, at least initially, for the cause, what were they doing it for? We get an inkling of other notions of the good in Frank's comment that "nobody's mom" shows off ad banners at parties. Like many jokes, this was serious stuff. Their chief creative officer (CCO), Matt Eastwood, encouraged the duo to find something they could do:

> It didn't have to be a charity—it just had to be like a family connection or something, it's basically a smart way to... I mean, he called it "the Road to Cannes." And basically, the best idea was to win a trip to France that year.... We were kind of upfront about the reasons we were doing it, which was obviously... we wanted to help. But we also... a lot of people use pro bono work to, you know, maybe flex their creativity or for the pursuit of awards. So, we had a very open conversation of how it was mutually beneficial for both of us.

As Frank tells it, pro bono work is an opportunity to gain creative freedom and potentially win prestigious awards in the process—very different goods from the pure morality of noble causes. The chance to work on a pro bono project is a chance to do interesting work—to tilt the scales toward creativity and art. And then, at the end of the road, there is Cannes: the Cannes Lions is the most prestigious of advertising festivals and awards, with over ten thousand advertising professionals from all over the world flocking to the French Riviera to see and be seen for a week every June. A counterpart to the famous film festival, it is where prestige in the advertising world is allocated. The best work in a variety of categories is recognized by statues of lions—bronze, silver, and gold (titanium lions were recently added to the mix). It is the closest that the ad industry has to the Oscars. The road to Cannes is rarely paved with banner work.

When Frank talked to Kristine, the president of Water Is Life at the time, he was up front about his motives. He could help, yes. But he could also make interesting work, and perhaps a name for himself. She agreed, and the New York's Dirtiest Water campaign was launched. The project, as they mostly agreed in retrospect, was not an immense creative success. It was, however, good enough to be noticed. It was written up in the business magazine *Fast Company*. Eastwood was interviewed, telling the journal, "I love doing work that can make the world a better place—it's a nice change from selling burgers."[3] And, as he noted when we interviewed him, this was not bad for a project that came at a price tag of under

$800—virtually nothing in the advertising world. The campaign was also successful enough for Kristine to ask Frank if he and his team wanted to come to Haiti to help her in her next endeavor. And so the team came up with the idea for the First World Problems campaign and flew to Haiti.

Morality, creativity, prestige—these goods animated our respondents' understandings of what a good pro bono project was and which pro bono projects were worth doing. These are different siren songs, beckoning advertising professionals toward such projects. But then there are other, more practical and immediate ways in which our interviewees felt that pro bono work was valuable. Reminiscing about the First World Problems campaign, Menno, the creative director who held the light reflector in Haiti for Sam and Frank, talked to us about how the process "feels" different—that he experiences a deeper connection to these projects not only because of some touchy-feely notions of morality but also because he gets to see the work through to fruition:

> Sometimes advertising agencies are in the business of selling the process. Do you know what I mean? ... We cut out all that fat when it comes to charities and pro bono. ... So, the creatives come up and figure out what the strategy is and they figure out what they want to focus on and they do their own research and they figure out what the messaging is rather than having a bigger machine around.

Here, then, is another good inherent to the structure of advertising work. In a profession that increasingly divides labor among those who interface with the client, those who come up with the ideas, those who execute these ideas creatively, and those who actually make the ads, pro bono often offers a chance for advertising professionals to take over the process in its entirety. It offers them a path around approvals and pitches "up the chain of command." It offers them a carte blanche for a daring, self-directed process. Sam, Frank, and Menno came up with the strategic idea, sat with the client, came up with the creative way forward, and even shot their own video. In other words, the work was *theirs* in a way that it seldom was. Rather than different parties within the agency taking little pieces of the project—all of them feeling like their ideas and input were mangled in the process—the creatives took complete ownership over their work.

The advertising world is a pyramid with a broad base but very few places at the top. The ability to make a name for oneself is translated into six-figure salaries and into work on more creatively rewarding campaigns. To that end, Cannes isn't just a moment of sanctification of work.

Lions are converted into careers. Sam and Frank, like other interviewees who pulled off an awarded pro bono campaign, never did banners again. They moved to better positions within DDB, and then moved together to work at Deutsch, another prominent advertising agency, where they continued to work for Water Is Life, won yet more awards, and moved on to other prominent positions in the industry. Water Is Life, as they are the first to admit, brought them to where they are today professionally and economically.

Of course, this profusion of goods was obscured once the campaign made its public appearance. In articles in the *Huffington Post*, the *Guardian*, *Business Insider*, and CNN, the question of awards and creativity, of labor and careers, disappeared. Stripped of these elements, the campaign was discussed only in terms of the moral. Had the team misconstrued an ironic hashtag on Twitter as serious? Were "first world problems" not really problems at all? Didn't people in the "third world" also have petty problems, ones that were no less real despite being minor? And while these discussions are all well and good, they presume that pro bono projects are exclusively driven by advertising professionals' desire to do good, as moral agents pursuing moral causes.

The tension between purified and tangled goods was not simply an effect of the press. It also showed up in the interviews we did and throughout our interactions with advertising professionals. Some interviewees, even while going into detail about creativity and awards, made a point that, as opposed to others in the industry, *they* did pro bono work for the right (moral) reasons. More commonly, the professionals we talked to tacked between different goods. This was visible even in our interview with Matt Eastwood, who focused exclusively on the moral in his interviews with the press. When asked why he urged the advertising professionals who worked under him to seek out a pro bono opportunity, he first cited his moral motives: repeating, as he did years earlier, that it was "a human obligation to help and use those skills to help and use those skills for good as well as, you know... not just selling burgers."

But immediately after talking of morality, Eastwood acknowledged a second set of considerations, not only highlighting creativity but even noting how a pro bono account keeps advertising professionals sharper for their commercial, everyday assignments:

> From sort of a purely creative point of view, I think that some of the challenges that you have—working in a big multinational advertising agency, working on big global brands—can be tough. And the contrast of doing work like that versus something that's a bit more, I guess, "human," is

really great for the creative mind. I think one day you could be working on selling Kit Kat, for instance, which is fantastic and that's an interesting challenge. But if the next day at the same time you've got your brain working on... well, "How can I work with Black Lives Matter or Water Is Life" or whoever it might be... I think it's a nice contrast in your head of how ideas work. So, I always try to have people work on something like that because I think it keeps your brain fresh to have that contrast.

In reading this excerpt, as with many others, there is a temptation to erase all notions of morality as a thin veneer of talk over the "real" commercial and professional considerations at hand, to pronounce that, at last, the handmaiden of capitalism has removed the veil to reveal her true exploitative face. But that would be equally wrong, and not simply because the social world is always more complicated than any attempts to purify it. Rather, it is because to understand both the successes and the failures of pro bono work, we need to understand how different notions of the good become tangled together and fall apart, blur and clarify, how, at different moments, different narratives of the good come to the fore.

We can see this if we take a longer view. As Frank and Menno told the tale, going to Haiti changed how they saw their engagement. "After actually going to Haiti, we all were kind of... this is actually a *real* problem." While they may have thought about their foray into water problems opportunistically, long after their awards were won and their careers made, the team didn't stop working with Water Is Life. They cemented a relationship with the nonprofit and continued on, doing six more campaigns for it. They flew to Kenya, Ethiopia, and Thailand, and they worked with chemists who created a book whose pages double as an affordable water purification system. And although they were still very happy about the awards they received for this work—with more lions, some of them the coveted "gold lions" adorning their portfolios—their relationship to the nonprofit, and to the cause, changed. They were committed to Kristine's cause above and beyond the search for creativity and recognition.

Different goods, then, came together and drew apart in dizzying—but also highly patterned—ways. Through the ways that they came together and drew apart, advertising professionals like Sam and Frank could find meaning in their work, they could enact a moral position, and they (and their agencies) could both get recognized and get ahead. And while we have started our story with a pro bono project that succeeded in generating these different goods simultaneously, in the pages that follow we also encounter pro bono projects that floundered and ultimately failed to yield such an abundance of goods. By discussing the multiple ways in which a pro bono project can be viewed as unsuccessful in the eyes of the advertising professionals who execute it, the agency who oversees it, or the members of the advertising field more broadly, we explore how these goods emerge and how actors negotiate the tensions between them. On this level, this book is about the relationships between goods — and how those relationships need to be understood at the intersection of the existential relation to work, morality, organizations, and fields.

Yet if this is a core general problem in the sociology of culture and the theory of action, the case itself is important. For, through it all, these professionals sustained, on a level of everyday practice, the kind of corporate social responsibility (CSR) that critics often depict as a feature of contemporary capitalism. How can we understand both the ways that advertising professionals reproduce this world, and importantly, how the advertising world sustains and channels their actions?

Advertising and New York City

Advertisements are a pervasive feature of life in the United States. In various forms, they are densely embedded in our everyday worlds: they decorate the packaging of goods that populate our homes and workplaces, they can be heard on the radio and seen on television, they appear in catalogs and pamphlets that overstuff our mailboxes, and they decorate public space — flashing by on public transit, looming over us on billboards along highways, and popping up while we browse the internet. Ads push us to purchase specific products or services. They attempt to hold our attention in a world in which such attention is a coveted, and contested, resource. Moreover, ads serve to inform the public about issues of political, civic, or social importance — with both governmental and nongovernmental organizations vying for our attention.

Facilitating the success of corporations' sale of consumer products and services and driving online revenues that keep essential web services free, advertising is a key motor of consumer capitalism. Given its position, it comes as no surprise that the United States tops the global chart of advertising spending. The US advertising industry and advertising-related services produced an estimated $118 billion in revenue in 2018.[4] Total spending on advertising grew from $183.6 billion to $223.7 billion between 2015 and 2018.[5] Advertising, in short, is big business, one of the major economic engines of what is termed the creative economy.

And like much of the creative economy in general, advertising has long had a special place in New York City. At the turn of the twentieth century, New York City was already home to twenty-five advertising agencies, and that number grew rapidly. Several world-famous agencies were founded in New York, including George Batten Company and also Barton, Durstine & Osborn (which merged into the BBDO agency in 1928) and both McCann and Erickson agencies (which merged into Mc-Cann Erickson in 1930).[6] In the 1920s, "Madison Avenue" was synonymous with the burgeoning advertising industry that would give way to a postwar golden age of advertising that powered American consumerism. The city was also important in the later corporate transformations of the advertising industry. In the 1960s, McCann Erickson took steps to purchase other agencies and create a parent holding company, Interpublic Group; in 1986, three of the largest US agencies, two of which had their roots in New York, came together to form Omnicom.

The creation of Interpublic and Omnicom as large holding companies was part of a broad consolidation of power in the industry. Today, the global industry is dominated by a handful of corporate conglomerates that own numerous agencies and constantly seek to acquire new, rising stars. The so-called Big Four holding companies are the British WPP, the largest of "the Big Four," boasting a presence in 112 countries, over 130,000 employees and $16.86 billion in revenue in 2019; Omnicom Group, including over 1,500 agencies in 100 countries; the French Publicis Groupe, with agencies in over 100 countries and $7.98 billion in revenue in 2019; and the Interpublic Group, which reported $7.32 billion in the first three quarters of 2019.[7] These towering holding companies own several of the best-known agencies in the United States and substantially out-earn the next-largest organizations.

Yet, despite the transformation of advertising into a global business, place still matters, and New York City holds a special place in the ecology of the advertising world. As of 2017, the city was home to about 1,300 agencies, accounting for around 22 percent of all employed advertisement professionals in the United States, with a workforce of over 47,000 people. The industry is a crucial part of the cultural segment of New York City's core economic pillars, second only to film and television within the city's vast creative economy.[8]

Advertising and Corporate Social Responsibility

Advertising has had a changeable and often uneasy relationship with civil society. Although it has always been primarily an arm of market capitalism, its relationship to both governmental propaganda and philanthropy is long-standing. This is especially the case in the United States, where advertising's role in propaganda and its civil mission were instituted early on. The War Advertising Council, formed on February 5, 1942, after the bombing of Pearl Harbor, reflected the industry's desire to act as the government's mouthpiece in order to assist the war effort. Yet its mission quickly outgrew the war. In 1949, the Advertising Association published an analogous mission: "Advertising is a great industry, governed by scientific principles, guided by ethical purpose and capable of great national service."[9]

The spirit of wartime patriotism featured explicitly in the early work put out by the War Advertising Council, even when it was aimed toward public goods: the 1942 version of a campaign to prevent forest fires featured Axis stereotypes standing self-contentedly by raging fires. Two years later the campaign dropped these phantasms for Smokey Bear, the now-iconic character that reminds people of the dangers of forest fires. By 1946 the word *war* was dropped from the Advertising Council's name, and the organization that endures to the present day, commonly known as the Ad Council, solidified its purpose to "produce, distribute and promote public service announcements."[10]

This, however, was not—and is still not—the defining feature of advertising. During the ensuing postwar golden age, advertising performed the vital role of developing and diffusing a jubilant consumer lifestyle. As early as the 1950s the industry had already been reviled for using cynical manipulation to stand for senseless consumption and to serve a ruthless capitalist profit motive. In his campaign to win the presidency in 1968, Robert F. Kennedy decried that America's gross national product included "air pollution and cigarette advertising"—not elements of the economy that make Americans "proud that we are Americans."[11] In greater detail, Michael Schudson's classic study of advertising describes consumer society as one in which "human values have been grotesquely distorted so that commodities become more important than people... people sacrifice people to accumulate wealth... participants in consumer culture are seen as philistines; acquisitive and upwardly mobile, with sturdy character, perhaps, but *bad values*, working long hours and saving money to satisfy obsessive longings for whatever the next prestigious consumer good may be—the stereo, the home computer, the food processor, the videotape recorder. In the latter case, character has degenerated and values have, in a sense disappeared."[12]

This account lays out a seething critique of the industry, positing an antagonistic relation between advertising and human values. In its quest to turn a profit, advertising played an important part in forging late capitalism, turning consumption into virtue.

Still, the civic aspect of advertising never disappeared. While it may have been a relatively inconsequential part of the advertising world, campaigns like the Crying Indian ad for Earth Day, or McGruff the Crime Dog, continued to be produced by the Ad Council. It was these early efforts that laid the groundwork for advertising's particular form of corporate social responsibility.

Corporate social responsibility, of course, did not first emerge in the advertising world. The term was first used in the mid-1950s. It then received a boost from consumer protection campaigns in the 1960s and 1970s.[13] While the call to make business more morally accountable was far from new, the rise of neoliberal capitalism in this period gave corporations unprecedented power. And with such power, corporations also came under increasing scrutiny and were being called to take responsibility for their actions. Also critical to the growth of CSR were Reagan's explicit project of welfare state retrenchment, the growing privatization of public services, as well as budding awareness of environmental degradation and labor force abuses in global production chains. These culminated in a growing "sense of doubt in the moral integrity of the body corporate."[14] CSR thus challenged corporations to expand their mandate. Rather than worrying only about their bottom line, corporations were increasingly pushed to be socially responsible and to consider the moral dimensions of their business practices. CSR, then, represents a "third way" by which capitalism has recuperated the demand to do both well and good.

It is this relationship between doing well and doing good—what has become known as "the double bottom line"—that is at the heart of the current understanding of CSR. What started as a moment of critique, attempting to hold corporations accountable for their actions, has become fused with the self-understanding of modern corporations. As the sociologist Emily Barman notes, this "caring capitalism" has co-opted CSR to become not a moment of critique but of self-identification, exploiting these practices to organizationally expedient ends.[15] In this view, CSR is not simply a form of corporate "window dressing," but it is also a practice that allows firms and corporate elites to undermine state power by appearing to take on some of its functions.[16]

Given its prominence, over the past two decades a voluminous literature on CSR has emerged, trying to specify the phenomenon, map its local determinants, and trace its effects on corporate fields and organizations.[17] Beyond tracing its location in the modern political economy, such literature has attempted to show how the success of a company's CSR practices is correlated with myriad environmental factors, including national context, firm size, regulation regimes, state structure, and global pressures.[18] Complementing this macro-level approach, another body of literature focuses on individuals' motivations and processes of sense-making that make CSR desirable, or at least more likely. Here, researchers have mostly looked at CSR through the lenses of value systems and the sense-making attempts of individual actors.[19]

While these studies provide an important window onto the global reach and variations of CSR, they overlook an important aspect of it. Doing CSR is a practical activity—in terms of both the narratives it evokes and as practice.[20] Thinking about CSR in practical terms is especially important if scholars are to get a better handle on the dizzying array of different forms of CSR that corporate sectors opt for. After all, as many have noted, the notion of CSR describes a rather disjointed collection of corporate practices.[21] How do specific forms of CSR intersect with particular modes of work?

This book deals with the particular form of CSR that has taken shape in the advertising industry—pro bono work for nonprofits. While many corporations may opt to start a separate arm for their CSR work—a bank that funds education somewhere photogenic in the Global South, for instance—others stay closer to home. Some use their particular expertise in a new way. Thus, a corporation such as Shell or BP pursues efforts to develop renewable energy projects as CSR work, with one arm investing in fossil fuels and the other claiming to be part of the solution to the climate crisis. But in advertising, much as in law, pro bono work trades on the fact that both the powerful and the powerless need their services. In other words, pro bono is a form of CSR that works by redirecting existing expertise toward different clients and causes.

More technically, pro bono work occurs where individuals or corporations are "providing skills or services that are included in their occupational job description and for which the recipient nonprofit organization or client would otherwise have to pay."[22] Because advertising already had a market for its products in the nonprofit world, and as it expanded upon the kind of work that it already did with organizations such as the Ad Council, the 1990s saw an increase in the pro bono work that advertising agencies did, so much so that it became almost a routine facet of advertising work today.

All of the Big Four global holding companies we have introduced explicitly position pro bono work as an important part of their CSR portfolio. Publicis boasted over three hundred pro bono campaigns in 2013 alone, which it broadcast in a document called "CSR: Best Practices."[23] WPP estimated that across its agencies, it had negotiated pro bono work worth $55.2 million in 2009 alone, comprising the largest share of all CSR activities they undertook at that time—far more than other initiatives.[24] Omnicom's CEO boasted of the company's pro bono work in the very first page of the agency's CSR report, and Interpublic even started an internal publication called *Stronger*, featuring "advertising from pro bono and sustainably focused clients."[25]

In short, advertising has been swept up in the brave new world of CSR. Given the history of advertising, the particular output it generates, and the public attention that advertising can generate, pro bono is the main form of CSR that the advertising industry participates in routinely. Still, if we are to understand pro bono work as a particular form of CSR, we need to understand something about the actual work of advertising.

What Do Agencies Do All Day?

Studying advertising agencies, we quickly realized, meant very different things in the different agencies we went to. The agencies we visited ranged from small boutique shops of a few advertising professionals — where the distinctions between managers and workers seemed largely for the benefit of a professional-looking web page — up to massive multinational organizations of over ten thousand employees. Whereas some agencies occupied a few rooms in a nondescript building, other agencies we visited spanned multiple stories of high-rise buildings in Midtown Manhattan or the Financial District, with coffee bars (baristas included), pool tables, and other high-tech-industry-like perks. Many of the agencies we visited were arms of one of the Big Four holding companies, although others were independent.

These differences were somewhat reflected in the internal division of labor within organizations: in smaller boutique agencies, the division of labor was a little less rigid.[26] Still, the broad strokes of the professional structure of the advertising world were recognizable across agencies. When seen from the point of view of the actual work, "advertising" is not a single profession but a shared label given to a group of interlocking professions that work in tandem within an organization. Much as theater includes actors, directors, ushers, and stage workers, different advertising professionals engage in quite different forms of work — something that becomes important to understanding how they all make sense of their commercial and their pro bono work.

The labor process for producing advertising has changed over the years, as new technologies, techniques, and organizational arrangements have emerged. Advertising was transformed first by the era of television and then later by the arrival of the internet, which has surpassed television, to command more ad revenue than any other medium in American advertising.[27] But for all that, some of the basic professional boundaries and jurisdictions have remained relatively stable. For example, the fundamental division in the advertising world is that between account managers and creatives. Account managers ideally represent the client's interests within the agency—they work closely with the client and focus more on business needs than the actual form the advertisements take. The creatives are the professionals in charge of crafting the textual and visual language of the advertisement. Creatives in charge of the visual language of the advertisements are art directors; those who are in charge of the texts are copywriters. In most advertising agencies, since the 1960s, art directors and copywriters work as creative teams.[28]

The classification of advertising professionals as account managers and creatives was further complicated by the advent of account planners (sometimes also termed *strategists*). Emerging in the late 1960s in Britain, and diffusing into the United States and the rest of the world in the 1980s, account planners are a layer of professionals located between account managers and creatives. They have a double mandate. First, these professionals are supposed to be "consumer experts" as well as "cultural experts" within the agency. That is, they occupy the position of knowledge specialists; it is their job to know who the consumer is, what is going on in the larger cultural environment, and how the brand can interact with the challenges of its consumer base. They are meant to represent a stakeholder that is distinct from the client and the agency. In this capacity, account planners conduct research and craft what is known as the *creative brief*—the general idea for the advertising campaign that the creative team subsequently elaborates on.

This book, by and large, follows these professional distinctions. As we show in more detail, and as some research suggests, each of these positions comes with its own jurisdictional domain, as well as its own practical challenges.[29] But these horizontal distinctions are also complicated by agencies' hierarchical structure. In the largest, and most hierarchical, there is a seemingly infinite number of vice presidents, senior vice presidents, and executive vice presidents. Each of the different professions within the agency has its own hierarchical structure: account managers can become group account managers, the chief operating officer, and other management positions; there are senior planners, planning directors, and even chief planning officers; senior creatives may become creative directors, group creative directors, and chief creative officers. The distinctions among the work of planners, creatives, and account managers hold across our sample, but managerial titles can mean vastly different things in different organizations. What it means to be an executive vice president in an agency of fifty people is quite different from what it means in an agency of five thousand to ten thousand people.[30] Still, the position of management and the distinctions between higher-level managers and mid-level managers is useful—for, as we show later on in the book, managers have to think about different aspects of pro bono projects.

Theoretical Agenda

This book focuses on the everyday practice of pro bono as a particular form of corporate social responsibility, tracing the complex relationship between different modes of understanding these campaigns. But as we worked through our materials, we realized that answering the empirical puzzles we confronted led us to wider questions: about morality, about culture, and about the lived reality of political economy. What does "the good" mean in this social world? What does the perspective of those who worked on these pro bono projects tell us about the melding of philanthropy and the free-market economy that has taken the business world by storm?

In his *Sources of the Self*, the philosopher Charles Taylor offered a map as a metaphor for thinking of both morality and selfhood.[31] As we navigate life, there are certain images that stand starkly against the mundane background and according to which we situate ourselves and understand who we are. This metaphor is a seductive one. We can imagine ourselves treading in the wilderness, raising our eyes every so often to see how far we are from our image of the good life, of who we want to be. But what do we make of the multiplicity of goods that we see even in the short case of the Water Is Life campaign? Is the good really about saving one's soul, tainted by a life spent trying to convince people to buy one brand of shampoo rather than another? Is it about the ability to flex one's creative muscles and temporarily shift the balance between commerce and art? Is it a reprieve from alienated labor? Or is it traveling the road to Cannes and its coveted lions, and the prestige those lions promise?

The metaphor of the map begins to lose its utility. If we try to stay with such a metaphor, we must think about a multiplicity of maps and of goods. Perhaps, in the days before PowerPoint presentations, we could have imagined a bunch of transparencies stacked upon each other. But even that metaphor, dated as it already is, would be misleading. For it is not clear that the kinds of assumptions undergirding creativity can be simply laid over those of moral action; the assumptions engendered in careers overlaid on the intimate relationships that advertising professionals develop with their clients through campaigns. There are different constitutive assumptions at play here, different notions of what the good entails and of what kind of things "go together."

Instead, with Max Weber, we must begin with the "polytheism of values" that defines the modern world. As opposed to (probably mythical) simpler times when there really was only one map of the good, or when we knew at each given moment which map we were on, our times are marked by a separation of spheres such that "anyone living in the world... can only feel himself subject to the struggle between multiple sets of values, each of which, viewed separately, seems to impose an obligation on him. He has to choose which of these Gods he will and should serve, and when he should serve the one and when the other."[32] Such a polytheistic view requires a different vocabulary. Rather than thinking about culture as a coherent set of assumptions that supports a particular vision of the good, we must think about a world of contending ways to make meaning, different repertoires of action, grammars, or logics.

As these terms already attest to, we are not the first to chart these waters. Over the past decades a number of influential streams of sociological research have grappled with this multiplicity—from sociologists interested in the multiple modes of valuation in art to those interested in the complex array of goods in economic life or the challenges of modernity.[33]

Of these research traditions, two stand out by explicitly centering the question of the polytheism of goods. First, the literature spawned by Boltanski and Thévenot's work *On Justification* posits a multiplicity of worlds of goods at its center: organized clusters of meanings that are simultaneously available to actors.[34] Starting with moments of communicative contestation—in which people have to justify their actions—this perspective shows the justificatory power of historically emergent "polities," or "regimes of worth." In this rendition, each polity includes not only specific meanings and notions of the good (e.g., creative inspiration, civic duty, industry) but an entire grammar. That is, each regime of worth includes assumptions about its states of worthiness and unworthiness, which ideal objects and subjects populate the world, which evidence counts, and which tests allow actors to justify their actions as legitimate.

And while this line of work was criticized both for its baroque theoretical construction and for its fixed enumeration of worlds (one that the authors themselves could not sustain for long), it makes two crucial interventions.[35] First, it assumes that these historically emergent grammars have different evaluative criteria and disparate notions of the common good, so that they can't be simply compared by recourse to a common standard. But perhaps more crucially, they see the way people reach out for different goods as a practical activity that is mediated by the objects and tasks actors confront. As a practical activity, they assume that there can be both small victories of one polity over another as well as compromises between the worlds of worth as a result of contestation.

On the other side of the Atlantic, and more directly connected to the social life of organizations, a different theorization arose — that of *institutional logics*. Starting from Weber's separation of spheres, Roger Friedland and Robert Alford suggested that different macroinstitutions (e.g., religion, the state, the family) are constituted through a "set of material practices and symbolic constructions — which constitute its organizing principles."[36] These organizing principles, including what the good is in every such institution, can be thought of as logics. Such logics are theoretically looser than the notion of regimes of worth even as they are less precisely developed — more logics can always be constructed and their internal structure is never depicted in detail. In the broadest sense, institutional logics theory posits that goods emerge through actors' embodiment and engagement with mutually reinforcing points of a triangle: symbolic construction, ongoing praxis, and organizational pressures.

Importantly, while early studies of institutional logics largely assigned different logics to different societal and institutional spheres — and thus often depicted tensions and contestations among different logics — later developments have largely relaxed these assumptions, allowing for the ongoing interplay among logics to come into sharper focus in research.[37] This change, in turn, refocused the literature from an analysis of contestation and change between institutional logics over time to a study of open-ended, and ongoing, negotiation. In doing so, this approach came closer to analyses of intraorganizational multiplicity that have been developed in other research traditions in the study of organizations, as well as bringing Friedland into a closer dialogue with his French counterparts.[38]

Blending, blurring, or otherwise aligning different logics, as researchers following this tradition have noted, is an active organizational achievement.[39] In order to sustain contending institutional logics and goods, organizations need to develop an identity conducive to such blending, aligning, or other strategy of navigating multiple logics; actors, in turn, need to construct identities and narratives that allow for the resolutions of competing logics.[40] Indeed, many organizations are hybrid in that sense, holding onto multiple logics at once.

We are inspired by both the French notion of regimes of worth and by that of institutional logics. With both traditions, goods aren't a solitary symbolic object. When we invoke a particular good, we invoke other elements in its wake. There are, as the sociologist Gabriel Abend has put it, a host of background assumptions that go into any determination of the good.[41] It is in this sense that we believe it is useful to think about cultural grammars or constellations rather than thinking about a cultural repertoire, as some American sociologists of culture have developed.[42] And with both traditions, we see the different goods we trace in this book as made possible through material, organizational, and broader affordances of the field they are located within. Put simply, the material and organizational aspects of the social worlds in which we are enmeshed enable us, and even prod us, to seek out particular goods, as well as shaping and constraining our ability to make claims in relationship to those goods.[43]

Still, the position that we develop in this book departs from some of the assumptions that these research streams make. First, especially within the regimes-of-worth tradition, but also in early work on institutional logics, the assumption seems to be that the natural state of different goods is separate and pure. While actors can blend and blur logics, or arrive at a compromise among regimes of worth, doing so appears to take more work than holding on to one good.[44] There are some theoretical and methodological reasons for this assumption of natural purity. For those who are interested in justifications, beginning with a moment of contestation leads them to see things in terms of incommensurability. If we begin with a symbolic fight, we are apt to see the world in terms of semiotic foes. For those who write of institutional logics, the location of the goods in different institutional spheres assumes that goods, at least at this historical juncture, are more naturally considered apart from one another. Indeed, in the literature on hybrid institutions, much ink has been spilled on the ways managers need to construct a specific identity and narrative that allows for goods to be blurred or aligned.[45]

Rather than beginning with purity, we take a more pragmatist approach. We assume that both blurring and purifying goods takes work. Patterned situational constraints determine when actors take the blurring of goods for granted and when they assume that goods are distinct. In our interviews, we seldom asked advertising professionals about their concept of an ideal pro bono project. Instead, we asked about the challenges and opportunities they encountered in the context of their concrete work. Starting from the flow of everyday experience rather than moments of contestation produced a different theoretical image of the relationship among goods. In some situations, our interviewees worked hard to come to terms with the blurring of goods. How could they, to take a prominent example, portray themselves as purely intentioned moral agents while acknowledging that they were professionally invested in receiving awards? But in many other cases, it was the blurring and ambiguity that seemed to be immediately given. To evoke a metaphor used by the sociologist Viviana Zelizer, we tend to live in a tangled world, where different notions of worth and different spheres constantly bundle and unbundle as people engage in activity and interact with their fellows.[46]

Returning to Weber's famed notion of the polytheism of goods, and alongside Roger Friedland's later work, we believe that sociologists may not have taken the metaphor seriously enough.[47] Think, for example, of Greek mythology: A complex pantheon of gods, living side by side, with their shifting relationships, their petty jealousies, and their pacts. Although one god may nominally reign supreme, the gods around him often get their way, and even make him look the fool. The gods, in these narratives, have different personalities, different likes and dislikes; they accept different offerings from the realm of mortals (Athena, it seems, liked cows). In some situations, temporary conflicts emerge: Poseidon and Athena root for the Greeks to win the war on Troy, while Apollo and Artemis side with the Trojans. In rare cases there are wars among the gods themselves—as the generational conflict between gods and Titans attests to. And yet the Greeks often made offerings to "the gods," without clearly distinguishing among them. The scent of burned flesh wafted up to Mount Olympus, honoring different gods at once.

Less metaphorically, the question of when goods are ambiguously tangled and when they become well defined and separate is an empirical one. As the sociologist Dan Lainer-Vos shows in his study of Irish and Israeli government bonds, the ability to sustain ambiguity between bonds as simultaneously a nationalist project and as an economic investment was important in explaining the success of Israeli bonds (and the failure of the Irish bond drive). The relationship between specification and ambiguity is patterned, and that patterning is an important feature of the phenomenon.[48] While we sometimes try hard to distinguish among different goods, and while they sometimes clash and require us to "take sides" both in talk and in action, we often don't give ourselves a precise account as to which exact good we worship. Our actions often feel right precisely as they tangle different forms of valuation and action. The importance of ambiguity, of *not* specifying precisely why it is that we do what we do, is thus crucial.

Our second departure from current approaches to the multiplicity of goods is also rooted in our pragmatism. Inspired by the Chicago school of sociology, we focus on the situations in which people puzzle out the world confronting them. Actors' creative problem-solving efforts always occur within a social context. And given the ongoing pressures and affordances of both symbolic structures, interactional and organizational pressures, and material resources, these creative solutions often end up looking quite similar. In order to understand how creativity is patterned, then, we need to pay careful attention to the structure of situations.

So far, at this level of abstraction, we think everyone would concur. In recognition of these very assumptions, the French tradition is often dubbed a "neo-pragmatist" approach. In this literature, the key analytic moment is the one in which justification is elicited and actors and organizations are able to mobilize specific goods in order to work through the problems they face. In that regard, this tradition is agnostic about what the situation is. In some cases, it might be an organization trying to come to terms with its mission, or even trying to foster creativity; in others, it might be political mobilization.

Similarly, by focusing on organizational actors, research in institutional logics has shown that the success of hybrid institutions with blurring or aligning goods is a contingent, active accomplishment. Partly because it migrated from sociology to business schools, this tradition usually assumes that the organization is the relevant context of action that faces the challenge of a plurality of missions, and the site where these pressures become embedded in actors' ongoing processes of meaning making. While organization researchers such as Battilana and Dorado have shown managers' importance for navigating multiple logics, the mechanisms through which managers exert their influence are processes of recruitment and socialization—both of which presume that identity work in the context of organizations is the key dimension in which multiplicity is navigated.[49] And even as scholars have shown that the reaction to such multiplicity changes by actors' careers and even by the situation, the tension is located most crucially in the organizational context.[50]

Although many will thus agree that the multiple goods they describe are practically navigated by actors on the ground,[51] the question of the relevant level of analysis we should use in order to understand such ongoing navigations has been, we think, limited. The issue here is about how we think about the different layers that constitute a situation. While there is always an immediacy to any particular moment, situations do not exist in a vacuum. People and relationships extend through time, and there is always more to any situation than we first see. Actors' understandings of themselves, of their pasts and possible futures, impinge upon and define even the most mundane of situations.[52]

Put differently, as interactionist critics have long argued, we need to better account for how organizations, and institutions more generally, are "inhabited."[53] That is, we need to take the actual back-and-forth of action and interaction more seriously. But this also means that we need to attend to how other aspects of actors' lives—such as the moral pressures actors feel to define their worth in terms that are only loosely related to their professional identity—nudge actors toward certain understandings of the good and away from others. Readers of this book might be academics or advertising professionals, but their actions are defined by more than the organization they are located in. Our understanding of our own character and moral worth seeps into our actions; the importance of doing "good work" professionally may be temporarily located in the organization, but it is far from completely defined by it. Then again, our commitment and yearning for recognition in the field within which we are located pertains to so much more than what happens in the organization. Focusing on the organization as the relevant unit of analysis without attending to how organizational pressures and affordances interact with those emanating from other levels of analysis does not adequately capture how people understand themselves and how they navigate their professional lives.

In short, then, the approach we develop in this book traces the practical ways that both moments of ambiguity and moments in which actors clarify the tensions among goods occurs in advertising. As we show throughout the book, to understand how relationships among goods are patterned, we need to understand how the seductions and challenges of pro bono advertising emerge at the interstices of different levels of analysis—from the moral longing and guilt some advertising professionals feel to the organizational pressures that managers need to navigate; from the existential relationship professionals have with their work to their yearning to be recognized by the broader field of advertising and forge a career for themselves.

If pro bono advertising is a strategic space for studying the tangling and untangling of goods, it is because it sustains both a structural and a moral, existential assemblage. In this sense, this book outlines what we think of as a kind of existential fit between the world of advertising and pro bono work—that is, how different goods that are present in certain people's lives become tied together within a particular practice. But the existential fit—itself constituted by understandings of morality and of work—is coupled with a more structural one. That is, on an internal organizational level, at the level of the field of advertising, and even on the level of the global economy, there is a way in which existential concerns interact, sometimes uncomfortably, sometimes seamlessly, with a structural set of coordinates.

The way in which the different Greek gods were simultaneously worshipped is also precisely the one that defines the environment that advertising professionals inhabit. Rather than a specific story about a strange profession, then, this is a story of how moralities, markets, organizations, inspiration, and prestige all intertwine. Understanding how different goods come to be tangled and untangled, and how structural and existential considerations come together to form specific modes of action, gives us leverage to ask questions about the general contours of contemporary capitalism. It does so from the perspective neither of the critic primed to think that any talk of "doing good" hides baser (and "truer") reasons, nor of the free-market enthusiast, but instead from the view of those who, on the ground, struggle to find meaning within it.

Navigating This Book

This book follows different goods by moving between the contexts of action that define the situations that advertising professionals navigate in their projects. Following these different contexts, we show how goods are tangled and untangled, and what it means to "do good" in such a social world. We begin with the different aspects of the immediate situation—the moral, as well as the desire to feel that one is doing existentially good work, and the yearning for recognition in the field. Then, in the subsequent chapters, we show how these different aspects are set into motion—through managers' curating of projects, and through advertising professionals' boundary making and bridging of goods, as well as through their relationship to the measured effects of the goods they pursue. Although each chapter introduces new forms of worth as well as theoretical challenges and inspirations, we do so not in the abstract but by working through case studies of different campaigns, often from the point of view of multiple actors who worked on them.

Chapter 2 follows the stories of moral angst and the wish to do good that arose in many interviews with advertising professionals. As members of a mostly liberal creative class, interviewees often felt some discomfort with the fact that they grease the wheels of capitalism. As some of them told us, they worked precisely for "the bad guys." No less acutely, they often felt that, even if they didn't do bad work, their jobs felt meaningless: using their talents and their imagination to convince consumers to choose one brand of soap over another, for example. In other words, they felt that what they did—even if they did it well—simply didn't matter. And for many of our interviewees, they needed it to matter. Against this backdrop, we trace how advertising professionals sought out and volunteered to do pro bono work, how they poured time and effort into it as a way to reorient their own vision of themselves, and how they retained a sense of moral agency—feeling that they not only helped a cause but also embodied it. We trace how the place of doing good in these contexts led to a blurring of pro bono and paid corporate social responsibility jobs.

Chapter 3 moves from the vision of the moral good to the image of good work—that is, work that was not meaningful simply morally but also professionally. We highlight both the image of the creative-as-artist and the importance of the actual process of work—the creative and strategic control over the labor process. For a variety of reasons, not least of which is that clients did not invest huge amounts of cash into the campaigns, and also were usually thankful for the work as a gift, pro bono projects afforded professionals the opportunity to produce work that was less conservative. These campaigns were places where "crazy" ideas did not die at the first meeting; instead, they often came to fruition. And precisely because the agency did not invest too much money into such work, it was also a place where the work was led by a few people who became invested in it and identified with it in a way otherwise rare in the industry. Thus, we show how an existential relationship with work and the experience of alienation from labor plays into pro bono campaigns.

Chapter 4 changes lenses to look at the relationship between pro bono work and recognition in the field of advertising. To do so, it names the elephant in the room: the affinity between pro bono projects and awards, and the resulting definition of a good, awardable pro bono project. By following a number of campaigns, and the people who worked on them, we show how the awards won through pro bono work translate into both recognition and professional success. As such, these awards were the "goods" in the field—the moments in which actors gained esteem in front of their peers, and also turning points in their careers in the most practical way: in the kinds of projects they subsequently worked on, the positions they were promoted to in the advertising agencies, and their salaries. By tracing the history of awards, how people orient themselves to awards, and the tensions they experience, we focus on the field of advertising as a whole and on the fraught relationship between selfless morality and the self-interested desire for professional recognition that advertising professionals often contend with.

While the early chapters focus on the three main goods that professionals evoked in their narratives, chapter 5 explores how actors navigate the different goods. To do so, we begin with the work that managers— both top managers such as CEOs and middle managers who oversaw the work—do as they contend with their own set of tensions. Needing to manage pro bono work as part of the business portfolio of the agency and as an attempt to do good, managers engage in curatorial work. While managers themselves balance moral goods and the financial good of the agency, even the most business-oriented considerations needed to anticipate—and align—different goods. The imbrication of different goods was a crucial practical problem.

Chapter 6 turns from managers to the professionals themselves, and outlines two ways actors parse tangled goods. We first focus on the ways boundaries were made between "bad" projects, where the wrong kinds of goods were pursued, and interviewees' own projects. As we show, the cynical other was used to smooth the relationship between goods in interviewees' work. Even as the moral good may not have been pure—where the project is as an end unto itself—the comparison to these others allowed interviewees to see their work as more morally worthy. This, as we show, also involves moving to a consequentialist view of morality—that is, a view in which the moral is identified by its outcomes. The chapter then focuses on the importance of the language of "passion" in the interviews. As we show, passion talk enabled interviewees to connect and blur goods within the interview context. Because of how personal passion was, it implied authenticity, and as it was a term of investment with no clear referent in terms of the kind of good it denoted, it afforded interviewees the possibility to connect and seamlessly switch among goods.

In the last empirical chapter, chapter 7, we transition to an examination of how the question of "whether the campaign works" appears, and disappears, in pro bono work. Starting with the challenge of measuring success, we show that working pro bono was sometimes compelling precisely because advertising professionals could finally see the effect of their work. Both because they often work with small nonprofits where even small changes in donations or registrations translate into large percentages of gains, and because of the immediacy of such work, our interviewees often experienced the measured effects of their work in ways they could not in commercial work. However, without pressure from clients, and without resources for testing, the relationship between the measures and the campaigns' consequences was sometimes tenuous. The link between measurement and accountability was thus often severed, leading to what we refer to as consequentialism without consequences.

Last, chapter 8 comes full circle. First, comparing our findings to pro bono work in other fields—especially law—allows us to think again about what it means to live amid a profusion of goods. Rather than focusing on the moments in which the gods in our polytheistic world of values clash and contend with one another, we focus on the normal state of affairs: how we live through the profusion of goods. Examining the ways in which different goods are layered in a situation—and indeed, the ways that a situation itself is layered—is key to understanding pro bono work in the advertising world and questions far beyond it. Finally, we then return to the question of the everyday life of corporate social responsibility. Looking at the lived reality of advertising professionals allows us to examine how pro bono work is seductive from the point of view of the people who perform it: it offers them a pragmatic challenge and opens up a treasure trove of meanings to make sense of their efforts.

A Tangle of Goods

The complex relationship among goods that we describe in this book was not something that we saw behind the backs of social actors. It was something that advertising professionals talked about to one another, as Iddo saw when he conducted participant observation in a large advertising agency, and something that came up constantly in our interviews. When an account manager at the large global agency J. Walter Thompson reflected on the widespread practice of pro bono work at the end of a long interview, he noted this:

> I think that advertising people like challenges, creative and otherwise, you know? So, I think that they like taking on things. It's one thing to sell a package[d] good product. It's another thing to sell a cause.... [Y]ou often have to do more with less, so there's a little bit of creative problem solving involved, which is a good challenge. And I think also [that] a lot of times people take on pro bono accounts just to try and win awards somehow. And it would be disingenuous to suggest that that doesn't happen.
>
> And I think sometimes, honestly, there's a good business reason to say, like, "We will donate X amount of time to this cause with the goal of winning awards and then, therefore, we will be thought of as a more creative agency." So, therefore, the value exchange to us makes complete sense.... It can get a little bit weird.... [I]t would get weird if you've got agencies sitting there talking about how they want to win awards, and pro bono accounts talking about something different. So, you've got to make sure everybody's on the same page, but that seems like a valuable investment, you know?

Creative challenges, moral causes, business acumen, awards, careers—all came up in dizzying succession. And with them, the possibility that things may get "a little bit weird" as different people in the agency saw the pro bono work that they did differently—through the lenses of different grammars of the good. While pro bono work can be the perfect exemplar of successful CSR—the agency can "do well" by "doing good"—it is also an ongoing, contingent accomplishment.

The sociologist Marcel Mauss once described the gift as a total social fact—an institution that so tightly weaves together different dimensions of our lives that understanding it would allow us to approach much more than the phenomenon itself.[54] Pro bono work in advertising, we believe, is such a phenomenon. Pro bono work *is* a gift, but it is also much more. Both its structural location and its distinctive characteristics makes it a productive nexus for understanding the intimately existential dimensions of the lives of the people who perform it and the system of production and consumption in which it is performed. Equal parts a sociology of morality, of action, of culture, and of capitalism, the book examines the threads that comprise pro bono and how the interaction between those threads gives the woven fabric its distinctive patterns.

2. Morality in Pro Bono Work

In everyday talk, the term *pro bono* denotes work done for free. But rather than simply depicting the structure of exchange, the term actually connotes something more: the Latin phrase *pro bono publico* translates to "for the public good"—that good that transcends the narrow confines of work, a moral mission. This kind of good was highly salient to our interviewees. Joydeep Dey, a director of strategy and planning, spoke about his experience working on a pro bono account designed to raise awareness of mental illness. Ironically characterizing the campaign as "an extra credit project," he said:

> It's something that you get to do that makes you feel good about it but also takes all the skills that we apply to business-making problems—or, I'm sorry, money-making problems—into a real cultural thing.... The fact that I can use social media and an awareness-driving campaign and activate all of these people to then do something good, it feels good for me. So, [it's] extra credit in the sense that it's rewarding to work on, you apply the skills that you use every day, things that you're good at, things that we're good at, and it's something that's nice to talk to people about. It's something that kind of balances all of the commercial things that we do with something a little bit more human.

For Dey, as for most other interviewees, a pro bono campaign meant almost by definition working for a moral good, doing something that he would want to talk to others about, something "a little bit more human."

While different kinds of goods circulated in an ambiguous relation to each other, a crucial discourse of the good was the *moral* one—working to make a difference in the world, to make it better. When an owner of a small boutique agency was talking about one pro bono account she took on, the narrative she told was complex, with talk of creativity, awards, and internal politics. Still, there was something simple and straightforward about her moral narrative: "We want to do this type of work, because it's *worthy* of being done."

Other interviewees expressed something even more urgent and troubled. A middle manager in the strategy department at a multinational agency began by talking about his most important current client—a large weapons manufacturer. He used this commercial client to frame the subsequent conversation about pro bono work. "They make bombs," he said, becoming quite animated, "and so for people on that team [which he led at the agency], even if, creatively, they've done great stuff... they still need to cleanse their soul." While only a minority of the interviewees talked about their pro bono work in such a stark language of redemption, the chance to be a moral actor doing good in the world arose again and again.

But what are we talking about when we talk about a moral discourse? *Morality* itself is a fraught term. There is little agreement among metaethicists—the philosophers who try to define what kind of thing morality is—as to whether morality is even a thing out there in the world. Sociologists often gravitate toward a kind of descriptive relativism by which their subjects define what is morally good.[1] In such an account, it becomes difficult to separate moral language from other goods, each with its distinct vocabulary and grammar. Even if we think that we recognize a specific moral discourse that is different from other goods, interviewees did not stop their interview to tell us that they were shifting to a moral register. Yet, in listening to our interviewees, the moral good was quite distinct from, and sometimes even in tension with, other goods afforded by working pro bono for nonprofits.

This realm that we call *moral*—and that our interviewees recognized as such—is the realm of actions that define a person's worth beyond the confines of work. Moral narratives are those that define the interviewees over and above particular situations, are salient for their self-definition, and carry emotional weight.[2] While this is still a relativist position in that we do not purport to define what the moral good is, it allows us to remain true to the way that interviewees distinguished morality from other grammars through which they evaluated their own work, and provides us with a way to analytically parse out different goods. To put it otherwise, there was a crucial difference between being a well-regarded, or creatively good, advertising professional and being a morally good one. One can be a great creative professional and be a horrible person.[3]

Understood through this definitional prism, talk of morality abounded in the interviews. It emerged in the moments that actors talked about work that they did as advertising professionals—work that may have made their name in the industry, but also that was simultaneously beyond it. It was work that transcended its commercial and creative value; professionals imagined themselves as actors in a broader arena in which they defined themselves. In the words of one planner:

> I personally have kind of a love-hate relationship with the business. I have an existential crisis every now and again about "What am I contributing?" I'm aware of the culture of buying and needing and wanting, and I don't want to be contributing to that in a negative way. I don't want to be polluting, so … I feel like there's a lot of opportunity, that there is untapped [opportunity] in using advertising for good. And it just makes you feel better when you're working on something that's going to make the world better versus selling more chips, or ice cream, or whatever.

In strikingly similar language, a creative who worked pro bono on a medical account said:

> I think in every job, occasionally, you have some existential angst, which is, "Does what I do have meaning?" … Especially industries in the private sector…. And [pro bono work] is great, I can use this skill set to really good use. Not just good in the profitable sense for clients and stuff but actually good in the human sense.

This chapter follows these narratives of the broader "human sense," temporarily bracketing the relationship between moral discourse and the other goods it was entangled with. As we show, there are different ways to talk about the morality of pro bono work; there are narrative varieties of moral life. Whatever the narrative, we demonstrate that advertising professionals cherished the opportunity not only to work for a moral cause but also to become moral actors in their own right—to make the cause *theirs*. We then show how the language of morality often blurred the boundaries between pro bono work and other moments of doing good in their work, whether in crafting corporate social responsibility campaigns for large corporations or finding moral elements in regular, commercial campaigns.

Vocabularies of Morality: Power and Redemption

Pro bono work is an important vehicle of meaning. Like the planner and creative in the previous section who spoke about existential angst, the advertising professionals we talked to sometimes felt that their work was essentially meaningless, simply propelling consumers to purchase one brand rather than another in an undifferentiated ocean of brands. Against this backdrop, interviewees returned again and again to a tension between what they usually did in their line of work and their work for pro bono clients. As a senior planner recalled when talking about one of the first pro bono campaigns he worked on:

> When I worked on the child protection on the internet campaign it was like "This is great!" I genuinely felt for the first time that actually I might save someone's life today. And my wife, who is a doctor, who did that every fucking day—you're always like... I know [that] what I do is slightly less important, but there are these moments when you go, "Actually, I'm going to make a difference" and... that's true of a lot of the kind of pro bono work that you get to do. So as a strategist, as a creative, as an account person... you feel good about yourself in a way that you don't necessarily feel about other work.

Some aspects of this confession are unsurprising. After all, people in many professions have bouts of angst. Especially since the turn of the twenty-first century, it has become imperative to find transcendent meaning in one's work in "the creative economy."[4] And as we have noted, advertising as an industry has been particularly denounced for driving unnecessary consumption.[5] Given such a stigma, advertising professionals' search for transcendent meaning through work is made difficult and potentially more urgent—especially in comparison to a medical professional.

Two other things are noteworthy about the senior planner's comments. First, the meaning that advertising professionals derive from pro bono work is distinct from the meaning they derive from doing great creative work. As the senior planner suggested, although creatives can "feel great" about their craft as creative work, there is still something lacking in such an image of fulfillment.

Equally important, if less visible, is his assumption of efficacy: an internet campaign that can save lives. As we return to in a later chapter, interviewees were at times cynical about certain aspects of pro bono projects, but they usually presumed that such campaigns were successful.[6] In this context, it is not surprising that the most common narrative we heard was using advertising's powers in order to do good. Advertising professionals' self-image was often a little romantic. They were "hidden persuaders" and "attention merchants" who had grown all the more prominent in the era of social media manipulation; they were powerful—if wily—cultural agents.[7] True, the correspondence between this powerful persona and the reality of advertising work is less obvious. As the sociologist Michael Schudson documented, advertising's effects on driving consumer behavior are often quite unclear.[8] Still, our interviewees shared this image of the all-powerful manipulator of public opinion and private preferences. As one executive creative director said:

> I think we just believe in the power of great ideas to solve problems and I think this is probably a very personal thing. It's like, we just need advertising to be more aware of its power, even more now in the times we live in. I think we need to just help people to think more often and to question themselves a little bit more. Advertising has such a wonderful power. It's everywhere, and with the right brands I think you can tell people things that can make them reconsider something—anything from your neighbor to what you eat to many different things.... I think it's a little bit of... I don't know... I feel a particular responsibility in the times we live in that we should be more aware of that. We should try to do more with what we have. Obviously, I know there's advertising for alcohol and cigarettes and that kind of stuff, but in reality, there's also the possibility of doing great things and communicate great things and make people a little bit more aware of other things and value other things and appreciate other things. In this case [a campaign for organ donation] it was just about celebrating bodies that are not particularly celebrated anywhere. I think there's always a big, big movement regarding body shame.... So that was a little bit of the essence of that campaign, just celebrating these people and telling them that they are beautiful and have this amazing potential to save lives, which was... the main message of the campaign.

This interviewee, and others like him, seemed to talk about the power of good advertising—that is, of pro bono advertising—in grandiose terms. Some of his words are reminiscent of comic-book superheroes. With great power comes great responsibility, or at the very least, the possibility of directing advertising's powers to the service of the greater good. Indeed, it was the tension between the image of advertising professionals as wielders of cultural power and their perceptions of how they used that power that provoked an urgency in their moral discourse. Using such power only in the service of corporate interests was reckless, even immoral.

When such moral language emerged, some interviewees felt that it wasn't simply their own insignificance they were confronting. In one interview, we talked to Federico, a senior strategist in one of America's most illustrious ad agencies. Federico, an immigrant from Argentina was

in charge of some of the agency's campaigns for pharmaceutical industries. Big pharma paid the bills. Asked about his work at the beginning
of the interview, he grew pensive: "My job is, historically, ... to help the
bad guys. So, yeah—I work for the bank, I work for pharma. Maybe next
will be oil. Somebody has to do that, and increasingly, it's been me." As
the interview went on, Federico spoke about the pro bono campaigns
he worked on and how he saw the work aligning with both awards and
creative pursuits. He was cynical and self-deprecating when talking about
his own work and motivations. Yet when asked which pro bono project
he was personally most excited to work on, he grew animated:

> I actually feel good doing any of that compared to what I do—definitely
> the bad guys.... I don't care. I feel equally good.... Water in Africa,
> blood donations... I'm happy to take them because it's a good balance
> versus working for corporate America, corporate pharma. So, it doesn't
> matter, it really doesn't matter... I mean, my passion... Yes, I think usu-
> ally helping third world countries probably gets a little more interesting,
> because, naturally... but it doesn't really matter. If we're helping here
> with [Hurricane] Katrina or something like that, I like it as a change of
> pace. It helps me, you know? ... It makes you a little more... It gives your
> job a little more meaning. You find more meaning in what you're doing.
> Oftentimes you're working on how to sell shit that nobody cares [about]
> or wants. So, here comes an opportunity to do something and make it a
> little different. You want to do it. In general, most people want to do it.

While this is not a purely moral discourse (note the "change of pace"),
Federico nevertheless bubbled over. He described his work as selling "shit
that nobody cares about" and working for "the bad guys." In contrast,
working pro bono allowed him to "do something" and think deeply about
different causes, about things that mattered. As the interview went on, he
spoke at length about his attempt to understand the real problems that
nonprofits try to solve: the moral stakes, the obstacles they face, their
very identity and mission.

Constructing Moral Agency: Three Cases

Taking on pro bono accounts allowed advertising professionals to define
themselves beyond the confines of their work and sometimes against the
grain of the campaigns that they usually worked on. But what kind of
moral action was this? It wasn't, after all, their nonprofit. Yet it was, to

an important degree, their campaign. How did these professionals conceptualize the kind of moral action that they engaged in?

Working on pro bono accounts took up only a fraction of workers' time. Even as many interviewees averred that they treated pro bono accounts just as they would any other account in terms of time and effort, such accounts made up only about 2–5 percent of their total work. They may have taken the work seriously, but they took it seriously for only a sliver of time. Yet the interviewees made clear that the short time they got to work on these accounts was morally meaningful. While it may in part have been meaningful because advertising professionals got to execute an account on behalf of a cause that they believed in, they also actively *shaped* the account's moral claim.

Having the opportunity to do so was possible because of the ordinary habits of advertising work. To be a good advertising professional, interviewees told us that they needed to deeply understand—and even identify with—the client. This was especially the case for planners, but also for creatives and, to some extent, account managers. The professionals we spoke with learned everything they could about a client's product category, about the brand, and about the client itself. In most instances, this process included generating a reason to care—both for the advertising professional and for the campaign's intended audience—which was much easier to do in a pro bono account. As an account executive at a midsize agency said:

> I think a lot of our jobs are pushing products that we may or may not be super-personally involved in. And you find things with every client that you can genuinely get behind and you believe in and you push forward. But at the end of the day, you're working for someone else's brand as opposed to something that you truly, genuinely believe in. So, I think using our voices for something that we care about is a very different, wonderful thing.

An important part of advertising professionals' work is therefore a kind of emotional labor. They need to find an aspect of the account to identify with so that they can forge a temporary commitment to the work and the brand. Like the emotional labor demanded of flight attendants and other service industry professionals that the sociologist Arlie Hochschild identified, this advertising work requires a kind of deep acting.[9] Our interviewees needed to find something about the brand that could move them, could motivate them personally, so that they could "genuinely get behind" the work. While performing this emotional labor was not required in the same way that service professionals must perform cheerfulness for their customers, advertising professionals nevertheless tried to construct an emotional investment in the brands they represented, and they saw such investment as an important part of their work.

Yet, as this interviewee expresses, becoming personally invested in goods like chips or ice cream is not always easy, and identifying with the client's interest is often fraught. In work for many paid clients, advertising professionals struggled to genuinely care, even as they needed to convey an idealized version of the client's brand identity. While advertising professionals usually did not spend their days discussing brands' and corporate clients' moral shortcomings,[10] they did oscillate between attachment and detachment—completely immersing themselves in a client's mission and product benefits in one moment, only to wryly comment about the meaninglessness of the brand in the next.[11]

Pro bono work, though, was a different story. If the usual imperative to identify with the client's perspective often seemed difficult, in pro bono accounts this was precisely what was so compelling about the work—what made it "a different, wonderful thing." In the ways that interviewees talked about these campaigns, they were not only aiding a moral cause; they were also sharing in deeply felt, meaningful action, thereby actively becoming moral agents.[12] That is, professionals felt not only that they were moving a worthy moral vision forward but also that they were taking part in envisioning the moral project, even if for a limited time and in a limited fashion.

This showed up in a number of ways. First, even as some pro bono accounts came from clients who approached the agency or came through the Ad Council, management took on the campaigns only when there was enough buy-in from professionals within the agency. Moreover, of the 108 pro bono accounts we followed, 28 came from employees rather than management. Some arrived through personal networks that advertising professionals were already enmeshed in; others came about when a creative or a planner had an idea for a campaign and then went fishing for a compatible client. While not all of these employee-generated campaigns were about doing moral good—sometimes they were just a favor for a friend or a stellar creative idea waiting for execution—in many cases it was professionals' personal commitment to a specific cause that initiated the process.

One example of this process was the Barton Graf agency's Climate Name Change campaign, done in 2013 for 350.org, an environmental nonprofit focused on climate change. In what became a viral campaign,

FIGURE 2. "John Boehner Ravages Coast" is the header for this image from the Climate Name Change campaign, which petitioned the World Meteorological Association to change its storm-naming system to the names of policy makers who deny climate change. The campaign was created in 2013 by the agency Barton F. Graf for 350.org.

the agency produced a satirical online petition and videos demanding that the meteorological service change its naming practices for superstorms. Instead of using arbitrary first names in alphabetical order (e.g., Katrina, Sandy), it called for using the names of politicians who deny climate change, such as Hurricanes John Boehner, Marco Rubio, or Michele Bachmann.

The campaign was very successful, at least by some measures. It was highly awarded—the seventh most awarded advertising campaign in 2014. The nonprofit 350.org saw a surge in media attention. The campaign was written up in newspapers such as the *Guardian*, which called it "one of the most unique and visually impressive environmental ads" ever made,[13] and it was talked about on major television channels such as ABC.

Unlike many pro bono projects, no client reached out to Barton Graf with a request; it was the agency team that reached out to 350.org after developing an idea. Dan Treichel, one of the creatives responsible for the campaign, told Sonia:

We [he and his partner Dave Canning] had done pro bono projects in other agencies, but not for climate change–type groups. It was something we were really passionate about, and it was just really interesting because Hurricane Sandy happened in New York. So, it affected all of us, and then we kept sharing news about people's—about how they kept saying bad things about Sandy. So, it kind of came from there. It was like, "Oh, well, poor Sandy."

Like many creative ideas, it was sparked by connecting two observations. Treichel and his creative partner talked about climate change because it was something that they were "passionate about." And living in New York during Hurricane Sandy, they noticed how people—already cued to anthropomorphize the storm—ended up attributing undesirable characteristics to the storm name, joking about "poor Sandy." This observation about the discursive power of the storm's name allowed them to take the second step and connect it to climate-denying politicians. As an account executive who worked closely on the campaign recalled:

We had all these discussions at work just between the few of us at how outrageous it was that some politicians just deny that climate change exists. There's scientific facts, there's all these facts... How are you just sitting there in front of people saying "Oh, I think it's a hoax." It's so silly! And we kind of wanted to flip that on its head and expose that in a really big way. So, [Dan] had ideas around it for a while. And I think he and his partner started just concepting and came to me very quickly, asking if it was something I would be interested in helping them with. I was all for it. It was that simple. So, myself, those two creatives, and a strategist just dove in and spent months dedicating ourselves to that in addition to all of our [commercial] clients.

To effectively execute this, they needed approval from management. First, they pitched the idea to the company's founder, Jerry Graf, asking for permission to work on the project. As they recalled, he proceeded to quiz them on the science of climate change. He wanted to know whether they knew what they were talking about, to be sure they hadn't simply landed on a tantalizing creative idea they wanted to pursue. Satisfied that they knew their science, Graf gave them a green light to pursue this idea on their own time, saying that the agency would help them produce it if they sharpened the idea and found a client. He even gave them comments and ideas on how to improve their script. Over the following few months, they did the work—writing scripts, ideas, and storyboards—before approaching a nonprofit. So the nonprofit in this case was decidedly not the driving moral agent. As the account manager noted:

Our biggest goal was picking an organization with someone that people recognized and knew already, even if that was a subset of society [that] recognized [the nonprofit]. We wanted to make sure that it really did add a stamp of legitimacy to the work, especially if the work was a bit of a satire. We were overtly making fun of politicians. So we didn't want it to come off as a silly stunt. We wanted to [ensure] that it felt real and that the point was very much driven, in that we were also hopefully driving donations to this organization.

At least as this account manager recalls it, the nonprofit itself was partly a means to an end. In a reversal of conventional advertising's roles, the campaign was the action's end and the client the means.[14] The team members recognized that partnering with a nonprofit would allow them to do two things simultaneously: legitimize the project so that it would be taken as serious political action rather than written off as a satirical stunt and leverage the campaign to mobilize donations to the cause, something they were not equipped to deal with. The agency and the production company they approached paid for the production costs, not 350.org. While 350.org certainly took part in the campaign and benefited from it, the driving moral agents of the campaign were the agency's team members.

This case, however, was atypical: the professionals who worked on it were not directly paid by the agency for their time; the agency and the production company shouldered production costs; and the bulk of the campaign was worked out before the nonprofit was even contacted. Yet even in more typical cases, when the nonprofit was the key actor in defining the target message and the client shouldered production costs (albeit reduced ones), advertising professionals still often took ownership over the campaign and over defining and crafting the moral cause. This was especially true when they volunteered to work on causes that they already cared about.

An example of this is a pro-LGBTQ campaign focused on gay men's rights to donate blood. The work was done by Saatchi and Saatchi, a well-known midsize agency, for GLAAD (formerly Gay and Lesbian Alliance against Defamation), an LGBTQ media-monitoring nonprofit, and Gay Men's Health Crisis, a New York AIDS service organization. The campaign started off by targeting a regulation by the US Food and Drug Administration (FDA) barring gay and bisexual men from donating blood. Yet, as Jonnie Ingram, the creative who led the campaign, explained to Shelly, when FDA rules changed mid-campaign, it turned out to be pivotal in determining the direction of the campaign:

So, throughout my career, I just sort of got to see a lot of people doing things they were passionate about on the side. It was definitely things that were, you know, anything from domestic violence, to helping the homeless, to everything… There were just all kinds of different passion projects people were doing. It was really inspiring. I, myself, am a homosexual, so I have been able to sort of find my passion and help our community in the best way I can. I've actually done a lot more than just the Celibacy Challenge, but that one was definitely a really terrific experience, and I think got to execute quite beautifully, and a really fun one, so to speak.…

[At the time] a gay man wasn't allowed to give blood based upon supposed scientific data that sort of regulates… and prevents gay men from donating blood… saying we're more promiscuous. And in this case, it was really disappointing because I find that any policies—what the FDA had on the questionnaire—made it look like we were less than everyone else.… I think that anyone, wherever you come from, and you go fill out this questionnaire you see "Oh, it asks if you're a man who has sex with another man," and then suddenly, I think, people presume that we are these beasts or animals that spread disease. It just really, really bothers me, and I think if we were able to change that, starting obviously with gay marriage legalization to any other little policies that are out there, is something that really stood out for me.

So, what I did was—this was actually kind of a long process. We started this campaign before the FDA put in the regulatory ban for a one-year sex abstinence ban. So, we had a whole campaign that was really just about actually overturning the lifelong ban. And then I come into work one day and someone showed me an article saying the FDA changed the policy and now it's fine, and everyone is like, "Oh, it's fine. We can't do this [campaign] now."

As did other interviewees, Ingram took on pro bono campaigns that he felt strongly about—particularly for causes affecting LGBTQ people. Indeed, years prior he had spearheaded a campaign promoting safer sex practices among gay and bisexual youth. When the agency took on GLAAD and Gay Men's Health Crisis's project to target FDA regulations, he was excited to take on an active part. Yet, at least as others in the agency envisioned it, the work became moot when the FDA changed its regulations. After all, if the campaign was against the ban, and the ban was lifted, wasn't the problem solved?

It is precisely here that Ingram's own definition of the problem became instrumental. If the problem was stigmatization and gay men being made to feel like "beasts or animals that spread disease," then the FDA policy change made no difference. The FDA did not simply lift its ban. After the regulatory change, gay and bisexual men were technically permitted to donate blood, but they were required to sign an attestation that they had not had sexual intercourse with other men for the previous year. It was not a total ban on gay men donating blood, but a ban on sexual activity was no less problematic; it implied that these men were dangerous and needed a yearlong quarantine. Thus, immediately after being told by his colleagues that all was over, Ingram pushed back:

> [I said:] "Are you joking? Because this is actually even worse." A one-year sex abstinence ban is the exact same thing, and there's still that stigma you're attaching to gay men, and that's what we want to eliminate.
>
> So, I got the team back together, and then we came up with the idea to make fun of that a little bit and encourage people to take [the] Celibacy Challenge as a ridiculous way in an effort to save lives, which is how the campaign came to life. Obviously, just saying a one-year sex abstinence ban is kind of humorous out of context. It just sounds ridiculous, so I was like… "this is the idea." …
>
> So, I want to rewind a little bit. I got our CEO and our chief creative officer to back the idea, and they said they would help us fund it, which was really terrific. If it was good enough, obviously, because there's a bit of a caliber of execution that we have to stand up to, have the agency put money into it. So, then we just went with it, and when I read the script, the CEO laughed out loud and he's just like "Do it!" So we did it, and we got our team together to sort of help execute it and craft it.

The final campaign received a host of media attention and a silver Clio award—one of the most important awards in the industry. It featured actor Alan Cumming as head of the satirical Abstinence Bureau, telling gay and bisexual men to give up sex for a year so that they could be eligible to donate blood according to FDA regulations, while recommending "fully-approved activities" they might engage in to pass the long year without sex. Cumming narrates these mundane activities ("practice yoga," "clean your house," "take up pottery classes") as suggestive images of these activities flash before the viewer. A pottery wheel bears clay in the shape of a giant penis, a man frantically jerks a long drill bit back and forth through a plank of wood, and so on.

In terms of moral agency, the crucial point was that Ingram's definition of the problem shifted the campaign to focus on the experience of stigma in a way that was divorced from the specific FDA regulation the

FIGURE 3. Alan Cumming stars as the head of the Department of Sexual Abstinence in a satirical video lampooning the U.S. Food and Drug Administration for banning gay and bisexual men from donating blood unless they have been celibate for a year. The campaign was produced in 2015 by Saatchi & Saatchi for GLAAD.

agency was meant to tackle. While this vision aligned with that of the two nonprofits, neither the decision to perform the pro bono work under the changed regulations nor the specific form it took—a jubilant celebration of gay sexuality mocking the idea of a celibacy requirement—was preordained.

Even in cases where advertising professionals did not already have a personal affinity for a specific cause, they often developed moral agency through the process of researching and working on the campaign. In the following case, centering on food insecurity in the United States, the campaign came to the agency through management and was handed to a team that did not volunteer to work on it. Yet during the work process, some planners became so enmeshed in the work's moral mission that they tried to push the nonprofit to take a different—more radical—moral stance than it was prepared to commit to.

Riad, a senior planner at a large agency, narrated this shift as he told us about the campaign.[15] He began by showing the final result: an evocative television commercial that highlighted people's innate goodness, tugging at heart strings—and hopefully purse strings too. Yet without being prompted, Riad went on to say that while the campaign was successful and he was happy about the work he ended up doing for it, it wasn't what he and his team envisioned. Commenting that his team had "wanted to take it in quite a different direction," he explained:

We got very excited about moving away a little bit from the charity piece, like, "I should give some money," and more.... We were thinking about it more in terms of the injustice of it. And so, the fact that we live in the US and people are going hungry is kind of wrong. And there is a social injustice element to it. What was really interesting is, you look at this separation.... On the one hand we have people who are obsessing over what they eat, are Instagramming every meal, looking at where it was sourced, where it's come from. And so we've got this... we've got more and more interested in our food.... And so you can kind of see that trending that way. [And] at the same time, going the other way, is a whole load of people who actually have zero choice in the food they eat.... And out of sheer necessity because it's now the cheapest way you can feed a family.... All—all the wrong food is subsidized and so it just manifests into this "Huh, it's cheaper to eat that than to eat fresh fruit?" So yeah, you know, the reality of food deserts and environments... even if you have the money to get fresh fruits and veggies you can't even get it.

IDDO: Did you actually do a spot?

RIAD: Oh, well, we... we had a whole lot of work that went in that direction. It never got to creation, but there was a... we ultimately went to them with about three or four different strategic routes. But the one we preferred was all about people: you take the people that are at the other end, who are now obsessing over food, and then you start to bring to life some of the stark realities of people that, kind of... you don't necessarily see every day but the moment you realize that goes on...

And it was also to stop people-blaming. So, part of what tends to happen with child hunger is people go, "Well, I blame the parents. They're obviously not working hard enough and they're obviously not..." You know? This part of the American culture is to kind of [assume that] if you are successful then you've obviously worked hard, and if you're unsuccessful then you haven't. So, part of that route was to help people understand that child hunger isn't due to bad choices that people have made. And, systemically they're... it's unfortunate but the reality is that: no, they had no real option but to be in that position. And then that starts to feed into kind of your like... well, that's just unjust.

In effect, Riad and his team were invested in a deep politicization of how people can and can't eat. Rather than the campaign inspiring charitable sympathy, they wanted to expose what the social theorists Richard Sennett and Jonathan Cobb called "the hidden injuries of class," as those injuries are reflected in the food we eat.[16] Malnutrition in the United

States is a matter not of bad choices and irresponsible parents but of structural forces: farm lobbying, crop subsidies, urban segregation, food deserts. Instead of inviting viewers' compassion, the team wanted to awaken their outrage. Tellingly, Riad later said that in the version he and his team envisioned, "the end point wouldn't have simply been 'I think I'll go on and donate some money'" but rather would have "start[ed] to shine a light on the issue more broadly and have it as a conversation."

While the team presented different possible directions to the client, as agencies often do, they pushed for the one they wanted. But the client would have none of it. In one of only a handful of cases we encountered where a pro bono client declined a proposed campaign, the nonprofit was wary of politicizing what they wanted to position as a universal (and apolitical) moral imperative: give money to feed the hungry. Yet at least for a large part of the process, the advertising professionals working on the campaign envisioned the moral cause differently. Rather than simply asking the nonprofit what they wanted and executing that strategic idea, the advertising team recrafted the moral good in their own way.

This is not to say that all the advertising professionals we talked to were enthusiastic about each and every pro bono account they worked on. Some were cynical, while others made a point of saying that they didn't feel any difference between pro bono accounts and commercial ones. What's more, in almost all cases — including those we presented above — narratives were tangled and complex. Yet an overwhelming majority of the interviewees also spoke in these existential, moral terms about their pro bono work. Given the nature of the work, they needed to take on the client's dilemmas and challenges. A cause that they felt deeply about afforded them the opportunity — even nudged them — to become active moral agents rather than relatively passive executors.

The Moral Neighborhood: On Second-Order CSR

Part of what crystallized the narratives we depict in this chapter into a recognizable discourse was the typical way of talking about how pro bono work relates to commercial work. In addition to patterned talk about what pro bono work is, another relationship is just as crucial: there are also ways to talk about what it isn't. As students of culture know well, meanings are relational. To a large extent, we define what something is by what it is not. At the same time, we also define objects by imagining them as part of the same group, or neighborhood, of things. That is, things that may not be quite the same but that we lump together. In mathematical terms, we place these things in the same set.

The pro bono morality tales evoke other, neighboring morality tales. As such, they point to the location of pro bono work within the broader political economy. There were also other — rarer — opportunities for professionals to feel that they were doing moral good. In some cases, interviewees spoke about morally compelling work they did as part of their regular paid work for corporate clients. But morality more regularly arose in another kind of work: advertising campaigns for clients doing their own corporate social responsibility projects. We call this *second-order CSR*.

In an era when "doing good" is often part of corporations' branding, advertising professionals sometimes found themselves working on campaigns that seemed very similar to those they did pro bono — except these were for corporate clients. These campaigns were performed as part of a portfolio of client representation (e.g., when the agency of record representing a large bank also crafted the bank's CSR campaigns) or when corporate clients approached agencies to handle a CSR campaign because the agency had particular experience with "cause-based" campaigns.

There are substantial differences between a pro bono campaign for a struggling, community-based nonprofit and a corporate CSR campaign, but the differences were not so vast to the professionals doing the work, at least not in moral terms. When interviewees talked in the moral register, they sometimes slipped into talking about these commercial, second-order CSR campaigns. In some cases, we asked about pro bono accounts, only to receive long, detailed descriptions of fully paid accounts that the interviewee worked on. When Sonia asked the founding partner of a small agency to describe his most recent pro bono project, he launched into a description of a paid CSR campaign, describing it as follows:

> [There is] a general trend... for several years, in our industry, that we're looking for opportunities within existing clients where the output is actually having a positive effect on our society one way or another. For instance, with Stella [Artois, a beer brand], that we were working with... we came up with this program called Buy a Lady a Drink. [The typical Stella beer glass is a chalice] which Stella actually sells these days.... We came up with a program that [when] anyone who buys one of those, it actually provides some more unfortunate folks in our globe with clean drinking water. So there are opportunities within a brand to actually do... or get the same feeling as you get when you do pro bono work.

Although there were differences between pro bono and CSR campaigns in the actual work process — professionals weren't expected to work on second-order CSR campaigns on their own time and the campaigns were more creatively limited than pro bono accounts—this interviewee and others noted their fundamental similarity in moral terms. As another interviewee put it, "People want to believe their work matters, and then they get to work on things that they believe matter" and "psychologically, it [feels] the same." Most advertising professionals did not parse out the structural differences between pro bono work for nonprofits and paid CSR work for large brands. But even if they had, the differences would not have been as straightforward as they may seem at first glance. After all, advertising agencies often presented pro bono work as their own form of CSR.[17] More to the point, these kinds of work felt the same. As with pro bono work performed for nonprofits, in second-order CSR campaigns professionals could envision themselves as moral agents and feel that they were using the tools of their trade for the good.

The importance of second-order CSR as a kindred—and sometimes equivalent—way to access moral agency also came up when interviewees talked about the other side of doing good: morally dubious campaigns. We asked all interviewees if they had ever declined a pro bono account and which accounts they wouldn't accept. The answers for the latter, more speculative question were invariably couched in moral language. The New York–based advertising professionals we talked to by and large supported the Democratic Party. In describing what they wouldn't do, they almost all listed hot-button political issues championed by the right wing: anti-abortion, weapons manufacturing, pro-gun lobbying, and big tobacco.[18]

However, when we asked about actual campaigns they had declined to take on, the answers were rarely couched in the same moral terms. Anti-abortion organizations hadn't approached the New York agencies we sampled; the National Rifle Association did not come knocking. And the fact is that some of our interviewees *did* work for clients they had moral qualms about. Rather than pure moral tales, there were a host of other considerations and goods in the stories we were told, and most of these considerations, like the promise of a creative challenge, were not really about the morality of the client's business.

In the very few cases when interviewees declined projects on moral grounds, it was precisely such second-order CSR campaigns. For example, one planner had refused a CSR campaign for a mining company working in sub-Saharan Africa that approached his agency because he didn't feel that the effort was genuine; he suspected it was a disingenuous way to manage public relations:

We got a request from them that said, "Hey, we need to rebrand our mines," and we said, "OK, why?" They said, "Oh, well, because we have some perception issues and reputational issues that we need to conquer, so we need to reposition ourselves." And I was like, "OK, tell me a little more about the reputational backlash you're facing." So, it became very obvious from two clicks on Google that the company we're talking to was ranking number one on every list around the world of the planet's most evil companies out there. So, there were things like entire villages being evaporated and people disappearing because they [the company] wanted to establish a digging ground. Working conditions were the worst I've ever seen or witnessed. So, just horrible, horrible stuff. And they had a new CEO at that point and he said, "We got to change our perceptions around that."

I said, "Well, OK, the only way you're going to change perceptions is if you change the way you behave, right? So how committed are you guys to actually changing your processes and the way you do things?" And I didn't get a very clear sense that they were really committed to doing that. So, we turned down the project, and said, "No, we will not work with you," which wasn't easy internally because there were two different schools of thought. One was "They're totally opponents, just basically evil, and we will not work with them because they're trying to put lipstick on a pig and it's not happening." Then there were others who said, "Well, we should specifically work with the most challenged companies because if we can move the needle a little bit on those, the impact is probably higher than us working with companies or NGOs that are already doing pretty well." So, it was very interesting, even for me from an internal perspective, to see those discussions unfold.

SHELLY: Did you fall on one side or the other of that debate or were you just kind of witnessing other people articulating what to do?

PLANNER: Oh no, I made the decision at the end of the day to not work with them, because while I recognize we want to have an impact with the type of work we want to do with companies, I'm very uncomfortable doing work where I feel that we are enabling a company who's not fully committed or is not doing enough at least to correct some of the wrong that they're doing.

It was not that advertising professionals in the agency categorically refused to work on this account. But the planner felt that it would be, in effect, "putting lipstick on a pig"—a phrase advertising professionals often used to describe shallow attempts to mask a brand's flawed nature. While advertising professionals routinely lament that they needed to put lipstick on pigs in their commercial work for corporate clients, doing so in a CSR campaign was more problematic. The integrity of the work was wrapped up in the campaign's moral nature.

Pro bono work, of course, isn't only about morality. It comprises the pattern of entanglements and tensions between moral narratives, business objectives, narratives of creativity and labor, and opportunities for recognition and advancement. Yet in moments where interviewees were enraptured by their moral narrative, the elements in the set of projects they talked about shifted. Thus, although a second-order CSR campaign for a corporate client and pro bono engagement for a nonprofit entailed structurally different work, they were both ways of doing something morally similar. They were part of the same moral neighborhood.

Conclusions

The moral discourse among advertising professionals was one of the most important ways for them to make sense of the pro bono work they performed. It was often the first thing advertising professionals reached for, and clearly it was the first thing that they expected us to be interested in. It was also largely the official discourse of campaigns themselves. When advertising professionals talked to the media about their pro bono campaigns, other goods mostly faded out of sight. In situations in which the tangle of goods was purified into an official narrative, it was the moral good that held sway.

Some of this is about the presentation of self and agency branding. Nevertheless, the vocabulary of morality was not a superficial gloss or justificatory vocabulary that hid the "real" draws of pro bono work. Working pro bono accounts afforded people in the advertising industry a seductive field of action. It wasn't only that conducting pro bono work allowed them to further causes they felt strongly about. An advertising campaign was not simply a vehicle through which the nonprofit transmitted a moral credo. Rather, the nature of advertising work meant that advertising professionals were afforded the opportunity—and even felt an imperative—to identify with the client and the cause. Rather than just transmitting a moral good, they felt that they could shape it, acting as moral agents. The causes they worked for were not just means to mission-driven ends; they were also ends in and of themselves. Part of the powerful seduction of pro bono work is precisely this moral opportunity to not only do something but also to be someone.

Still, morality is not the only good that shaped advertising professionals' relationship to pro bono accounts. While professionals' moral commitment was important—traveling among situations and defining the self over and above the work they did—this was only one good among several. Dimensions of the work itself and what the work meant for

people's careers and reputations were also important, sometimes aligning with and blending into the moral, sometimes creating moments of
tension or breakdown.

To return to the metaphor of the polytheism of goods, morality is but
one god within a pantheon. It is to these other gods that we now turn.

3. Good Work; or, The Gift of Unalienated Labor

While speaking to a planner at McCann Erickson, we asked whether he had ever declined a pro bono project. He thought for a second before sharing one such case during his time at a previous agency. Perhaps surprisingly, his narrative did not draw on the moral registers that we documented in the previous chapter. He had not declined to work on the campaign because it was a morally objectionable mission or a cynical abuse of his time and labor. Instead, his answer pointed to another grammar.

As the planner recalled, he had an opportunity to work with a client through the Advertising Council of America. The Ad Council, mentioned in the introduction, produces public service campaigns on behalf of other nonprofits and US government agencies. Since the Ad Council creates relationships between civic organizations and advertising agencies, these projects are effectively equivalent to pro bono work, except that they also come with Ad Council funds. Such work is thus quite coveted, as funding affords higher production value, and having a budget for media purchases means the work can also be highly visible, at times becoming iconic. Despite this promise and the client's noble mission, this planner and his agency had summarily declined:

> [The situation] was like, "Here, we've got it, it's yours to take." But what it was, they already had an idea developed from a previous agency, they wanted to stick with that idea and ... do like a "round two" of that idea. We were like, No! ... Because there's no ... that's the complete opposite of a client where you can do something creative and interesting, and so we're going to do this second round of another agency's work *and* not get paid for it?! ... There was obviously no creative opportunity. On some of the others [clients] in the gray area it would be around work they've done in the past, and from a simple conversation you can start to assess

their appetite for new work.... And so, if you don't get a sense of that, and particularly if it's not necessarily a cause that's very close to people's hearts, then it's going to struggle.

A moral mission alone, it seems, is not enough. In this case, it wasn't that the cause was not worthy. The planner's hesitation to take on the project was not based on how deserving the cause was.[1] Rather, pro bono work also needs to present a creative opportunity, to be interesting to work on. The client's request breached a basic expectation: pro bono work needs to be fulfilling not just morally but also as a work process—as *labor*.

Beyond being a moral good, pro bono work constitutes a peculiar gift exchange. The agency supplies strategic and creative labor free of charge to the client—an obvious gift. Yet the nonprofit provides a countergift. Good pro bono campaigns allow advertising professionals the opportunity to be moral agents, as we've established. But it also provides the opportunity to do good work, as in rewarding, high-quality work. As such, it offers an escape from the frustrations of routinized work with paying clients. Whether this is because pro bono clients can't control what the agency does, or because they know that they shouldn't, it nevertheless results in a different work experience for professionals.

But what kind of exchange was this? As anthropologists have long observed, gifts are ways of managing relational positions. Gifts are intimately tied to social standing, so how and how much one gives in a gift-giving relationship determines one's relative power in that relationship. This entails a practical artfulness, as people employ a strategic calculus to navigate gift giving, including when exactly to gift and how much to give.[2] As anthropologists and sociologists have also observed, such a calculus operates just as much—if not more powerfully—in situations of unequal exchange. Writing about unequal exchanges, the sociologist George Homans suggested that the countergift for unrepayable gifts is deference.[3] Without much to offer, the only thing the weak party can provide the gift giver is the gift of social status.

Seen through this lens, pro bono work sits in the interstices of a radically unequal, distant exchange and a more straightforward and direct one. On the one hand, pro bono work fits the form of gift giving seen in philanthropy—a "pure gift" to needy recipients who wouldn't usually interact with agency professionals. But this gift is complicated by the relationship's practical structure. While the final gift supposedly goes to the people or causes served by a nonprofit, the immediate exchange takes place between agency workers and nonprofit staff. As clients, staff are a step removed from the final beneficiaries of the work. The gift, then, is doubled. As an intermediary between beneficiaries and the agency, the nonprofit allows advertising professionals to perform a moral good. But within the immediate exchange relationship, the nonprofit also provides professionals with a different experience of work. The plurality of goods is reflected in a doubling of the gift.

It is for this reason that the Ad Council's request for the planner's agency to rehash somebody else's campaign was such a violation—an "easy no." Without the countergift of original and creatively satisfying work, the Ad Council (and the client) broke the unwritten terms of the relationship. Focusing solely on the campaign's moral dimension, they reneged on the premise of exchange in which they were supposedly engaged as a nonprofit. A very different grammar of goods was at play. Thus, in some cases there can be possible trade-offs between pro bono work's moral valence and its experience as labor. The planner in this case revealed a fuzzy arithmetic that pitted the two goods against each other. If the pro bono work was morally compelling enough, then perhaps it would be worth it. But without the case being really "close to people's hearts," rote execution would struggle to survive the trade-off.

Analyzing our interviews, we noticed a cluster of different work-related considerations that advertising professionals weighed as they discussed pro bono work. They talked about their creative freedom, about the kinds of work they got to try their hands at, and about how clients treated them. The cluster focused on advertising professionals' working conditions and their existential relationship to their labor.

The Creativity of Labor

Advertising is a conflicted calling. It is a creative industry, but one in which creative expression directly serves a paying client. This does not make it unique. No creative profession is entirely free of material constraints. Think of designers or architects, for example. Even what's often understood as "pure art" was produced by artists who had to sustain themselves—most early modern painters, after all, worked for a patron who commissioned their work or otherwise supported their creative endeavors.[4] The very notion of unfettered art for art's sake is a latecomer to the scene. In interviews, as in our ethnographic fieldwork, advertising professionals did not complain about being hired guns. This was their work. Indeed, as Shelly found in another project, designers talked about the mix of industrial commerce and art as one of the things that actually drew them to their work rather than an unfortunate dilution of pure creative expression.[5] Advertising professionals talked in much the same way.

Producing creative content for clients necessarily tied together clients' business objectives and the artistry of advertising professionals' skills. As a craft, they did not experience doing creative work for a client as a lofty, theoretical issue. It was both more immediate and more prosaic. In other words, it was a labor process with all its practicalities and challenges. Here, advertising professionals frequently complained about their clients. Their frustrations reflected a desire to do interesting work to showcase their talents and allow for masterful expression. They wanted to produce pieces they could be proud of as aesthetic and rhetorical objects. Even while they had no qualms about doing such work for someone else, they wanted to control what they did.

Retaining such control was typically rare. Paying clients, after all, put a large amount of money into the campaigns they contracted. They needed to pay the agency, pay production costs, and pay media dollars to publicize the work. They also had a crucial stake in their ever-looming perceived return on investment, or ROI. A campaign might be creative, but it will be largely worthless if it fails to drive sales; even worse, a controversial campaign might hurt sales instead of boosting them. As agency professionals griped again and again, this meant that clients were usually conservative. While clients often said that they wanted to see "bold" work to make themselves heard amid the overwhelming buzz of competing consumer goods, the fact was that they usually dialed down creatives' more risky work and gravitated toward well-worn advertising clichés.

Advertising professionals thus constantly complained about the constraints of cautious clients with whom they had to negotiate. "Good clients" allowed advertising professionals more freedom to produce riskier and more interesting work, having what advertising professionals talked about as an "appetite for disruption." Yet most clients did not, nixing ideas that creatives and planners thought were best or toning them down so much that they became unrecognizable. As one account manager said when describing his own work mediating between the client and the agency's creative and planning teams:

> There's always a struggle between yourself and the client, and that's the hardest part about the job. And that's also really grinding, [the creatives are constantly saying] "Oh, we think our idea is right and they [the clients] don't see it and they're making it worse." That's every day, all the time, the most constant struggle at every single point in the process. And it can be really frustrating.

Professionals understood pro bono work against this background. As one creative put it, the frustration with most paying clients stood in sharp contrast to the way advertising professionals experienced pro bono work—as creatively liberating, perhaps cathartic. "It's not a burden," said one of the creatives who we interviewed about the long nights and weekends spent doing pro bono work. "It's more like you're actually exorcising your creative demons when sometimes you can't on a daily basis."

The opportunity to exorcise one's "creative demons," as two other interviewees also described it, was a structural issue. The following planner explained the seduction of pro bono campaigns in her work:

> From a creative perspective you get to do things that you're not... they're more pure from a creative standpoint.... It doesn't get muddied down with all these client mandatories [required aesthetic, rhetorical or tonal elements] or all these politics or all these things you have to deal with where the work gets diluted because the client thinks, "Oh, I'm a marketer and that's not the way it should [go]." You know, we're always struggling back and forth with our clients in terms of... like, they take a great idea and then they slowly push it to where it's mediocrity....
>
> Honestly, I mean, there's this climate that we're in now... CMOs [chief marketing officers, on the client side] look for new jobs every eighteen months. So, ...if you don't turn around sales, if you're hired and your brand is in the toilet and you don't turn around sales, or [if] you are bonused on this much percentage of increasing brand awareness or whatever, that is not good motivation toward driving you to do good work. Sometimes it can be .... [G]reat CMOs... trust the agency or they work in partnership with the agency, but a lot of them—out of fear—it's like, "No, no, no we gotta stick with this traditional thing, we need more shots of the products," you know? "We need more product shots..." [T]hey just end up making decisions that are based on "We gotta sell the product, we gotta sell the product."

This interviewee, like many others, actively tried to understand the client by putting herself in the client's shoes. Under constant pressure to increase sales and with extremely volatile careers, the client's marketing department pushed to have what it perceived as safe, effective campaigns. As another planner sympathetically put it, "They're in a difficult situation." While this planner admitted that these kinds of campaigns may actually have some of their desired effect and nudge sales upward—something that most interviewees denied vehemently—it meant that bold, sophisticated ideas were usually declined. Clients would rather have another unremarkable, flattering product image—which is not very exciting from a creative standpoint—and a small uptick in sales than an original, emotionally compelling, but riskier piece of work that may make more of an impact.

Moreover, as she mentions with "client mandatories," clients also need to think carefully about the brand's aesthetic precedents. Some colors and fonts, for example, are mandatory. Coca-Cola, for example, has its own visual language, a recognizable brand crafted over decades. Agency professionals are held to past decisions; clients often prescribe the mood that the brand should evoke, its visual and emotional identity. As advertising agencies and campaigns came and went, clients often felt like they needed to keep the brand's identity intact, very rarely opting for a major overhaul or "rebranding." In short, there were a lot of good reasons clients were conservative and why purely creative work was routinely muddied or compromised.

Against this background of ongoing frustration, pro bono work felt very different. For one, this was a matter of jurisdiction.[6] For all but the biggest nonprofits, advertising professionals do not need to contend with a client-side marketing department. Even when there is something like it (e.g., a large nonprofit's public relations arm), it is much rarer that such a department intervenes in the advertising professionals' work. What's more, a pro bono client allows professionals more freedom because a nonprofit does not have media dollars invested, and so has less to risk than a corporate client does. In essence, even a relatively ineffective campaign will not hurt a nonprofit. It may be disappointing, but it will be mostly harmless.

At a more basic level, in all but a few cases where nonprofits felt that the agency went too far and declined a campaign proposal, pro bono clients understood the terms of exchange. Julia Zeltzer, the founder and creative director of Hyperakt, a small "boutique" agency that describes itself "at the frontlines of social change," captured this point.[7] Describing a recent successful pro bono campaign that her agency led, Zeltzer explained:

> So, [the pro bono client] said, "Push the boundaries!'" They've given us the freedom, but after years of working with clients you kind of know where your freedom ends and you could push it as far as you can... [but] I felt that we pushed it pretty far. So, two ideas came up.... We presented two ideas. One was a beautiful but safe choice. Another one was more rough, unusual, weird... and that's the choice they ended up going with, which is great.

To be told by the client to "push the boundaries"—and to actually have the client stand by that invitation when the time comes to approve a campaign—is every creative's dream. While extolling such a campaign's advantages later on in the interview, Zeltzer noted, "If you have the time, why not? Why not continue polishing your craft and pushing your boundaries?"

Zeltzer's narrative is telling: it shows two facets of the terms of exchange. As we return to in chapter 5, managers curated pro bono work, selecting nonprofits open to "disruptive, bold" work. As one CEO put it, they needed to gauge whether the client would allow creatives to "flex their muscles." At the same time, the client needed to follow through. What made the above campaign so good, from the interviewee's perspective, is precisely that the client delivered on the promise of creative freedom. Faced with two options, the client opted for the one that was riskier and that the agency was more excited about implementing.

A final way that pro bono projects enable more fulfilling work is the very nature of the causes that nonprofits represent. As one planner quoted earlier argued, the difference between the kinds of products she usually sold and nonprofits' causes ran deep. After noting that the directive in paying accounts was "We gotta sell the product," she added:

> In a pro bono that's not really the case, right? Because that's not what you're selling. You're not selling the product per se. It's more selling an ideal or a value system or a service. You're tugging on . . . [I]t's inherently more emotional and so the work is inherently more emotional, and most creative people want to work on more emotionally based things than functionally based things. Because again it's not as satisfying to say, "Well, that coffee was 100 percent dry-roasted arabica beans and it's now only ninety-nine cents." That's not creative, but it might be good business.

While telling, the planner overstated her case. The advertising industry went through a major shift in the 1960s, when data-driven advertisements came to generally be seen as less effective than emotionally driven campaigns. Indeed, in the history of the industry's craft, this is often described as a crucial historical change.[8] The consequence is that arabica coffee beans are now usually advertised in highly emotional ways. Rather than price or measures of quality, campaigns routinely sell camaraderie or familial bliss. "Emotionally based" campaigns are the rule rather than the exception. On the flip side, pro bono campaigns are not altogether devoid of facts.

Nevertheless, the planner's narrative captures an important difference between campaigns. While emotional associations are prevalent in the industry, pro bono accounts come closer to providing a "pure" emotional experience. If one imagines a spectrum of advertising campaigns' emotionality, pro bono work tends to fall far on the emotional side of the spectrum. Working for the sick, the poor, and the orphaned is not only good because it foregrounds a moral cause that advertising professionals find important; it is also good because it lends itself to effective emotional appeals. Advertising professionals who are able to engage in such work have immediate, practical consequences for their work experience.

Even though creatives did not cherish any notion of themselves as pure artists, they often felt that creative labor necessitated some degree of emotional connection between themselves and the product. Consequently, many interviewees spoke about the pragmatic challenges associated with generating emotionally driven campaigns for some commercial products. One creative described it this way:

> In some ways advertising is an art of essentially taking a product and then having to come up with a philosophy for that product, a reason for that thing to exist, why they did those things. If you say, for example, Nike, you made a shoe about trying harder or just doing it or getting out there every single day. You have to create this mythos, right? That has to be invented in some way. That has to be manufactured.... That becomes a little bit more of an additional hurdle, because you have to basically come up with that, sorry for the term, that bullshit, in some ways. That's the art of creative bullshit. You have to marry that in some sort of a semitruthful way, or marry it so there's some kernel of truth—versus, in the case of a pro bono client, that philosophy, that's already embedded in what they do. That *is* them. That's their cause. You don't have to lie. There's no lie or things that you have to attach to a kernel of truth. They want to help refugees, for example. That's the philosophy. Go. Or, say, UNICEF, you believe in the sanctity of children's lives. Go. That's all you have to do. You have to figure out some way to make people care about the philosophy versus the two-step of "OK, I have to come up with X philosophy about Nike shoes and then figure out some way for people to buy into X philosophy of go out and Just Do It [i.e., Nike's campaign slogan and strategic positioning]."

Although many creatives we spoke with welcomed the challenge of generating a "philosophy" for a product like Nike and might not have described the process as involving deception, this creative's account does reveal the additional burden of responsibility that a creative team assumes in commercial advertising. Before generating creative content for the campaign itself, creatives had to generate "the kernel of truth" that would enable potential consumers to connect emotionally with the campaign's message. In contrast, the nature of the causes taken up in pro bono work spared creatives the moral work of coming up with "bullshit... in some sort of semitruthful way," or worse, having to "lie." But this was not only a moral matter: not only do pro bono projects remove the need to generate half-truths; they also afford easier pathways to present a compelling creative brief and are thus more conducive to emotionally moving work. As another creative told us, "It's easy to like a campaign that's doing good and there are so many issues that it opens the door for a lot of creativity."

Following the Labor Process

Studies of factory work often begin with the division of labor. In premodern times, so we're told, artisans created a world of objects by dint of personal activity, making the product from beginning to end. Although they often needed to buy the materials for whatever they were making, they took the raw materials and personally crafted them into finished products that they then exchanged on the market at a piece rate. While it was still an exploitative system, the work that these individuals did remained a part of who they were.[9] The product and work did not immediately belong to another, and so represented no loss of self. It was not "alienated" from one's being.

The emergence of capitalism changed all that. The new system of production cut up labor into little roles and parts. The prophet of classical economics, Adam Smith, started *The Wealth of Nations* with a well-known paean to the virtues of dividing pin production into many discrete tasks, allowing factory workers to produce an overflowing abundance of pins. Divided action and the deskilling of labor were some of the hallmarks of the rise of industrial capitalism.[10] It was a division of labor so complete that it turned—and sometimes still turns—work into monotonous physical movement. Yet if all workers did was turn screws all day, would the finished products be "theirs" in any way? If the task becomes a repetitive movement that any laborer can reproduce, will it have any deep relation to the specific worker? If people are creating animals, do such work arrangements strip them of their humanity?

At first glance, these labor processes seem to bear little relationship to the work of advertising professionals. Whereas the loss of creativity is clearly relevant for those who do routinized manual tasks, the division of labor and the alienation it brings feel more distant in a creative, white-collar profession. Yet as in other creative industries operating at the interstices of art and commerce, the division of labor has made an important imprint on advertising. Especially in larger advertising firms, but also across the industry, organizations divide the labor of advertising into discrete parts.

As we noted in the introduction, the interviewees in this book are managers, creatives, planners, and account managers. These roles, however, have not always existed as they do today. In the industry's earlier days, there was a key division between account managers—businesspeople who worked closely with the clients and whose job it was to represent the client's interests in the agency—and the "creatives," whose job it was to create the advertisement's textual and visual language. In both advertising circles and popular culture, this was most commonly thought of as the distinction between "suits" and "creatives."

In past decades, this division was further divided. First, the role of creative was split into "copywriter" and "art director," one in charge of the text and the other working on the visual elements.[11] A second rift, beginning in the United Kingdom in the late 1960s and disseminating to the United States in the 1980s, was the creation of "planning" departments and the role of planners (or "strategists") in the advertising world. These professionals were brought in to serve as local experts and researchers. Their job was to conduct primary research, review secondary research, and come up with general strategic guidance for the campaign, which they then gave the creative teams to "execute" in whatever way they saw fit.[12] The process was coordinated among different departments responsible for different stages. Moreover, as advertising work moved to television commercials, it generated another division: conceptualizing the advertisement's creative blueprint versus building it. As advertising professionals know well, some of the most important decisions happen at the moment of production, whether in casting, photography, or directors' work on set.

In short, especially in midsize and larger companies, advertising work has been cut into pieces, Taylorized into discrete parts. With the diversification of advertising in the digital age, agency departments may now also include design, search optimization, social media, and user experience alongside account management, creative, planning, and production. In commercial projects, those who worked to win an account were usually not the same as those who would devise, design, or produce it if the agency won the account. And those who worked on the account usually had narrowly demarcated roles. While advertising professionals' work is far from the routinized motions in a pin factory, what they create sometimes feels only distantly theirs, as it does for workers in less creative trades.

Here, pro bono work was once again different. Because interviewees told us that pro bono accounts were staffed with a skeleton crew of professionals often working on their own time, people on the account would usually follow the campaign from its inception to its production—crossing jurisdictional boundaries and breaking the conventional division of labor. As one creative put it, one of the benefits of pro bono work is that it allows her to experiment with other job tasks and professional positions, "wearing hats that we don't usually wear."

This was most visible in the case of creatives, who often talked about two important kinds of professional opportunities for jurisdictional forays: performing planning work or executing production. To return to the comments by Menno, the creative executive who led the Water Is Life campaign at the start of the book:

> Sometimes advertising agencies are in the business of selling the process, do you know what I mean? ... It's like the bigger machine in the process [is there] also because the client wants that, right? And the strategy sessions ... and so we cut out all that fat when it comes to, like, just creative work with charities and pro bono.... The creatives come up and figure out what the strategy is, and they figure out what they want to focus on, and they do their own research, and they figure out what the messaging is rather than having a bigger machine around.

What Menno alludes to is a common jurisdictional battle waged between planners and the creatives who specify and execute their strategic ideas. While the relationship often runs smoothly, and planners take care to present ideas that are general enough for the creative team to make its mark, at times creatives feel they are being forced to execute somebody else's vision. This friction may seem especially notable because planning is a relatively new profession that has encroached on creatives' occupational territory. In Iddo's ethnographic fieldwork, he witnessed many moments when creatives pushed back—either saying that the planner's idea was too specific and interfered with the work or complaining that they couldn't work with the strategy the planners suggested. Pro bono projects allowed creatives like Menno and his team to assume the role that he felt should have been creatives' domain all along—he delighted at the chance to "cut out all that fat."

But there was more to it than the ability to finally craft strategy. Further downstream, creatives also got to take part in the production process—to realize their vision in a way that they seldom could. Talking about the Water Is Life campaign, Menno and his coworkers, Sam and Frank, all independently gushed about how they had to learn to hold the camera and do the lighting when they went to Haiti to shoot the ad for First World Problems. As Frank tells it, when they got the green light from the agency to produce the video, the three just "grabbed some beers that weekend and made the film."

It was a "war story" of sorts, a way to construct the campaign as a personal struggle that highlighted the team's tenacity and ingenuity. Scrappy though the team was, they drank beers to steady their nerves and undertook an immense task, emerging victorious. But more than just a narrative of personal ingenuity, this war story also celebrated the team's chance to take on unfamiliar roles as part of the production. This feature of pro bono projects was echoed in many of our interviews with creatives.[13] One creative talked about this as "the opportunity to expand yourself." Gretchen, an art director who worked on a fashion show that acted as a fundraiser for unhoused youth, noted that she got to do parts of the creative process that she didn't usually perform, like hire the production team and participate in the actual production process:

> I got to handpick a photographer and the director that I wanted to work with to make the video and the photography. . . . So, I took him for drinks and I said "I want to do this thing and I want you to shoot it, would you come and shoot it? Or can we come to you? Or, you know, here is my vision . . ." And he just ran with it. . . . I couldn't even finish the concept thing and he was like, "I love it! I want to do it!" . . . From a creative standpoint, I got my first choice, cream-of-the-crop perfect person to shoot this. Which makes the work so great. And then I got to direct a little bit and write a little bit . . . in addition to the art direction that I do on a day-to-day [basis,] which I love. . . . I really got to dig into [it]. I didn't have a copywriter until the very end to write some of the ad stuff. So, that was really fun and exciting.

The ability to take on new aspects of the work came up most prominently in creatives' narratives. Managers, after all, preferred lean, small teams to lead pro bono accounts; they always included creatives on these accounts, whereas account executives, planners, and production staff were often deemed unnecessary. Still, talk of other responsibilities and porous jurisdictional boundaries also emerged in interviews with both planners and account managers, who spoke about rare opportunities to have input into the creative process. In the case of Barton Graf's Climate Name Change campaign, one account manager who was deeply involved in the campaign talked about how she enjoyed the creative process:

> It wasn't why I went there [to Barton Graf] by any means, but once I got there and started talking to creatives about things they were interested

in doing, it was very quickly apparent that "Oh, I could be involved in this…" And it's not like they were out doing things for these causes already. No one was volunteering for anything. It was just more: this is something that I really care about, and my job is creating a form of art out in the world.

What was striking in the account manager's reply may not be immediately obvious: account managers almost never depicted their job as creating an art form. What the engagement with pro bono work allowed this account manager to do was talk about her job much in the same way that creatives often do. Since she was so engaged in the process, she was "creating a form of art" rather than acting as a liaison between the client and those who create the art.

Returning to the division of labor, while we may be less convinced than Marx that people are as crucially defined by what they make, it is clear that the more that advertising professionals could follow the project from its inception to its completion, the more they felt that it was theirs. Talking about how he saw the role of creatives in pro bono accounts more generally, Menno summarized:

> Creatives on pro bono assignments take on a bigger chunk of it. [We will do] the planning, we will do the account management…. But sometimes we take on stuff from production so it becomes more personal. So, if the project becomes more personal and then something great comes out of it and then the world sees it and then the world goes like, "Oh my God, this was great!" … Is it an ego boost? Is it just more satisfying? It's more satisfying than when it comes out [in regular client work], because when it's a big-money production for a client, you are a small percentage of the overall thing.

As we will return to in the next chapter, following the entire pro bono process is so seductive in part because "the world of advertising" can see that the work is theirs and identify them with its success. But the satisfaction of pro bono work *qua* work in interviewees'—and especially creatives'—narratives cannot be reduced to recognition. Simply put, the work defined them because it was theirs in a way that other work simply was not.

Working Relationships

So far, we have analyzed how interviewees talked about their work in terms of the relationship between advertising professionals and the campaign itself—what they produced and the internal division of labor. Yet this leaves out a crucial aspect shaping the work: the person for whom work was directly being done, the nonprofit client.

The client always loomed large in advertising professionals' narratives and ongoing concerns. This was especially true for planners and account managers, who faced the clients more often than creatives did. The difference between good and bad clients was immediate and crucial for the everyday work experience. At a minimum, it was here that pro bono's countergift of unalienated labor was most pronounced. Julie, a planner at a midsize agency, explained that client relations were a crucial factor in the draw of pro bono campaigns. For Julie, advertising work was "a rollercoaster of feelings":

> Sometimes the job is not so great. The clients are not always open, and they're not appreciative. There's a level of—*abuse* is not the right word, but it can be very tough on certain days.... [Yet in pro bono campaign work] it just makes me feel a little bit more useful. I feel clients are mostly grateful, or gracious, and appreciative. On a day-to-day [basis] you don't always feel that way, so some of it is because I feel I need emotional fulfillment. When I go to these clients they're really engaged and excited—they're just lovely.

Or, as another planner put it:

> No matter what we do for them, even if it's a quick two-minute turnaround because it's a rush job, at the end of the fire drill they're like, "This is phenomenal. Thank you guys so much. We know we made you hustle and pulled you off of the two other assignments that we actually had you working on, but this is a huge help." So, having clients who are like that, who show their thanks, and [this nonprofit] did... they loved the work that we were doing and were happy with everything. It makes those super-hard days a lot more bearable because you don't feel like you're just slaving over the work, and it's not going anywhere.

In other words, the countergift's most basic currency was gratitude. Our interviewees talked about how grateful and "simply wonderful" most pro bono clients were. On the flip side, they were highly dismissive—even outraged—in rare instances in which clients failed to honor this aspect of the exchange.

A pro bono client's failure to appreciate the work can even derail a project. Much like the "easy no" case at the start of the chapter, when pro bono clients failed to honor their end of the bargain, the agency sometimes declined or even "walked away" from a project. One such case involved a pro bono account that an agency was initially excited to work on. It was for a good cause and the nonprofit's head was "a fairly high-profile... charity worker. And she was thought to be really up and coming, and getting like MacArthur grants and stuff like that." It seemed like an interesting opportunity to do "good work" in multiple registers. And yet as the work commenced, it quickly became clear that the relationship would be different from what the agency had envisaged:

> When I actually got involved with everything, I realized that she [the nonprofit's president] really wasn't engaged with what we were doing. She was delegating to a consultant — a strategic consultant — and that consultant was trying to tell us what to do, and it became one of those weird situations.... [N]umber one, the person that we're trying to say is the huge value for us actually isn't that interested in working with us. She's concentrating on her charity, and on the promotion of it. Fine. But number two, this consultant person, who you start to realize in the ecosystem of pro bonos — and that was something that I was actually spending a lot of time learning — there's a lot of people who work in it, and I think, some of varying level of skill... let's just put it that way, passion versus skill....
>
> We had a couple of awkward conversations where [the consultant] was, "Here's what you need to do." And I was like, "You know, with all due respect, I don't need you to tell me what I need to do, because, number one, ...we are offering our time, you know? And number two, we kind of do know what's better." So, that was a weird situation where I'm like, "There's no way that we're gonna bang our heads against the wall to try and get through this consultant, because it doesn't make any sense."

Rather than engaging the agency directly, the nonprofit hired a consultant, which introduced an additional organizational layer between it and the advertising agency. Much like in paying clients' marketing departments, this consultant had her own vision of the work and ideas about how it should be done. On one level, this is a betrayal of both gratitude and creativity; advertising professionals were being told what to do by someone they felt was unqualified. They felt that they were both better than the consultant, and they were "offering" their time — which meant that dealing with the consultant was especially onerous.

Reading this case carefully, however, the betrayal was not only a matter of reneging on the promise of creativity or a particular consultant's incompetence. It was also that the client who the agency was excited to work with didn't engage with the work. Instead, she spent her time focused on other aspects of her nonprofit. But why is this narrated as a betrayal? After all, paying clients' upper echelons very rarely interact with agency professionals.

To understand this part of the planner's sense of outrage, we need to focus on the relationship's very definition. Like gift exchanges in other contexts, the gift of pro bono work often changed actors' relational definitions. Beyond clients' gratitude, interviewees consistently depicted work with a pro bono client as a partnership. Rather than working *for* a client, advertising professionals felt that they worked *with* the pro bono client. The problem in this situation was not simply that the client was a bad one but that she remained strictly a client.

This same issue can be seen in the way that our interviewees discussed successful pro bono work. One example is how Evan Vogel, the CEO of a small boutique agency called Night Agency, described his work for Keep a Child Alive, a nonprofit that provides affordable access to HIV drugs and medical care across Africa. After discussing the campaign and the nonprofit's mission, Evan talked about working with the nonprofit's CEO:

> She's just a force . . . she's a creative activist. She's a part of the fabric of . . . every single one of these ideas and campaigns, and it's not like [she's just] supportive, but she's contributing to the ideas. . . . You know, I think that would be the way we would love for all of our client relationships to be — less agency-client. Because the way the best work gets done [is when] you're in full partnership. . . . And we believe more so than ever, especially with the environment as it is today, that if you can treat your client and agency as partners, then you're going to find that you're going to be so much more successful in terms of your creative endeavors versus "my team versus your team," which sometimes is the case.

As Evan made clear, the ideal of advertising work as a partnership spilled over beyond pro bono work. At least during interviews, it often seemed like a more general ideal. For most commercial clients — even "good" clients — such an ideal remained a pipe dream. Indeed, given that advertising professionals also wanted to have their riskiest ideas approved and their expertise carefully respected, we may wonder whether a real partnership would have been desirable were it possible. Nevertheless, Evan's ideal pro bono collaboration entailed an active client both partnering in the work and being amenable to the agency's ideas.

This became more apparent when interviewees spelled out exactly what such partnerships entailed. In an interview with a boutique agency's CEO, she talked about a current nonprofit account that she was particularly excited about and thought was a good example of successful pro bono work. Describing the work, she fondly joked about how the nonprofit often apologized for any requests, then added that they were wonderful clients:

> [In] nonprofits, everyone is super-emotional, everyone gives a huge shit whether things go right. But I think it's all just resulted in us getting a lot of context and information we wouldn't have otherwise had because people care, and they'll take the time to write you that ten-paragraph email, which in some cases is annoying but, in a nonprofit, it can just be really helpful because you can get a lot out of that.

While the ideal pro bono account was thus a partnership, it was a partnership of a particular sort. It was one in which the moral project became shared and agency professionals felt that they were truly an appreciated part of the nonprofit's mission and work. In other words, it was a partnership that allowed professionals to feel the moral agency we depicted in the previous chapter. As such, the planners and creatives we talked to emphasized long conversations they had with their clients and how the clients shared information about pro bono cases. At the same time, it was a partnership that gave them freedom to produce their work instead of constraining them, to work without clients' attempting to push their own creative or strategic agenda.

The gift's reciprocity also cemented relationships over time. Indeed, the difference between market exchange and a gift is partly the gift's anticipated temporality. While the market operates in well-defined rhythms, the gift has an element of indeterminacy. A gift is a constitutive "element in a relationship";[14] as the client transformed into a partner, the relationship's temporality often became less defined. Once again, the Water Is Life campaign is instructive. The creative team who worked on the campaign continued to work with the same organization, taking the client with the team as they moved together between three different agencies. As we talked about the different campaigns, the creatives Menno, Sam, and Frank often seemed puzzled by how long they had been at it. Menno reflected:

> It's tough to pull these projects off. Whether it's paid or pro bono or client, whatever, it's always tough. But at the same time, I don't know... Water Is Life we've been doing for a long, long time and then every time when

we are through it's like, "Oh, that was a tough one." But then a month later we go, "Oh, we should do another. This was actually kinda fun when you think back."... Because we try to do something different every time, it just keeps it interesting, keeps it engaging.... [O]ur Water Is Life client [Kristine Bender, executive director].... It's like you're stuck.... [I]t's hard to say no to her because she is a super-brave individual.

It was important for Menno to be able to do interesting creative work, as it was to enjoy the work in the ways we have outlined throughout the chapter. Yet even as each time the team did another campaign they vowed it would be their last, their relationship to the executive director kept pulling them back in. As Frank noted in an interview: "I'm still texting with Kristine all the time." Agencies had long-term engagements and complex gift relationships with commercial clients too,[15] and many relationships with pro bono clients did end after one campaign. Still, ending a pro bono project was difficult precisely because the gift exchange turned the engagement into a partnership, stretching it in time.

Conclusions

Pro bono work is philanthropy of sorts—an unreciprocated, free gift in which one party receives the goods and the other seems to receive nothing but moral satisfaction. But to think in those terms is to consider the exchange only as one between advertising professionals and the ultimate beneficiaries of the worthy causes they worked on. This was, of course, how advertising professionals talked when they gave purified accounts in media interviews; it maps onto a major pillar of the official discourse of corporate social responsibility. And yet as advertising professionals were the first to note in our interviews, while this moral discourse did capture aspects of pro bono work, it gave only a partial view. Once we attend more closely to the relationship between the nonprofit and the advertising professionals, we discover new terrain. From this perspective, it is more fruitful to see the work as a set of reciprocal gift exchanges.[16]

As we have shown, work on pro bono campaigns tended to be work that professionals found compelling *qua* work. While advertising professionals supplied their labor, they also received the opportunity to engage in a form of work that was theirs in a way that most work for paying clients simply wasn't—it was a gift of unalienated labor. Given the unwritten terms of exchange and the lack of monetary investment, nonprofits allowed agencies to be bolder in their work, accepting most of the ideas they presented, with few exceptions. Further, because the work was usually done on a shoestring budget and with skeleton crews, advertising professionals often found that they followed the campaign through the labor process, performing tasks that were ordinarily divided among different positions and jurisdictions in the agency. Last, because of the clients' debt of gratitude and because the pro bono causes usually lent themselves to emotionally driven campaigns, professionals felt as if they were working with an ideal partner rather than a client. Taken together, pro bono campaigns allowed advertising professionals to feel that the work was conceptually theirs, theirs in terms of the work process and theirs in terms of feeling like they were not working *for* a client but *with* them.

These gifts, like all gifts, were somewhat ambiguous. While they were anticipated and expected, projects could always go awry. Nonprofits sometimes operated like corporate clients or tried to have a strong voice in creative decisions. It is telling that, when these breakdowns of the gift exchange occurred, especially around work relations and questions of creativity, interviewees were outraged. Something deep in the fabric of reciprocity had broken down.

This chapter delved into the structure of the work itself. Rather than taking the intersituational self as the level of analysis, as a moral discourse presumes, this chapter focused on how advertising professionals experienced their specific labor process. In a sense, it was an occupational analysis, to the extent that occupation refers to people's patterned relationship to the specific kind of labor that they do. Still, such an analysis overlooks an important part of pro bono work and work more generally: the significant professional audiences that the work is aimed at beyond the client or the diffuse public. This requires us to shift our analytic lenses once more, this time toward the occupational *field* in which advertising professionals are embedded and the way that goods in the field are distributed.

4. The Elephant in the Field: Awards and Recognition

In 2018, just as we began writing this book, the Cannes Lions International Festival of Creativity, the most important advertising awards festival in the world, was making some changes. First, entry fees for award submissions were slashed. With revenue growth slowing in the advertising industry, some agencies had begun to complain about how expensive it was to submit work to the competition and send their employees to southern France, questioning whether the price tag was worth it.

Beyond cutting fees, there were structural changes to the awards themselves: the festival's award categories were reorganized and expanded. The new system placed awards into nine tracks. In addition to tracks such as Craft, Reach, and Impact was a new award track: Cannes for Good. This track contained two awards: Lions for Change and Sustainable Development Goals Lions.

But how did restructuring award tracks and categories fit into changes that were largely driven by questions of cost? And why did the Cannes festival add a new track that specified the "good"? As we have come to see, these changes were intertwined. For, exacerbating the tension endemic to advertising between the industry's business goals and its artistic acumen was a curious fact: a disproportionate number of Cannes Lions seemed to be awarded to pro bono campaigns. Murmurs about this perceived imbalance, which had already been prevalent for a while, became more pronounced after the 2015 awards, when some advertising professionals noted that pro bono projects appeared to dominate every single competition.

Ad Age, one of the two main advertising trade journals, cited some complaints from the industry's clients who were always skeptical of awards given by advertising industry insiders to fellow insiders. Especially given the costs of attending various award festivals, they felt that the event would be better if it focused on paying clients' concerns. Advertising agencies "have to acknowledge," mused one executive from Coca-Cola, "that their clients are more than ever concerned about driving revenues and profits." The disproportionate number of awards given to pro bono campaigns encapsulated this disconnect. "I wonder," he added, "if the results would be different if the jurors were all CEOs, or if the success criteria for the campaigns were economic value generated for the respective brands."[1] Not only was the festival exorbitantly expensive; it was also, from his perspective, awarding the wrong things.

Some advertising professionals shared this unease about pro bono work's apparent dominance at the awards festival, if for different reasons. Whereas client-side professionals like this Coca-Cola executive felt slighted by the consecration of work that had little commercial value, some advertising professionals saw pro bono work as "low-hanging fruit." The same article in *Ad Age* also quoted the chief creative officer of DDBO Worldwide—one of the most respected and awarded advertising agencies in the world—who noted that it was creatively easier to win awards with pro bono work, since it is "usually a very single, simple problem that needed to be solved as opposed to a complex, tiered business issue."[2] From his perspective, the problem wasn't that awarding pro bono campaigns was awarding the wrong kind of thing, but that there was something too easy about the definition of such work.

The Cannes Festival went on the defensive and tried to explicitly deny the charge in a news story written up by *Ad Age*: "'There is a misconception that lots of charity work wins awards,' a Cannes spokeswoman said, but added that it's a growing issue and one under review. 'Not-for-profit work historically has won about 10% of Lions,' she said. An anomalous rise to 22% in 2015 was followed by only 6% last year."[3] Yet even winning 10 percent of the awards meant that pro bono was overrepresented at Cannes. With pro bono work accounting for somewhere between 2 percent and 5 percent of agencies' work, even a conservative estimate would suggest that pro bono work was two to five times more likely to win an award than commercial campaigns were.

Under pressure from clients and some creatives in the advertising world, the Cannes Festival reorganized its awards. Instead of being able to send pro bono work to any category, pro bono campaigns could now be sent only to the designated track that honored such "charity" work, clearly differentiating pro bono and paid client work. After the reorganization, Cannes asserted that "all charity and non-profit work is judged separately from brand-led work during the festival."[4]

This episode hints at a number of themes and analytical puzzles. First, it locates pro bono work in the broader tension between advertising as creative work and advertising as business endeavor. Second, it highlights the close affinity between awards and pro bono work. Third, it provides a glimpse into some of the ambivalence that people in the advertising world feel toward pro bono work. But to understand the relationship between pro bono work and awards, we need to first understand the general place of awards in the advertising industry. Even if pro bono work wins awards, why does it matter? Why are *Ad Age, Adweek,* and Coca-Cola executives keeping track of the proportion of awards won by pro bono campaigns?

The simplest answer is that awards are important in the world of advertising; they loom large in the advertising professional's imagination. Pictures from southern France, posted by those lucky and successful enough to make it to Cannes, inevitably appear on Instagram and Facebook feeds in the early summer, serving as much more than tokens of a luxurious vacation. Even if academics, for example, like their awards well enough, they do not usually make or break professional lives. They are a form of validation that imparts status, legitimacy, and recognition. Yet except for the consecration bestowed by major awards like the Nobel Prize or the Fields Medal, academic awards are not the main way that reputations are structured and status allocated. In advertising, however, awards are arguably the industry's most important means of meting out recognition and designating worth. Alongside Cannes Lions is a host of other awards, including the Clio Awards, which mark "creativity and innovation in advertising, design and communication"; the Effie Awards, which reward "effectiveness in marketing"; and D&AD Pencils, which distinguish superior "design and art direction." Many of the offices where we conducted interviews featured trophies in central places: Cannes' winged Lions, D&AD Pencils, and emaciated Clio muses lined the shelves. As talk of morality or unalienated labor emerged during interviews, these trophies seemed to grow increasingly conspicuous.

This chapter looks at the way that awards figure into how agencies and professionals think about their work. In that sense, it shifts the analytical lens from self and labor to the level of the advertising field writ large. Doing so, it examines how pro bono work operates within a larger professional world where actors vie for centrality in a shared arena and how such work figures into the calculus of recognition and status that defines fields. First, by taking a step back from pro bono work, it traces how awards developed in the advertising world, as well as how organizational and individual actors engage with awards. Returning to pro bono work, then, the chapter shows how work on such projects sharpens some of the contradictory ways that awards play into the advertising field. Awards garnered by pro bono work act as a vehicle of recognition and consecration while also delivering its profane correlate: salaries and careers. In one sense, interviewees identified this as an unproblematic relationship: pro bono projects produced good work—in that the campaigns were often morally impactful, emotionally moving, and creatively bold—and such good work would then be recognized by others in the field. Yet we show that advertising professionals sometimes saw the obvious relationship between awards and recognition as a little shameful. Uncomfortably situated next to the notion that pro bono work is driven by a desire to do a moral good for its own sake, the promise of prestige and promotion seemed to imply that actors were self-interested, setting up a tension that advertising professionals needed to work through.

Awards in the Field of Advertising

Awards are a mode of consecrating actors within a field. That is, they are ways of recognizing and conferring both status and field-specific "symbolic capital" on actors.[5] In this sense, advertising is not too different from other creative occupations, where awards are also important. After all, Cannes' most famous awards festival is not the advertising festival but the eponymous film festival.

However, advertising's particular structural location makes awards more important in this industry than in many others for two complementary reasons. First, in an effort to establish itself as an occupation, advertising entrepreneurs brought in jury-based competitions of worth. Awards were therefore an official avenue for displaying the discipline's creative aspirations. Yet awards were also established to build agencies' reputations in the eyes of potential consumers. In other words, awards were a commercial activity designed to increase agencies' visibility in a situation where evaluating advertising's ability to drive sales was somewhat questionable. Propelled by these two dynamics, awards spread rapidly, in terms of both significance and sheer number. Beyond the international awards that this chapter focuses on, there are hundreds of smaller national and regional awards throughout the world.

While there were earlier advertising competitions on a local level, the oldest ongoing jury-selected annual award was the Art Directors Club Award, established in 1921 to explicitly "dignify the field of business art in the eyes of artists" and convey that "artistic excellence is vitally necessary to successful advertising."[6] Conceived by one of America's advertising pioneers to highlight art directors' role in advertisement, both the *New York Times*, which ran a story on the 1921 exhibition as part of an arts column, and the organizer of the awards and exhibition himself

FIGURE 4. The New York Festivals Advertising Awards reception, 2017. Photo by Marc Bryan-Brown. Courtesy of the NYFA.

compared the sad state of American advertising to that of France, where the ubiquity of modernist art nouveau and art deco seemed to attest to advertising's location within the realm of the arts.[7]

Awards ceremonies have since continued to emphasize advertising's association with the world of art. In the award competitions founded in the 1950s—among them the Cannes Lions Festival, the Clio Awards, and the New York Festivals Advertising Awards—the aesthetics and symbolism were far from subtle. The Clio award is named after the Greek muse of history, the proclaimer of grand deeds. Cannes' physical prize is the Venetian Lion of Saint Mark, imbuing it with European sophistication. Like the Art Directors Club Awards, these ceremonies sought at least in part to legitimize their craft as an art form. Indeed, the emulation of fine art is still evident in the ways that prizes are framed as awards for creativity and the embodied experience of award shows. Advertising stills are sometimes arranged in a gallery layout, with attendees ambling slowly, wine glasses in hand, past images of winning campaigns.[8]

Advertising's relationship to art is also reflected in jury composition. While most competitions do not have artists as jurors, juries for awards such as the Clio and Cannes are dominated by creative figures from within the advertising field: senior art directors, planners, and CEOs of well-known agencies.[9] As the Clio's website put it when describing their juror selection process, "Clio selects individuals whose own creative work epitomizes the best of their respective fields, ensuring that each juror has an in-depth understanding of the industry's evolving marketplace."[10] Similarly, the Cannes website noted, "Our Jury Presidents are pivotal in this process, themselves having demonstrated their creative credentials in guiding teams, organisations and brands to set exemplary standards."[11] Just as wealthy collectors are not usually chosen as jurors for major art awards, advertising awards signal their field purity through jury composition.

If anything, awards have become more important to recognizing creativity in advertising than in other fields. As opposed to visual arts and literature, the advertising field *qua* creative field (rather than commercial endeavor) has fewer alternative modes of artistic consecration such as gallery shows or museum exhibitions. Unlike literary awards, for example, advertising professionals cannot trade the refusal of awards for status. There can be no advertising Jean-Paul Sartre, who scathingly declined a Nobel Prize, or the early writers who won the Man Booker Prize only to pummel the award and its provenance in their acceptance speeches — paradoxically imbuing it with legitimacy through these displays of repulsion.[12] In terms of creativity, awards are the sole mode of official consecration.

Yet this is only part of the story. While advertising awards were modeled on art awards and exhibitions, the field still could not be considered "pure art" — and never really wanted to be. This can be seen in the structure of awards. Advertising is a hybrid form. While some advertising professionals we interviewed were dismissive of awards and declined to submit their work for consideration, it was not because they thought that awards sullied art, but for precisely the opposite reason: for them, advertising should not be considered an art form to begin with. As the Coca-Cola executive we began the chapter with noted, things would look much different if more client-side corporate managers were represented on the jury.

This ambivalence can be seen in the history of the industry's awards festivals. While Cannes rewards creativity and is juried by industry insiders, it was also established to promote the industry to clients. Cannes' advertising award was established by British cinema and TV advertisers who wanted the same kind of legitimation — especially public recognition, including from potential clients — as the filmmakers who established the Cannes film festival a few years earlier.[13] In an even clearer example, the Effie Awards were established in 1968 precisely to reward perceived effectiveness rather than treating advertising as an artistic field.[14]

Much as the attempt to construct advertising as an art was a halting one, the institutionalization of awards to showcase advertising's effectiveness in the market was a response to ongoing ambivalence about advertising as a profession. In one of the first books laying out the new profession of advertising in the United States at the turn of the twentieth century, Calkins and Holden used seductive language to depict how the "profession of an advertising man steadily rose until now it aspires to rank with that of the three 'black graces'—law, medicine and divinity."[15] Only a few pages later, however, some cracks appear in that confidence: "Advertising, at present, is an Art... It has not yet reached its place as an exact science. There are many men who know how to play skillfully upon the prejudices, tastes, likes and habits of a nation; but there is not yet a man who can tell definitely how much publicity any given dollar will buy. Possibly, there never will be such a man."[16]

This ambivalence, with moments of elation followed by deep uncertainty, is a recurring theme in both the history and the present state of advertising. There is, on the one hand, a brash confidence that advertising molds the public's hearts and minds. This is the world of the "hidden persuaders" that Vance Packard wrote about in the 1950s, when advertising was emboldened by its brush with World War II propaganda and depth psychology.[17] On the other hand, the uncomfortable realization that it is still very hard to prove that advertising increases sales has been a gnawing uncertainty at the heart of the profession.[18] As we return to in a later chapter, while this has partly changed since the advent of web advertising and the possibilities for consumer tracking that it engenders, this is only a partial advance. Uncertainty still weighs heavily on anyone who makes claims about the effects of advertising.

Given such a situation, awards have another property. While acting as a way of allocating recognition to other insiders, they are also a way to signal to clients—both existing and potential—that advertising works. In this capacity, awards are "a surrogate for agency performance."[19] Bringing these two paths together, the limited research on awards in advertising shows that agencies send work to award competitions for two reasons. First, a survey of agency managers in the 1980s found that the item they most agreed on was that winning awards made it easier to recruit creative talent and improved morale within the agency.[20] Second, even if some managers were unsure whether awards would actually help them secure future clients, such potential promise was still one of the most common reasons they entered work in award competitions in the first place.[21]

In short, then, advertising awards simultaneously act in two ways. As a vehicle of recognition, they confer symbolic capital within the field. Yet awards are also a signaling mechanism oriented toward clients who value a different definition of good work: high return on investment for their advertising dollars.

Awards and Pro Bono Work: Between Organizations and Individuals

With awards playing such an important role in the field of advertising, pro bono work is both ideally located to receive them and magnifies some of the dynamics that make awards so central. Throughout the interviews, we found that interviewees—both those who celebrated pro bono work and those who lamented it—maintained that pro bono work won a disproportionate number of awards and that the awards were an important reason professionals did such work in the first place. One New York agency made it all but official: while employees usually filled in their worksheets with the client account number, pro bono campaigns were designated by an "awards number"—a constant reminder that pro bono work was the best chance of winning coveted awards.

To better understand how pro bono work plays into the dynamics of awards, it is useful to make a further distinction: to whom are awards given? At first blush, the answer is straightforward. Major industry awards invariably go to the agency that has produced the campaign.[22] After all, the agency contracts the work, and campaigns often receive input from a large number of professionals within the agency over the project's life. Especially for clients, the agency is the relevant actor rather than any particular professional. In this sense, actors in the field of advertising were organizations, not individuals.

At the same time, agencies are often quite large. Even if some of the recognition for awards falls to the organization as a whole, it is specific—and highly mobile—professionals within the agency who craft award-winning campaigns. Thus, while the Cannes or the Clios publish only the winning agency's name, advertising professionals' trade publications such as *Adweek* or *Ad Age* also publish the names of the key advertising professionals who worked on the campaign—the creatives, art directors, planners, and account managers who were primarily responsible for the campaign. Moreover, individuals are acknowledged even within the context of award ceremonies; while awards are presented to the agency, the agency usually sends the people who worked on the campaign to collect the physical trophies. Thus, while the agency as a whole takes credit for a campaign, recognition is also afforded to specific actors within the agency who were understood to have been responsible for the work.

This distinction matters. Awards operate differently for individual and organizational actors, and pro bono campaigns play into these consider-ations in slightly different ways. For organizational actors, awards act as an index of worth for two primary audiences. First, echoing advertising research, garnering awards is seen as a way to signal to potential clients that the agency is successful. This is especially the case for smaller agen-cies. As Ellis Verdi, one of the founders of DeVito/Verdi, a relatively small agency, explained, "I mean, when you win awards... sometimes [it] is associated with winning business, right? More awards, you bring more business here, you can potentially get those people impressed. 'Oh, you're an award-winning agency?'"[23]

In this context, pro bono work provides an opening for smaller agen-cies to produce work they may not have been able to land with paid clients. One account manager in a midsize agency captured this when he talked about why agencies, including the one he worked in at the time, take on pro bono accounts:

> The biggest thing that can happen to a small agency is that they win some gigantic award, and that's more likely to happen [with pro bono work]. If you're a small agency, you sign whatever clients you can, and some of them are different, some of them have creative prestige early on... but a lot of times you're dealing with smaller, more local products.... [So] if you get a good nonprofit and win some awards with that...

Working with smaller clients and local brands, who many interviewees perceived as conservative in terms of the work they would approve, small agencies could leverage pro bono work to put themselves on the map. Since work on pro bono accounts was done on a shoestring budget, agencies also used such accounts to showcase what they could do with very little, with the implicit promise that with a larger budget they could do so much more.

These considerations are mostly relevant for less-established agen-cies, but others are more universally acknowledged. Thus, perhaps more important, awards are seen as a recruitment mechanism for advertising professionals — something we return to in the next chapter. In this capac-ity, awards signal both the prestige that potential employees can accrue by working in an "award-winning agency" and the interesting work they may be able to do. Awards, then, are the icing on the cake of a good job at a good agency.

But thinking in these terms, we have to move from the consecration of organizations to the consecration of individual actors — to the profession-als who crafted the campaigns. Here, the client is by and large irrelevant:

individualized consecration is aimed squarely at other professionals and agencies in the field. It is a way to garner recognition from one's peers, as well as from potential employers in other agencies. Importantly, it is something to put in your portfolio (traditionally called a "book," the advertising professional's version of the résumé).[24] One creative at Ogilvy laid this out when he listed the different reasons pro bono is so prominent in the advertising world:

> Whatever the opposite of cynical is, on that end you're doing good and it's creative and it's something that's worth doing—that's certainly a factor. But I think it's also equally a factor that a lot of creatives do it [pro bono] because, hell, . . . it gets a lot of press and it's good in a book. It's good in your portfolio, and if it gets enough recognition, that's your ticket to doing a lot of big-name projects later on and more money and more bonuses and essentially reputation, too. That's the ultimate currency that creatives look to get. . . . You get your name for free, pretty much, in the trades [trade journals] and agency blogs, and that's going to get you jobs later on at, ultimately, a higher pay scale.

Shifting between a cynical register and "whatever the opposite of cynical is," this creative noted that doing something worthy is all well and good, but at the most basic level, press or awards from pro bono work translate into career moves. For example, recall that the Water Is Life campaigns acted as an important step on the career ladder for the core team that worked on them. Frank, Sam, and Menno moved together from agency to agency as a team, mostly based on the awards and reputations they garnered on the campaigns. They also found themselves working on more interesting accounts at these agencies. If Frank complained that in his early days at DDB he was mostly "doing banners" for the internet, something that he didn't enjoy or find creatively satisfying, he never again did banners after the Water Is Life campaign's success. As he put it, "Everyone was kind of like 'All right, maybe you guys aren't best suited for banners. We can use you for something else.'"

As we show later on, managers often treat pro bono accounts as a training tool that allowed creatives and planners to expand their professional horizons, while creatives talk about pro bono work as enabling them to "tell a bigger story" than they usually did. The awards they won validated their work and allowed them to transition to bigger client accounts and more compelling campaigns. As one senior creative put it, "Especially if you're a younger creative person, they're going to really be given the opportunity to do something on a scale that's seen by people for a larger client. And the chance to tell a story about that brand or that particular thing."

In some cases, winning awards led to even broader payoffs. Oliver Maltby, a British-born executive creative director at Interbrand, credited the awards that he received (for both pro bono work and paying clients) with opening global opportunities to him:

> [Awards] highlight real talent in the industry: people actually thinking differently.... [And] they're a great way to... So, I've moved around the world a few times basically because I have awards. And that's part of the stipulation if you're looking for, say, an O[-I] visa. It's about your award by the industry. So, they have practical reasons, as well as being something nice to put on the mantelpiece.

Awards were a legible currency. The O-I visa, for example, is a US work visa given to "individuals with extraordinary ability or achievement." Awards served as a signal of achievement, transferable even beyond the world of advertising.

Last, whereas awards are always important, pro bono campaigns also imply a closer association between the professionals and the campaign they worked on. As we have already seen, pro bono work was usually done with reduced, ad hoc teams. Thus, the work was more legibly the team members', for both others within the agency and for actors across the field. John "Ozzy" Osborn, the American CEO of BBDO, highlighted project ownership as a good reason to take on pro bono work, especially at early career stages:

> If you have an opportunity when you're young in your career to grab a pro bono thing because other people are too busy or whatever, grab it! Because it might be a great opportunity to, with little oversight, develop in your own sandbox; something can be seeded and sprouted and be beautiful and amazing.

In short, the same reasons that make pro bono work compelling morally and as labor also make it a prime candidate for receiving awards. Managers and advertising professionals alike emphasized that they got to do work that was creatively interesting and in which they would be morally invested, while also underlining that the topics lent themselves to compelling, emotionally driven work. This work was then judged by advertising insiders who rewarded what they considered bold, interesting campaigns. Moreover, because of pro bono work's structure, awards' reputational and career outcomes were further heightened; small companies got to demonstrate their talents and small, dedicated pro bono teams within larger agencies didn't need to share the glory and recognition.

War Heroes without Wars: Awards and Work

So far, we have depicted the relationship between awards and the world of pro bono advertising as a happy meeting between field dynamics and a particular form of corporate social responsibility. Yet the fit between the discourse of awards, careers, and recognition and the grammars of morality and professionals' existential relation to their labor was not always so straightforward. When the Cannes festival came under fire for the preponderance of pro bono campaigns winning awards, some of the most vocal critics came from within the advertising world—rather than from the client side.

This is not to say that grammars did not become tangled, at least sometimes. Take the grammar of field recognition and professionals' relationship to their work. Awards, after all, were given for interesting, creative work. As one creative commented, he often strove to "elevate the creative to the caliber of winning an award." The award was simply recognition of "good work." A creative director further explained:

> It's something in our industry that propels careers forward and it's important, you know? It's a mark of good work. And so people are thinking about awards whether they're working on a pro bono piece, or whether they're working on any [other project].... I mean the best way to go about it—and when I'm trying to go about my career, I try to think of "What's the best idea? What's the best idea I can think of? What's the great work I can do?"—and then hope that in a year's time someone on a jury somewhere also thinks it's a great idea. So, I'm not really usually thinking about the awards while I'm concepting on an idea ... I'm just trying to think of the best idea I can.

In the ideal world this interview depicts, awards would flow naturally to great work—the field's consecration of work would seamlessly fit actors' experience of field-specific goods. The same sentiment emerged in the words of George Tannenbaum, an executive creative director leading the IBM account at Ogilvy and Mather who had also worked on a few pro bono accounts throughout his career:

> I think the best work. For instance, the thing that did so well last year from R/GA about "Love Has No Labels" ... I think that was good work,

period. And it happened to be for a good cause, and they know how to milk the award system better than anyone to their own benefit. I think they put a tremendous amount of time and care into everything they do, as most agencies do. So, I don't think there's any real difference in the best work.

Funded by the Ad Council, R/GA's campaign to encourage the public to question implicit bias and spread inclusion came up in other interviews as well. It was cited as a perfect example of pro bono work that hit the mark on all accounts: for a good cause, creatively impressive, and award winning.

But implicit in these accounts was a tension: while awards should flow to good work, for many campaigns "good work" and "award-winning work" were not synonymous. Some professionals we spoke with explained that advertising work was sometimes made more with an eye toward receiving awards than toward simply crafting good advertising. As Tannenbaum continued:

> I think that some of the award work is directed at a very small audience, is not practical, it "doesn't scale" in the parlance of today, and is, you know, for pro bono businesses that may or may not have existed before the awards show. It's kind of like the work is done before there's a client relationship even, and that's different than a pro bono account, where you get a proper assignment, proper brief, proper reviews. . . . Advertising in a stupid way is like writing a sonnet. You're supposed to have rules and regulations to stay within—I don't mean it's formulaic, but if it's really advertising, someone's paying to run it or someone's paying to do it. Otherwise it's not advertising, it's showing off. . . . I don't say it out loud to many people, because like I said at the start, the currency today is winning awards whether they're real or not. [But . . .] it's kind of like a war hero without a war.

Tannenbaum's point is that first coming up with an idea and then approaching a nonprofit client, as was the case in quite a few of the campaigns we have already outlined, subverts the rules of advertising.[25] It is easier to win awards since the work begins from a compelling creative idea and thus does not operate by the same rules of the game that other work in the industry needs to follow. Beautifully capturing the paradoxical quality of being consecrated for work that doesn't represent the field, Tannenbaum describes this as war heroes without wars, medals given for valor without a war being fought.

Our interviewees' perceptions of the tension between award-winning pro bono campaigns that just "showed off" and the rest of the work in the advertising industry also depended in part on an agency's location in the field. Smaller agencies explicitly yearned for awards (although some, perhaps conveniently, claimed that they didn't need awards since that wasn't what their work was all about). But those already located at the center of the field also had a complicated relationship to such consecration. For example, a manager who had worked at Wieden+Kennedy claimed that he wasn't enamored of awards:

> I think it's a little silly that we create our own awards for our industry when there's so much that goes into it that shouldn't be about awards, so that's my own thing. Again, that was a Wieden+Kennedy thing, even though at Wieden+Kennedy we won a ton of awards, it was never the goal. It just sort of happened. So, I take it with a grain of salt. As far as awards go, I think it's silly in our industry.

Of course, no one wins awards accidentally. Agencies must actively apply for awards, a process that is actually quite costly—both in terms of money and in terms of the time and effort it takes to prepare some submissions. Rather than take this excerpt as a statement of fact, therefore, it is more useful to read it in two ways. First, like the excerpts above, it hints at the relationship between work-for-awards and the more structured and constrained ongoing work of advertising. Simultaneously, despite the good-natured criticism of awards, the excerpt naturalizes how goods are allocated in the field. It is an expression of Wieden+Kennedy's (and by extension the interviewee's) central position in the field—evidenced both in awards and in major clients. Wieden+Kennedy counts Nike as a client and has been responsible for iconic Nike campaigns like Just Do It! From such a central position, with a cabinet full of awards as a background, awards were at once "silly" and abundant.

Awards and the Moral: Finessing the Background

The tensions between the discourse of awards and recognition and that of good work (*qua* labor) were less poignant than other tensions in interviewees' narratives. A sharper tension arose between the way that many interviewees talked about awards as a vehicle for career advancement and reputations on the one hand, and as moral work on the other. Despite the messiness of these different discourses, each bundled together different background assumptions and thus gave rise to discursive grammars that sometimes seemed incompatible.[26] Given awards' centrality in propelling careers and affecting salaries, awards were almost by definition narrated through the lens of self-interest. On the flip side, the moral discourse posited that people do work at least partly for selfless reasons. One creative captured this tension: "Selfishly we are trying to elevate creativity, but at the same time selflessly doing work for free."

This possible tension between moral work and awards came up in patterned ways. First, there was straight-up cynicism. At least in some moments, many interviewees spoke about pro bono work as hypocritical, undermining any authentic claim to "pure" morality. In the words of one creative who asked to remain anonymous:

> If I had to tell you in full honesty what I thought about a lot of... pro bono work... I think there's this predominant attitude toward that kind of work in advertising where it seems very, very, very much as opportunities to do stuff that can win advertising awards. So many advertising creatives are hungry to win awards in Cannes and other type of advertising award competitions. And, those types of briefs [requests for work], I think a lot of times, the reason they get so much attention within the agency, the reason so many people want to work on them, sometimes maybe even... I can't say this, you know—I don't have proof of this—but I think maybe even sometimes the reason agencies bring them in is because they see it as an opportunity to do something like to win an award.... They're doing stuff that they think has some social currency to it you know? It's... it's hot-button issues, hot topics in society they want to do, things that they think are relevant... things that they think could get attention.

In these moments, pro bono campaigns were described as devoid of any moral dimension. They were chosen as "hot-button issues" to "get attention" for the agency and the professionals crafting them—or crassly for the awards and recognition they might garner. Pro bono work was simply a means to an end, and the end had nothing to do with the nonprofit's cause.[27] As another creative director put it succinctly: "It's 'make us rich or make us famous.' That's sort of the mantra." In these cynical moments, the gap between the moral dimension and the structure of the advertising field seemed unbridgeable.

However, this sharp tension was by no means inevitable. First, some (albeit few) interviewees argued that beyond merely the quality of the work, pro bono work won awards precisely *because* the causes were moral and therefore emotionally compelling. Imagining themselves in the shoes of a juror, one creative explained: "Naturally we're all humans. If you're a juror, watching all these things, and you watch something about selling tofu burgers or something about saving children, you're going to vote for the children." Still others noted that when pro bono campaigns won awards, press would follow, eventually raising the profile of the worthy cause being highlighted. Awards thereby extended the life of pro bono campaigns and raised their effectiveness. In this rendition, awards added to the moral good, such that "when work is more recognized, it's more of an economic multiplier for the [nonprofit] clients that we serve."

These interviewees attempted to diffuse possible tensions between the grammars of awards and of moral work by claiming that they aligned in practice — saying either that recognition directly aids the good or that awards are given to moral work precisely because it is moral. However, such narratives were rare. Most interviewees recognized that being written up in trade publications and blogs usually did not serve as an economic multiplier for a nonprofit. Though theoretically plausible, the idea that jurors awarded pro bono work because of its moral dimension was also not widely shared among our interviewees. The complete blending of morality and recognition in the advertising field was doubtful.

At the same time, cynicism was not the predominant register through which interviewees struggled to align awards and morals. Even in the few interviews where it was the dominant register, it was seldom the only one. Most interviewees who talked about the relationship between morality and awards didn't make awards subservient to a moral good. Rather, although we have so far treated the moral grammar as a unified discourse, they aligned the two goods by moving back and forth between different ways of talking about morality. This can be seen in the words of a strategist and partner at the small boutique agency CG34, Dominik Prinz, who made much of his career, both in Europe and in the United States, through pro bono work. Reflecting on the place of awards in the industry, he noted:

> Well, look, I'm a little torn on that one because I feel genuinely [that] this space and whatever type of work is being done requires a lot of genuine commitment to the cause. So, I think that's important just from an ethical perspective.... [S]ometimes I see a little bit of lack of that interest in the advertising space, because a lot of the people working on these projects, they don't always start there [from an ethical perspective]. I think sometimes the main motivation is around "OK, cool, this is the type of client that allows us to do whatever we want to do, right, so I can win an award," which I get, but to me there's a bit of a moral, ethical component that's missing a little bit.

I do recognize what the work does, though, from an impact perspective for a lot of organizations. So, really great, creative work can mean a lot to a nonprofit, especially ones that have no media budget and no budget to do these types of things, and if it's done well, it can create massive awareness and fundraising, so that's great.... I guess the only criticism would be if you are an advertising agency, make sure that you don't only have the best creators on that work but also the best intentions.

Mid-interview, as Prinz discusses pro bono work, a significant shift emerges in the background assumptions at play. Not only is there an unstable tension between discourses of morality and awards; he also grapples with another, even deeper tension: how to even conceive of morality in the first place. In the span of two short passages, Prinz switches between two different modes of thinking about the moral.

At first, Prinz begins with a discourse that places purity of intent at its center: pro bono work needs to arise from moral considerations. Since awards sully such purity of purpose, there is an irreducible anxiety—even hypocrisy—at the heart of most pro bono work.[28] Until here, we are squarely in the realm of a cynical narrative. Instead of treating pro bono work as an end unto itself, it is but a means to a self-centered project.

Immediately afterward, however, Prinz switches to another mode of argumentation, one that makes quite different background assumptions about how to evaluate the relationship between morality and self-interest. Whereas in the first paragraph the question is about the purity of internal intent, in the second it is about the consequences of pro bono campaigns. If the pro bono campaign works, if it creates "massive awareness and fundraising," then it is by definition good. The questions of intent and of the relationship between means and ends become secondary. If we evaluate projects by their outcome, internal considerations don't necessarily matter. Indeed, they matter only if the work that wins awards did not deliver on its promises.

This second narrative also draws on the tensions between awards and labor we have outlined—whether this is simply work that is designed only to please jury members or whether it abides by the usual rules of advertising. But the more important question is whether the work is just highly awarded, gimmicky, and doesn't actually further the nonprofit's mission or whether it aids the client's objectives. By shifting the grounds to the client's objectives, the relationship between ends and means ceases to be a question of intent and becomes a question of effects.

The latter, consequences-based alignment between awards and morality emerged in many of our interviews. And yet the question of intent still lurks in these narratives. Even in his interview, after Prinz switched from emphasizing internal motives to focusing on the fruits of pro bono labor, he still returned to intentions by imploring advertising professionals to make sure they work from "the best intentions." In other words, the move to consequentialism was not complete. Even as they focused on effects, advertising professionals still needed to craft different ways to depict pro bono work as a site of convenient alignment instead of tension. As a copywriter at Grey agency described it, pro bono should be "kind of like the unselfish and the selfish com[ing] together in a really good way."

Conclusions

The centrality of awards, we speculate, varies across fields in a patterned way. In situations where standards are obvious and transparent—such as who can run one hundred meters the fastest—awards recognize a more or less obvious outcome. For example, for figure skating to become an Olympic sport, a complex codification of rules needed to be developed (how much does a triple axel count for, exactly?). In situations of high uncertainty like those found in the advertising industry, where there has been very little agreement on "what works," awards take on a different importance: they work to establish the good.[29]

If awards are central, pro bono work magnifies the chances of receiving an award and the field-specific symbolic capital that awards generate, as well as that capital's potential conversion to careers and salaries. Given that they are less constrained by client mandatories, pro bono projects favor creative, bold work. Since they are usually centered on broad humanist issues, pro bono campaigns also afford the opportunity to do "emotionally compelling" work. Moreover, since it is usually done by small teams, recognition for pro bono work is more focused, at least on the level of the individuals crafting the campaigns.

Still, aligning or blurring the grammars of awards, labor, and morality is not without its tensions. First, because pro bono work operates with little client oversight, some interviewees saw the awards as somehow "emptier." If work can start from the creative idea and then look for the client, does it play by the same rules? Is it then consecrated by the field precisely because it doesn't need to obey the rules of the field? Second, most interviewees faced a tension between seeing awards as a vehicle for reputation building and careers on the one hand, and pro bono work for nonprofits as an act of selfless benevolence on the other. The most common way that actors worked through this tension was by shifting from an internalist, actor-centered view where the good was known by pure intentions to a consequentialist view where the good is known by the fruit it bears. Yet this move was not complete. None of our interviewees moved to a purely consequentialist grammar. Instead, the actor-centered grammar of intent constantly reemerged.

These patterns and tensions give rise to two broad sets of questions that we explore in the next three chapters. First, as we see in the case of awards, navigating goods is often fraught. How do managers and professionals alike smooth out these tensions? Given that they do not simply move over to a consequentialist standard for the good, how do professionals circle this narrative square? How do they talk themselves through this dilemma? Second, however, there lurks an even more basic potential problem. Consequentialism, after all, assumes that we know something about the consequences of our actions. How do advertising professionals determine the consequences of their pro bono campaigns? Here, we must ask how projects are evaluated and how consequences are tallied.

5. Curatorial Work: Managers and Organizational Pressures

In one of our early interviews, we sat down with Gretchen, a senior creative at a midsize agency. As we were told by an account manager at her firm, Gretchen's personal creativity was instrumental in the agency's pro bono work for Rochester Fashion Week, a fundraiser that benefited poor and unhoused youth. In her colleague's words, Gretchen "really poured her heart and soul into" it. Gretchen spoke about the project at length, remembering how the agency's partner offered her this opportunity, reasoning "it was up [her] alley." As she recalled, "she [the partner] didn't even have to get the entire sentence out, I was like, 'Yes!'" Inspired by street fashion and eager to connect the fundraiser's fashion show to the cause, Gretchen told us:

> We mixed real models and adults who are spending a lot of time on the streets... we mixed a really expensive beautiful coat with the jeans that they came in with, with a T-shirt from Salvation Army and we were really blurring those lines like, What is fashion? ... So, we did this sort of really dark, moody, fabulous, tonal monochromatic photoshoot mixing models... Mixing the fashions, mixing, blending and doing that whole thing. And with lines like, "Compassion is the new couture." Or "Apathy is so last season." And "Philanthropy is the little black dress." And we had all these lines. And then the tagline on everything was "Walk the walk." Because we want you to walk the walk down the runway and walk your walk in your life and do your thing, but also like put your money where your mouth is.... So, all of the pieces that we made were playing with that tension and we also developed a whole new logo for them. And we did these huge posters, we did billboards, we did ten-second TV spots, we did animated GIFs and then we did this engagement piece.

Gretchen's enthusiasm for the project, both moral and in terms of the work itself, was palpable. Then, after talking effortlessly for almost an hour, we asked if she had ever declined a pro bono account. This time she hesitated:

> I don't know if . . . *I* haven't . . . I think that if it's in our vertical [i.e., within the agency's expertise], we'll probably always say yes. If it serves our local community I think we'll always say yes. I can't imagine . . . *I* don't . . . not that *I* know, *me*, *personally*, no, *I've* never heard of the agency turning away a pro bono account.

While Gretchen was extremely articulate throughout the interview, this question seemed to leave her lurching for an answer. As far as she knew, the agency always said yes. But how often did her agency actually say yes?

All agencies, we discovered, had to decline some pro bono requests, if not most of them. Indeed, as the account manager at Gretchen's agency had told us only moments earlier, given the agency's workload, it capped pro bono projects to one or two a year. Gretchen may have never declined a pro bono account, but her managers certainly had.

Thus, while rank-and-file advertising professionals attempt to align goods in their work, they do not do so from scratch. When the advertising professionals we talked to accepted a pro bono account—even if they were the person who came up with the idea and brought the account to the agency in the first place—they couldn't just get to work. As with any campaign, projects needed to be vetted by management, including the company's CEO, even in the biggest agencies we approached.

This raises two intertwined questions. First, what are the differences between how managers and agency employees perceive pro bono projects? CEOs and middle managers—no less than their employees— invoked multiple goods when they spoke of pro bono projects. Indeed, since they were usually removed from the work itself—especially in big agencies—their moral narratives often seemed cleaner, more purified. Yet for all the similarities between the C suite and the professionals who managers employ, we found that managers also had other things on their minds. Taking the organization into account as a whole, they thought about pro bono projects in terms of the agency's entire portfolio, corporate image, and workflow. In other words, they needed to think in terms of the organization. Interrogating managers' calculations brings us to a second question: since there were usually more pro bono ideas and requests than time (and therefore employee work hours), how do managers decide which pro bono projects to take on? On what grounds do they say no? In a very practical sense, managers are gatekeepers of goods, but how do the pro bono projects they choose interact with managerial considerations?

As we show, given the effort and the resources that pro bono accounts require, managers needed to choose projects that would be successful—to engage in careful curatorial work. More theoretically, the chapter asks how such managerial curation facilitates employees' experiences of potentially clashing goods as entangled or blurred, and when these practices fail. Since both entangling and disentangling goods is a practical activity, it is work that can be made more or less easy. In what follows, we explore how managers curate projects so that different, and potentially contradictory goods, seamlessly align.

Pro Bono as Organizational Challenge and Resource

Managers needed to evaluate pro bono work not only as a good unto itself but also within the context of the agency's larger portfolio—in terms of what it meant for their other clients and campaigns. This brought with it a host of challenges, perhaps the most obvious being the potential of conflicting client interests, or what some considered "politics." Was the choice of pro bono projects shaped by the agency's roster of clients? Did managers think about the nonprofit's mission in relation to their paying clients' politics? Some certainly did. Requesting that we anonymize this part of the interview, one manager of a large agency explained:

> A lot of very worthy not-for-profits, they may actually run counter to, perhaps, some of the interests of some of our clients. So, that's another thing that we take into consideration. So, for example, if we work with [big oil], and it is an excellent client of ours, and they do a lot of really great things from a business perspective. But let's say the agency were to go off and do a whole pro bono effort with like Greenpeace. You know, Greenpeace, they're active detractors from [big oil]. We can't have the agency developing advertising that slams big oil. That's like crazy. We just can't do that. [Big oil] helps keep us employed and in business. There are occasions when you have to be smart about making sure that the interests of our client come first, which is why any pro bono cause that gets into taking a stand on issues or policies—issues, policies, or politics—we have to stay away from.

Even more bluntly, a president of an advertising production agency noted:

> I'd say we're attracted to most pro bono causes as long as they're not seriously political.... But when you have someone calling you saying we want to do an anti-abortion ad or an abortion ad, you know, that's where, we kind of, eh ... we gotta really think about that.... Anti-drugs, cancer—

those are things that everybody's interested in. There's no political bent either way, you know? You have people that were supporters of Trump that buy the products, you have people that were supporters of Hillary, so you don't want to draw that line. And you'll notice that when people do draw that line, you know, it causes certain divisiveness, you know when you have folks that are heads of big companies and they decide that they're gonna donate a lot of money to anti-abortion or abortion it affects and offends part of their constituency.

Perhaps this avoidance of politics should come as no surprise. Given their client roster, these CEOs opted only for seemingly apolitical goods. "Issues, policies, or politics" were dangerous territory, best avoided. Thus, these agencies had an explicit bias toward "human" causes: poverty, health, hunger in the developing world (though without talk of any systemic causes), bullying in schools, and the like. They opted to try and help alleviate the kind of suffering that most could agree on and that ruffled no feathers.

Yet, interestingly, only a handful of CEOs and higher-level managers brought up these considerations. Of the 108 pro bono campaigns that we have good data about, there were quite a few pro bono projects that would be considered political, at least by US standards. Work for environmental concerns and global warming, LGBTQ rights, gun control, and women's reproductive rights were common; one large agency did a pro bono effort for Black Lives Matter. While it is always possible that other CEOs opted to remain silent about moments of conflicting interest—after all, the CEO quoted above asked to be anonymized—this is unlikely. In some agencies, CEOs explicitly talked about how pro bono work allowed them to make good on their political commitments. For most agencies and accounts, the question of political risks simply did not emerge, as the chances of pro bono work conflicting with clients' interests was not an issue. After all, not every brand carries the same activist opposition as fossil fuel companies, weapon manufacturers, or pharmaceutical industries.

If most managers were not primarily thinking about the political ramifications of their pro bono engagement—and some even performed pro bono work precisely as a way to engage in the political—what did they consider? The answer was much more mundane and, at least sociologically, much more interesting.

Managing Time, Experience, and Careers

In all the pro bono accounts we followed, the burden of pro bono work was not borne by the agency's resources alone. Both agency managers and rank-and-file advertising professionals often talked about the fact that taking a pro bono account works only if employees are willing to put in some of "their own"—meaning unpaid—time. For example, one of Night Agency's founders, Evan Vogel, described how he took on Keep a Child Alive, a nonprofit that helps children living with AIDS in sub-Saharan Africa and India. This was a project that Evan was clearly invested in. It was a long-term relationship rather than a one-off campaign, and Evan had been a member of the nonprofit's board of directors since its inception. Still, while working with Keep a Child Alive brought the agency attention and perhaps even some corporate clients who knew the campaign or the nonprofit's celebrity founder, it was a serious drain on the agency's resources, a drain that could be sustained only if it was partly shouldered by employees:

> You know, you are asking people at some points in time to go above and beyond, and we have [paying] client work and we need to get that stuff done, so we are asking them to double up and take on more responsibility since you can't just throw more people at the equation. We're asking people to do more, so when we ask them to raise their hands at the beginning and say, "Do you want to be a part of Keep a Child Alive?," we're saying, "Yes, this is going to be fun, but this is also going to require potentially more work. Are you on board for that?" And this is not ... the type of work where you're going to get paid or get bonuses for our end of it. So, you're asking people to contribute more of their day and time, and people are here in New York City and have other things to do. So, we're also asking people for that as well.

Pro bono accounts are therefore sustained not only by the agency but also by employees who work on the account during their free time—nights and weekends. As one senior planner in a large agency explained:

> I can't be sure [how long I spend on pro bono accounts]—it's officially 5 percent. Unofficially, it's more, because that is the type of work that people want to do and don't mind doing it on the weekends and after hours and that's a lot of time that's not being captured, right?

Despite this unpaid work that employees shouldered and despite receiving tax benefits, pro bono work was still costly for the agency. While production costs tended to be low (and were sometimes paid by the client or donated), they added up. And even if workers volunteered free time for pro bono accounts, the company still lost some paid employee work hours. CEOs and middle managers alike repeatedly told us that they needed to be mindful of such costs when they agreed to perform pro bono campaigns. Some managers complained off the record about the amount of resources that certain pro bono campaigns swallowed up.

For the most part, however, CEOs seemed to find a balance they could sustain. Asked when they would refuse to take on a pro bono client, one CEO replied, "If I take a look at the organization... and I'm like, 'Holy smokes, this is going to be impossible.'" Since pro bono work cannot directly pay the bills, managers need to assess whether the company has the bandwidth to do good. This was not a binary matter of having or not having time. CEOs needed to assess how much time the pro bono accounts would shave off from paid work. In some cases, nonprofits asked for something small, but the scope of the work quickly ballooned. Even as he talked proudly of all the pro bono work his agency performed, Frank O'Brien, the CEO of a small agency called Conversation Agency, noted:

> Pro bono projects are usually sold in such a way where it's like, "Oh, it's not going to be that much work. We've got this guy, this client, that's got this brand. They just need a little bit of help. Let's hop on a call on Monday." [So, we say,] "Cool, no problem, let's have breakfast." The next thing you know it's six weeks later. Your whole team is stressed and one foot out the door. That little carrot [i.e., asking the agency for a small and "fun" assignment], I would say, comes up more often in pro bono specific "asks" [requests] and after a while you just learn how to set your boundary and say, "I'm sorry, I can't do that."

What is at issue here is a form of mission creep. With paid clients, mission creep was precisely what the agency strove for. Agencies often take a small part of a big client account, hoping that a small campaign will be a foot in the door and lead to a larger share of the client's brand. Pro bono, though, needs to be approached much more carefully. Either the boundaries need to be set in advance or—given the nature of mission creep—the agency needs to make sure that it actually wants to commit its work to the nonprofit. As the interview continued, Frank noted that "fun little assignments" tended to be "a big red flag." Chuckling, he added skeptically, "'It'll be fun...' Really?"

In our interview with upper-level executives at Mother, a midsize agency, we learned about how they had struggled to establish and maintain boundaries in their relationship with a nationwide reading nonprofit, Reading Is Fundamental (RIF). This case offers an instance of an agency failing to control pro bono mission creep. After being completely defunded by Congress in 2011, RIF reached out to a junior creative at Mother for help obtaining alternate funding. The junior creative went directly to a managing partner, Paul Malmstrom, to ask if the agency could help. On his decision to accept the project, Paul said: "A lot of things are happening here organically because people here want to do them ... They just bubble up from anyone in here, we take them on. It's the same with RIF in particular. It wasn't any specific outreach we did, or anything like that. It wasn't as organized as that." When we asked Paul whether he knew from the outset what the scope of the agency's involvement with RIF would be, he replied:

> I think the answer is no, we didn't know that. But also, we brought it on ourselves because I remember trying to close—it was like any kind of problem solving here. Your objective is X, we don't treat this just as a communication brief. We actually think you should do a complete rebranding to make it feel fresh and new. I think that came from us. "Take this advice. This is what you need to do to solve, or to get closer to solving this problem." And so, I think that things swell, and they swell because you're going to believe that's the right solution, but also people working on it, they are excited—"yeah, this would be awesome to rebrand the whole damn thing." I'm going to make this typeface just for RIF and then people spend night after night just creating this typeface ... But, that's based on enthusiasm and the sense that you are doing something great. So, it's *slow*, if that's the right word ... it kind of expanded as an assignment, it kind of dragged out maybe even longer than it should have.

The engagement with RIF swelled so much that, Paul revealed later, at one point the head creative on the account was dedicating his time exclusively to the project. When asked if he felt that the work for RIF was intentionally donated at a time when the agency had excess bandwidth to donate, Paul explained it had not been intended:

> For one, we are lousy businessmen, and two, we didn't predetermine, and maybe we should have, "This is how many hours, days, months that we can work on this." It was, "All right, that sounds cool," and then "Oh, now we have to do this thing, too. Should we do this? Oh, OK. Let's do that." So, it just becomes this Tantric relationship with your client. So, I think we couldn't really foresee how much it was, but we said what was, "yes," at every turn. And so, it got extended more and more.

In most cases, however, managers did not simply look on as mission creep inflated a pro bono project's scope. Instead, they proactively minimized pro bono work by carefully selecting projects they deemed likely to stay contained and simple. To help with their assessment, some considered the potential client's organizational structure. As John "Ozzy" Osborne, the American CEO of BBDO agency at the time, put it:

> It's very hard to say no to things. We would say no—we'll look at an opportunity on a number of different levels.... Is it an opportunity to work with great people and are they easy to work with? What I mean by that is, sometimes these not-for-profits and sometimes these causal [cause-based] things, they're made up of a lot of big committees and large boards. And because they're not-for-profits and because these boards rely on the volunteerism and the philanthropy of the people who run the board, there's sometimes a tendency to let everybody have an equal voice. That's a really difficult situation for us, because it's really, really hard to get everybody on the same page, especially if we're doing it for free. So, if it's a clear line of decision-making, then that actually will factor in.... You know, is the process of partnering with them going to be a hair-pulling exercise or is it going to be kind of a fun, productive, efficient kind of experience? Those are factors that we take into consideration.

At least for Osborne, one of the most important considerations in evaluating a potential pro bono effort was not the content of the work but the anticipated logistics of interaction between agency and nonprofit. The more centralized the nonprofit, he reasoned, the easier it would be to work with it. Fearing long discussions and changes of opinion, Osborne favored structurally simpler nonprofits.

This is not surprising or particularly Machiavellian. Indeed, advertising professionals often complain about indecisive clients—whether corporate or nonprofit. Sometimes clients are beset by internal power struggles and underlying vision and decision criteria seem to shift depending on who is present that day. Account managers often strategize about which manager in the client company they should approach and when, or speculate about how dynamics in the client's company may pan out. Such clients, as advertising professionals often gripe, too often ask for one thing and then opt for something else when another power broker in the client company reviews the work. Consequently, such "difficult clients" tend to ask for multiple revisions of both creative directions and executions. For paying clients, this is an expected part of the work process. After all, advertising professionals may hope for clarity and consistency, but not all clients are exemplary. In their commercial work, they very rarely decide against working for a paying client because it would be difficult or even risky. Putting up with difficult clients is part of the job.

A pro bono client, however, is a different story. Here, some managers felt that they must factor in whether the potential client has a "clear line of decision-making" at the outset when determining whether to accept a project. A difficult pro bono client who requires many revisions and re-revisions might cost the agency more work hours spent on the campaign. Put simply, an easy client would use less of the agency's resources.

But Osborne's language was not only couched in work hours and cost. A good pro bono client was a "fun, productive, efficient kind of experience." There was an implied smoothness to the relationship that being an "easy client" afforded. As another CEO at Doublebit Narrative, a smaller Brooklyn-based company, told us when talking about a current pro bono client:

> It's funny 'cause they [the nonprofit client] think they're our most difficult client. They really do. They're always apologizing for asking for changes and things. And they're wonderful. They're just lovely, nice people that we like. So, I think I just wish they wouldn't think they were bad clients.

As we wrote in chapter 3, the tenor of the relationships with pro bono clients is crucial. But these relationships are not only a matter of the structure of the gift-exchange relationships between advertising professionals and the nonprofit client. As managers opted to work with what they anticipated to be easy clients, they simultaneously ended up shaping their advertising professionals' work experience. A good pro bono account was time effective, but in managing that aspect of work, managers also ended up optimizing their workers' relationship with the nonprofit. While it was always hard to know in advance if a client would be fun to work with, managers' practical concerns tilted the chances in their favor.

Managers also did much more than make sure that pro bono work did not take over the agency's resources. First, pro bono work offered a chance to flex an agency's muscles in domains it hadn't yet ventured into, especially for smaller agencies. After all, even pro bono work is still work: one small agency's CEO talked excitedly about pro bono work without so much as mentioning nonprofit causes or morality. Instead, he talked about taking on a beverage brand on a pro bono basis in order to expand the agency's portfolio. While this CEO was the only one who completely conflated pro bono work with offering free labor in the hopes of snaring a client down the road, and the only one who did not talk about the moral seductions of pro bono work, there were more subtle ways working a pro bono account could prove useful for the agency's commercial business. As another small company's CEO told us, even as he also stressed the moral side of things:

> It's part of their credential spec [i.e., the agency's capacity]. And so, when you go into a pitch you need to show that you have a diverse portfolio. And so, showing that you are able to create a campaign with limited resources especially on pro bono work, and that you are successful with it, shows that you're able to really move the needle on, let's say, driving organic traffic [i.e. visits to a website or social media engagement not generated by purchased ads]. And so, the thing is, it's all about... it's a numbers game. It's like, if you're able to be successful with limited resources, then we know that we can trust you, say, if we were to cut our scope or if our budget were cut in our department.

This CEO turned the shoestring feature of pro bono work into a strength. It became a rhetorical tool to convince paying clients to hire the agency. "If we were so successful with so little," he suggests, "imagine what we can do with actual resources."

But second, and more frequently, CEOs talked about pro bono work as a safe training tool for inexperienced employees. As one agency founder told us:

> Staffing it [a pro bono project] with a junior team and getting them to roll up their sleeves in a way they might not otherwise with a marquee [important, influential] client—I think there's something to be said for that.... I think historically agencies felt like doing that is a good breeding ground for young talent who may not be ready to go on big, high-paying accounts but could absolutely cut their teeth on stuff, and [pro bono] clients would be more willing to accept that younger talent.

Sending in younger talent to "roll up their sleeves" and "cut their teeth" was possible because of the relative safety of pro bono projects. Normal failures in a pro bono campaign—whether a failure to gain traction or achieve any benchmarks of success—held no consequences. There was no real danger of losing a client or hurting the agency's reputation—unless, perhaps, it would be a spectacular failure that would draw attention for the wrong reasons. As a senior planner at Interbrand who oversaw staffing put it:

> A little selfishly, one thing we wanted to pay attention to is that we bring people into the room who have never had the opportunity to run a project

like that, or sometimes very junior people, to be honest, who had a high level of affinity for that type of work, but who are just too junior to run a session with the CEO of a company themselves. So, we wanted to create opportunities for people to gain experience and learn. So, it's a mix... making sure we do right by whoever the client is and also making sure we do right by the people [employees] to be able to train them and give them the experience they want, because it was pro bono.

Again, pro bono is a useful training ground for junior people or people who haven't had an opportunity to do a particular kind of work (e.g., an interactive web campaign). As opposed to a paying client that may not take too well to a junior team managing the account, the last quote implies that the pro bono client cannot be choosy about who works on the campaign. It must be grateful to receive even inexperienced help, and so it "would be more willing to accept that younger talent." While most CEOs repeated that they allocated as much time as possible to a pro bono campaign and treated it "like any other account," these accounts could nevertheless be leveraged as training grounds for personnel, often making them quite useful.

Indeed, some CEOs stressed that this aspect of pro bono work made them valuable as career-makers in the industry. As Ozzy Osborne put it immediately after talking about the value of taking on a pro bono account:

> I tell this to young people everywhere I go. If you're ever given an opportunity to do something where there's no downside [risk]—so, it's an incredibly broken thing where it [the brand] looks absolutely horrendous and there's no upside—grab it because if it goes out the door or it goes south, you're not the one that's going to be blamed. It's only upside.

What is particularly striking about this response is the implicit equivalence that Osborne makes between pro bono work and difficult brands that seem to be beyond redemption, a "broken thing." The equivalence here is about the place of the work in a budding advertising professional's career. Much like a "broken" brand, with a pro bono account, if expectations are not met, then nothing is lost. A pro bono project that fails to deliver carries effectively no reputational or economic consequences—at least for the professional.

Pro Bono as CSR, Recruitment, and Retention Tool

According to many of the CEOs we spoke with, the pro bono accounts' moral stakes were valuable for business reasons. Working pro bono and other cause-driven projects, such as the second-order CSR depicted earlier, was a way to both manage their agency's image and to recruit talent. We spoke with Mark Kaminsky, cofounder of SS+K, an agency known for cause-driven projects including President Obama's election campaign. The agency is explicitly committed to devoting 20 percent of its work to corporate social responsibility and pro bono accounts. Kaminsky said:

> Advertising's an odd industry. It's home to a lot of people who I am not sure would have a very comfortable resting place in a modern capitalist society, were it not for advertising.... Capitalism can be very heavily about profits and machinations, for better or worse. But suddenly you've got this commercial art of advertising where you have people with skills in music, and writing, and design. It's just a wonderful, it's a wonderful environment to be in. But it doesn't attract the same people.
>
> So, I think there's that self-image, and out of the 1960s and all that, ...I think advertising, far more than your average business, had people in it who were fueled by idealism... [P]articularly given the underbelly of advertising, which is about manipulating people and prompting frivolous sales, when you couple that in there as well... We have to occasionally do something for the common good and nobly take no fee and put our efforts into it. So, if you're Leo Burnett [a large global advertising agency] and you do no pro bono—and your profits are public, because you're all part of public entities—you look kind of churlish. You look kind of nasty, right? So, you also have that. So, I think it's the self-image, it's the public image. It is an image business....
>
> But you do have a lot of people, I mean, we attract them like flies here—we have had strident politically motivated artistic people here.
>
> IDDO: The kind of people who already want to do issue-based work?
>
> KAMINSKY: We do. We've had people just like... As I was saying about advertising, there but for the grace of God I'm not sure where they would go. For some people we've been that agency *within* that industry. You know... really true believers in causes and in changing the world, and in living a more virtuous life... You know people like that. And they're 20-something and they live in Brooklyn, they're hipsters, they ride bikes, they're vegans. You know these guys, right? ... What happens if they leave is then they split their life. They'll be freelance at a big agency selling who-cares-what. And then they'll have their private lives. But at SS+K we offer them the chance to have an integrated life where they can be that person [who works on cause-driven work], or at least to a greater degree. Nothing's perfect, but they can be here and still live by their code of ethics as they define it in work as well as at home. And that's an unusual thing. Now, do we always live up to that? Of course not... And

sometimes we have these discussions, Lenny [Stern, his partner] and I
you know, we're hustlers as well.

In this paean to advertising as a refuge for artists, musicians, writers,
or designers otherwise unhappy in late capitalism, Kaminsky raises two
main benefits for doing pro bono work. First, pro bono is typical corporate social responsibility work, a way of giving back; the agency can take
a break from "manipulating people" and generating "frivolous sales" in
"modern capitalist society" to instead "do something for the common
good." Second, pro bono work is also a way to attract talented artists,
who as "true believers" might otherwise have struggled within capitalism. As we outlined in the previous chapter, the chance to win awards
for bold, interesting work was something that advertising professionals
saw as an incredible perk. But more than just attract talented employees
with the promise of possible awards, pro bono allows these idealists an
opportunity to live an integrated life, where they can achieve the rare
feat of living by their (we presume anti- or countercapitalist) code of
ethics at work.

Yet conceiving of pro bono work as a form of corporate social responsibility requires us to refocus our attention on advertising agencies rather
than the particular professionals who end up doing the work. The advertising industry is a multibillion-dollar industry, and large multinational
advertising firms may make more profit than some of their clients. In
such a world, and bolstered by the advertising industry's public image
as an unscrupulous motor of capitalism, doing pro bono work serves to
manage corporate stigma.[1] Indeed, as we noted in the introduction, large
holding companies that own advertising agencies often report pro bono
work as corporate social responsibility in their annual reports.[2]

Thus, much as a corporation like Shell invests in environmental pres-
ervation projects, advertising agencies donate their labor as pro bono
efforts. But there was a crucial difference. Corporate social responsibility
among consumer-facing corporations is, at least in part, a way to moral-
ize themselves in a world where consumers care about moral stakes and
would rather support a business that "does good." But this is not quite
true for advertising agencies, whose clients are corporations themselves.
As Kaminsky and others were acutely aware, while pro bono did have
a corporate social responsibility function, managing the agency's image
was an effort that pointed inward, aimed both toward the professionals
on their own workforce and toward those they hoped to recruit.

Precisely because SS+K performed more cause-driven work than other
agencies and saw themselves as less cynical about their pursuit of pro

bono work, "issue-based" political work, and second-order CSR, they could be more cynical during the interview. As Kaminsky joked, the advertising industry is populated by bike-riding, vegan hipsters. While it is unclear how true this stereotype may be, almost all the creatives and planners we talked to were likely liberal, as the term is used in the Unites States—suggesting someone who votes for the Democratic Party and supports women's reproductive rights, LGBTQ rights, controlling firearms, and addressing climate change. By performing pro bono work, SS+K and many other agencies implicitly promised workers a morally comfortable place in capitalism, even as they admitted that they were capitalist "hustlers" who couldn't, for basic structural reasons, aspire to any moral purity.

This leads us to the next set of factors in managers' curation of pro bono projects: the way managers needed to imagine and curate workers' experience. As with any of the goods we are discussing, even when managers talked about the organization itself—when they didn't speak of their own moral commitments and the way those shaped their pro bono work—they had to take other goods into account.

Curating Goods: Preemptively Tangling Goods

Managers performed curatorial work by preemptively weighing and aligning different goods. By considering the client's organizational structure and decision-making procedures, they laid the ground for a smooth work experience—something professionals yearned for with all clients. Similarly, when they took on pro bono as a way to recruit or retain talent, they afforded their workers the opportunity to avoid splitting their lives between their personal moral commitments and their work for corporate America, as Kaminsky felicitously put it. Managing pro bono accounts was also about sustaining creatives' and planners' blurring, or tangling, of goods. If managers wanted pro bono to "work," and avoid it becoming a burden on the agency's time and morale, they needed to think carefully about how different goods would interact in a particular project. Asked about when he declined pro bono work, one CEO said:

> Everybody's got their passions and everybody's got their interests. . . . We've learned to consider things based on the input from our entire management team. So, what I may want may be different from some-body else. Can we ignite the passion of our people? . . . So, if some really worthy causes are coming in here and saying, "Hey, we'd love for you to help us" and I've walked around this office and I've talked to people

and I can't get them excited about it, I have to unfortunately go back and say, "Look, I wish you luck but I can't offer you our creative firepower for this big effort."

Beyond the question of what this CEO thinks is a valuable cause, he needed to determine whether it is something his employees would be excited to work on. Especially since they would need to put some of their own time into it, they needed to be invested in it. Lacking such enthusiasm, the agency would decline the work. This meant that at some agencies—though not all—accepted pro bono projects were already vetted as a moral good in that the causes would ignite employees' "passions."[3]

Most CEOs were sensitive to the question of whether their employees cared about the nonprofit's mission. After all, in all but one or two of the agencies we interviewed, managers allocated creatives and planners to the account on a volunteer basis. In interview after interview, both low-level advertising professionals and managers described the process of offering the pro bono account to different teams and then letting the workers who felt strongly about the issue "raise their hands." As a president of an advertisement production company told us:

> You have to discuss them [the pro bono accounts] with your people and that decision about "somebody's for this or against this" and then you know who to work with. You have to take "no" as a partner in the company. We sort of have our philosophy but that doesn't mean that we inflict that on the folks that work with us and for us.

Even as he said that he had never had to decline a pro bono account he wanted to take on because he couldn't get his staff to work it, he was careful to assign pro bono work to the people who were invested in the account. To take another example, the Michael J. Fox Foundation for Parkinson's Research approached Deutsch advertising agency through a connection established by the agency's past president, Donny Deutsch, who became acquainted with the leadership of the nonprofit as they sat together on the board of directors of another institution. Yet while the past president had brought the opportunity to the agency, one of the account's leads was a creative whose father suffered from Parkinson's. Especially in large agencies, a cause could almost always be connected to someone's personal commitments.

At times, the rank-and-file workers' "moral voice" even led to an agency declining paid clients. This kind of moral spillover was rare, but it did sometimes occur, as SS+K's Kaminsky told us:

At one point I was pursuing the Ringling Brothers Circus. Like, what do I know? I knew that they were sending the elephants out to pasture. Did you follow this issue at all? Apparently, it turns out Ringling Brothers were mean motherfuckers with animals. And they were trying to make up for it, right? So they were in a very public relations kind of way sending the elephants to Florida to get massages and live out their days in pachyderm heaven or whatever, and it was quite splendid. And so, I thought, "Oh, good, they've come clean and they probably did because PETA was knocking the shit out of 'em, or somebody was, but they're doing the right thing, I'm done." So, they put out an RFP [request for proposals] and we were invited to compete. Then, the next thing I know, there's this backlash with some of these twentysomethings or thirty-somethings who think that they're still doing horrible things.... So you can be in that squishy spot.... So, you can have that when you attract staff like that. But good luck having a crackerjack creative staff and strategic staff and account staff in New York City circa 2016 if you're not dealing with these issues.

While Kaminsky seemed amused by the incident of failed second-order CSR, this excerpt points to the logical culmination of allowing his workers to have moral voice in the pro bono accounts the agency took on. This was the only case in our interviews where paid work was rejected "from the ground up," but it was telling that it could happen at all.

Creatives' and planners' moral stakes in pro bono work were thus important for management for nonmoral, organizational reasons. Moreover, much like the moral good, workers' existential relationship to their labor, and the ability to do interesting work feature prominently in managers' narratives. As one of the founders of Mother recalled when she talked about her earlier days, when she had worked a pro bono account at Ogilvy, a large and successful agency:

At Ogilvy, it was definitely [the case that] the pro bono projects were a little like a fun valve for you. And especially when you just have these massive accounts. IBM has an entire floor [of offices dedicated to the account]. And you work on that business for two or three years. And so, to have that little tiny valve, where it's like, OK, for a month this year, instead of selling servers, you get to think about whatever, the American Red Cross, or even the Tribeca Film Festival, or something like that. It was just very attractive because all of a sudden, you're like, "Oh my God, I don't have to think anything about diapers for a little while, and just maybe do this fun project."

As managers understood well, advertising work is often less than glorious. Much like other forms of work, the ordinary becomes a grind—the slow churn of a single campaign with the same visual language used over and over; variations on the same message driving copywriters off the wall. Some accounts allow for very little creative license. Others go on for so long that what used to be interesting creative and intellectual challenges have long become routine. Having a "release valve" offers a break from restraint or monotony.

In other professions, this ordinary grind might not be as much of a problem that managers need to think about too carefully, but the advertising industry is marked by extremely high employee turnover. According to the American Association of National Advertisers, the average annual agency turnover in advertising sits at 30 percent—almost a full third of an agency's staff is expected to turn over on a yearly basis.[4] This turnover rate is partly driven by waves of hiring and firing that agencies go through as they win and then lose clients. But it is also driven by personnel themselves. In Iddo's ethnographic work, in Sonia's work on advertising careers, and in the industry's common sense,[5] creatives and planners alike were constantly on the lookout for the next job, the next challenge. Some started sending out their portfolios within weeks of arriving.

Difficulty retaining staff was partly why so many agencies had perks such as a free snack bar, "Margarita Mondays," a barista, or a pool table. But more than high-tech inspired pampering, management also needed to attenuate employees' boredom. Pro bono accounts were another way to do this, and without needing to pull employees away completely into a new assignment. Given that most pro bono accounts were done "on the side" and didn't need intensive involvement—learning the brand's history, location in its business ecology, visual language, key creative ideas, and so on—it was a way to provide a quick and refreshing creative avenue. As the CEO of Doublebit Narrative put it:

> It is definitely, for a big agency, a way to keep talent excited and feeling like they are getting to try on new responsibilities. And sometimes a nonprofit will give you a little bit more creative license and sometimes creatively take more risks than a giant Fortune 100 company might.

As she put it, and as we discussed earlier, taking on pro bono accounts was not only about advancing one's career, although trying on new responsibilities was obviously also important. Pro bono accounts were also more interesting because creatives could try out things that would be shot down by a Fortune 100 company, for whom a small, incremental, and careful campaign was usually preferable to a bold campaign that might backfire spectacularly. The "little tiny valve" that one of Mother's founders mentioned was not only a moral outlet but also a creative one. As Lenny Stern of SS+K noted about the moral and the creative:

> I do think most people see it beyond the nobleness.... It's in the top elixir to attract people. It gives them a break from the more mundane. It gives a little shine to the agency. And the last thing is when people are not paying there is some belief that the clients are much more willing to say to the agency, "If that's what you think works, OK." So, there's an opportunity maybe to be more disruptive and more creative.

Management of the agency's image, the moral balancing act, and creative opportunities were all strung together, part of the "elixir" that made pro bono work such a good structural fit for advertising agencies. In other words, to achieve organizational goods, managers needed to consider workers' relationship to their work and creativity, their developing careers, as well as their moral commitments. Despite the obvious costs in terms of employee work hours, it was time well spent.

The Productive Power of Curatorial Work

Managers were not always as strategic about curating pro bono campaigns to satisfy their workers' blurring of goods. In a few cases, managers brought in a pro bono cause to the agency and unceremoniously assigned it to their workers. In one interview, a small agency's CEO talked enthusiastically about a pro bono account she had brought into the agency and had been representing for years. She was clearly deeply invested in it, both emotionally and in terms of the resources she devoted to it. After the interview, she referred us to one of the creatives who worked on the account. It was a short, and slightly painful, interview. The creative was taciturn. When we asked him about his work on the account, he said that there was no difference for him between regular client assignments and this pro bono work. He just did whatever the CEO asked him to do.

As we have shown, however, such instances were rare. Even when CEOs brought the account through their own networks and based on their own moral commitments, they often aligned pro bono work both with the agency's operations as a whole and with their creatives' and planners' personal concerns. At times, they consulted with workers; more often, they tried to assign the pro bono account to workers who cared about the cause, wanted the creative challenge, or needed the training. As we have already shown, many pro bono accounts also came through employees' own networks, so excitement from at least some of the agency's advertising professionals was a given.

By aligning the pro bono account with the goods that their employees cared about, managers could achieve organizational ends that went beyond their own moral projects and could ensure that pro bono work was smoother, and more fulfilling work. Their organizational aims were diverse: they managed the agency's image, trained and recruited talent, and gave their creatives and planners some respite from ongoing client work. As a by-product of their curatorial efforts, they determined the scope of their employees' moral and creative work.

In his classic essay on the three faces of power, the sociologist Steven Lukes noted that one important face of power is the ability to set the agenda.[6] Between the naked power of coercive violence and the concealed power of ideology is the mundane ability to shape other people's options. To an important degree, this is what management is paid to do. Yet in order to cull the options they presented to workers, managers had to take into account how they expected these goods to become tangled, or starkly contradictory, for their workers. This work was often invisible to the lower-level advertising professionals we talked to. When these advertising professionals were cynical, they were cynical about other things: the misuses of corporate social responsibility, the selfish motivation of awards, or how pro bono work was a way for managers to further foster the elite networks they nurtured as they sat on various boards of directors. But, critically, creatives' and planners' work to tangle and align different goods was shaped by managers' curatorial work. Whether one good was or wasn't at odds with another wasn't a theoretical question of logical entailment. It was a practical relationship. Managerial curation loaded the dice toward the tangling of goods.

6. Navigating Goods: Boundaries and Bridges

For the professionals who did the work, pro bono advertising was primarily organized around three grammars of goods: the moral good, the good of gratifying labor, and the good of prestige and recognition within the field. As we've shown, our respondents spoke about pro bono work's moral dimensions and found the chance to take on moral agency compelling. They talked about the existential seductions of pro bono work as unalienated labor. Within the advertising field, awards emerged as a powerful mode of consecration, converting pro bono work into symbolic capital that professionals could then translate into career moves and salaries both within and across agencies. Managers navigated between these key goods through curatorial work, that is, nixing ill-fated projects and approving those that were better aligned with their organizational goals. After all, managers needed to heed the market, limiting an agency's expenditures on pro bono work and using such campaigns as a recruitment and retention tool.

These different goods can be thought of as loosely patterned grammars grounded in different assumptions; each with its own genealogy and underlying background, each becoming most relevant at a different level of analysis, and leading to a predictable pattern of affordances and dilemmas. Returning to the polytheism metaphor, each of these grammars can be imagined as one god in a pantheon—sometimes laying claim to another god's followers, other times amenable to a shared offering. For, as we have depicted throughout this book, there are few "pure" goods to be had. Rather than analytically beginning with a pure good and then looking for "compromises," we have described a constant swirl of goods. Field dynamics flowed into labor, markets into morals. Indeed, goods were often co-implicated in ways that made them very hard to parse out in the interviews. Still, in some moments, the aligning and blurring of different goods became a pragmatic problem.

As Nina Eliasoph and her colleagues cogently put it, thinking about the tangle of goods requires us to think about actors' "navigation techniques."[1] This is because the different goods that we have outlined in the past chapters were not discrete units of discourse. As a grammar, discourses included a bundle of co-implicated elements. Talking about morality prodded advertising professionals to think about the relationship between means and ends, or about the imagined consequences of their actions. Talking about work evoked questions of creativity and their existential relationship to labor. Talking about awards evoked careers, but also seemed to nudge interviewees to think about pro bono in terms of motivations and consequences. To push the polytheistic metaphor a little further, gods in a pantheon were sometimes jealous of each other; their domains sometimes clashed.

In other words, the potentially clashing bundles of assumptions that each good carried with it created danger zones—places where the pragmatics of the projects they worked on could lead to uncomfortable contradictions. To navigate such treacherous moments, advertising professionals and managers needed to find ways to either distance themselves from the specter of contamination or blur the boundaries between different goods. That is, managers' preemptive curatorial work was not enough; advertising professionals also needed to navigate potential tensions between goods.

This chapter focuses on two discursive ways that our interviewees did so. First, following Erving Goffman's seminal work on stigma,[2] we focus on the work of stigma deflection—on the construction and discursive use of the morally cynical others, especially in cases where the tension between goods has overflowed the advertising world and entered the broader public sphere. Second, drawing on literature on ambiguity and polysemy in the sociology of knowledge, we focus on narrative bridges, particularly the ways that the language of passion allowed interviewees to flit between one good and the other.

The Cynical Other: On Boundaries and Stigma Deflection

One important way for advertising professionals to navigate the danger zones where goods might clash was admitting that the moral was often tainted by other goods, yet claiming that the worst of the impurities happened elsewhere. While few said—or seemed to want to say—that they were solely guided by moral considerations in their pro bono work, many interviewees noted that they were somewhat better than other advertising professionals and agencies. Such forms of deflection and boundary drawing are perhaps unsurprisingly common across stigmatized actions and identities. First conceptualized by the sociologist Erving Goffman to describe how people with embodied stigma go on to stigmatize others with a more pronounced stigma and who thus should be the "real" objects of stigma (e.g., a person who is hard of hearing making fun of someone who is deaf), such strategies of stigma deflection can be found almost wherever we care to look for them—from mental health patients to failed entrepreneurs.[3]

Stigma deflection among our respondents took on a few common forms.[4] First, although most rarely, some interviewees took pains to explain how they avoided the glamorous work that was associated with awards and even with existentially compelling creative work. Explicitly rejecting other goods, these interviewees stressed that they worked with one or two pro bono accounts year-round, spending most of their time doing "behind the scenes" and even "boring" work—redesigning websites, choosing fonts, and advising the nonprofit on structural changes. For example, one small boutique agency, Gluttony, worked pro bono with the Brodsky Foundation, which supported dissident Russian artists. Gluttony's CEO, Abby Honor, as well as one of the account personnel, related that the team never tried to do award-winning work or even exceptionally interesting work on the account. Rather, as Abby explained:

> It actually ended up being a very deep dive, because after looking at the way that they communicate to people, we went into fine-tuning what their mission was. So, really into the nuts and bolts of who they are. You know, it was a time when we needed to really decide who they were and what their mission was, even down to what sort of artists they were going to fund. Geographically, where were they located? So, it was a real reevaluation, but it took part in the fund and its mission. So, after working with them internally, we did not write their mission statement. We guided it more. So, after helping guide them and revising the mission with them, it went onto all of the traditional marketing, if you like. So, you know, looking at them from a brand perspective. What's their name? They had a much longer name. Shortening their name. Coming up with a logo. All very basic stuff, but... it was nothing magical.

The agency ended up spending an inordinate amount of time on things like email signatures, typeface, and business cards—"nothing magical." In Abby's narrative, the fact that the pro bono work was so mundane was proof of the purity of the agency's intentions. In pro bono work, Abby argued, she prioritized generating structural changes that would have the most long-term value for the nonprofit. As she said later in the interview: "Nobody is ever going to know about the work that we've done. It's probably more from a human perspective, and so, when I go to bed at night, I don't feel that I'm just trying to make money. I'm actually successful at giving back in some way as well."

In a similar vein, a few interviewees from Mother, a successful midsize agency, explained that they slowly realized they were working a lot for one nonprofit, almost as if they were operating as the nonprofit's agency of record. Over multiple years, they designed and redesigned the non-profit's websites and consulted on a plethora of structural questions; they did the kind of work that agencies often perform for ongoing commercial clients. Although they did produce one high-visibility campaign for the account, most of the work was far less visible—and therefore not glamorous or award worthy. In speaking about the Reading Is Fundamental campaign that we saw in the last chapter, one of Mother's cofounders said he never approached a pro bono account in such a way again because it drained too many resources, even though he was proud of the work the agency had done.

But more than just an illustration of the dangers of a spiraling client relationship and the expenditure of probably too much work and effort, this pro bono campaign allowed the interviewee to make a distinction between the intent propelling his agency and other agencies that worked only "for awards":

> Awards are a little bit like money. Do you do it for the awards? Do you do it for the money? Or is that a consequence of you just doing what you think is right? And I think we always had the latter view on things. That we are trying to do something as great as we can to solve a problem. If a consequence of that is that it won an award, that's great. But we haven't been as cynical as I know you can be in this industry. Some agencies have departments [that are] only making work to win an award. It's almost fake work where they persuade a client, to say, "Hey, can you run this once at midnight [an ineffectual time]?" And then it counts as a real thing and then you submit it because you have a chance to win an award. If you win an award you have a greater chance to get more PR for your agency and you have a greater chance to get other clients that you need to get your profit up every year.

At least within this excerpt, morality was incompatible with both awards and market goods. Both revealed that the work was a means to self-interested ends, whether to get more money or to get fame and recognition (which, as the interviewee notes, could generate future revenue as well). Even though some of Mother's work for the nonprofit did actually end up winning awards—and the agency would have had to apply for the award shows—the cofounder used the agency's ongoing, mundane work to draw a distinction between his agency and others. While his agency did pro bono work for the right reasons and won an award as a by-product of that, others performed pro bono work as a means to nonmoral ends.

To a certain degree, Gluttony and Mother were outliers in how they approached nonprofit clients and did their pro bono work. Yet it wasn't simply those who did unglamorous pro bono work who drew boundaries around their moral practices, adding a moral gloss to work that was "nothing magical." Narratives of contrasting character abounded. This cynical other was pursuing pro bono work for devious reasons of self-interest—perhaps even greed. This came up even in cases where the pro bono relationship was not in any way unusual. Interviewees often took pains to distinguish the way they approached pro bono work from how other agencies did the same work. Another CEO of a small agency noted:

> There are some agencies actually that their pro bono programs are pretty much hooked to their awards department. And larger agencies actually have awards departments. They don't call them that, but, you know, they look at a pro bono opportunity as a chance to do whatever kind of creative work they want to do and then win awards, right? I personally find that a little cynical. And we don't think of it that way. We just look at it as [an] opportunity to do something—to do some great advertising for an organization that's making the world a better place.

Generally speaking, it was the large agencies that served as this cynical other. Perhaps as a way to justify their relative status in the field, interviewees in some smaller and midsize agencies talked about large agencies as unscrupulous award mills that cared little for the moral good. After all, everyone knew they had awards departments, even if "they don't call them that." One agency partner referred to "the douchebags in McCann Erickson"; another CEO of a small company railed about "the Deutsches of the world"—both metonyms for large, morally suspect agencies. Others recalled how disturbed they were by the approach to pro bono work that they experienced at leading multinational agencies like BBDO or Grey. When we asked one advertising professional if he had anything to add at the end of the interview, he noted:

> The experience I had before at BBDO was very different, because I was handling a not-for-profit account where they did pro bono work back then, and all the work we did at that point was creating very creative campaigns, like very far downstream, like just get the story out there,

get the coolest photographer to tell the coolest story and make sure we win an award with this thing. So, the priorities were very different, and I think the level of sophistication in terms of the type of work that was being done... the priorities were different.

Implicit here is a claim that the pro bono work of large industry leaders is tainted, fueled by dishonest motivations, as they pursued hidden priorities that differed from the pro bono campaign's stated goals. Yet with very few exceptions, the narratives of interviewees at smaller agencies were not substantively different from those we heard at the dominant agencies like Deutsch, BBDO, Ogilvy, and McCann. Despite their assertions to the contrary, grammars of good were no less entangled and blurred in smaller agencies than in larger ones.

Cautionary Tales and the Societalization of the Tensions among Goods

Talking abstractly about "agencies that do it all for awards," and even naming specific large agencies presumed to be cynical others, were strategies of stigma deflection. However, interviewees also referenced specific campaigns, deploying them as semiotic focusing lenses. These were cases that allowed interviewees to sharply illustrate the cynical other—particularly egregious campaigns that served as an extreme measure against which interviewees could be judged. As George Tannenbaum, a creative director at Ogilvy—precisely one of the large agencies that other interviewees brought up as a cynical other—put it:

There was the thing last year that was a scandal that won an award and the award was withdrawn. It was an app that was going to help find refugees.... Maybe this is merely semiotic in that it casts a darker shadow over motivations and credibility than it should, but I'm influenced by things like that. I'm like, "You know what, show me that it's credible" because there have been enough of those where I am doubtful now about everything, and they're a little bit like campaign promises. Show me what you're going to do, and you see a few of those and you're like, "OK, or it ran three times on Bolly national television—the book that's also a water filter and things like that." I mean, come on, it's a terrific idea, but is it real? Is it real? And I'm not sure everybody is holding themselves to a tremendous high moral standard.

The careful reader will have recognized one of the campaigns that Tannenbaum uses as a semiotic focusing lens. The "book that's also a water filter" was one of the iterations of the Water Is Life campaign we started this book with. What for some interviewees was their signature achievement—a campaign they were proud of as a moral good—was for others a cautionary tale. Yet what is at issue for us is not adjudicating whether the filter-book was really a ploy for awards or a noble attempt to aid those without clean water. This case, like others, embodied different goods. Advertising professionals could read each other's work in varying ways, and through such readings construct a presentation of their own work and self.

While campaigns such as the book filter or large and cynical agencies were important resources for stigma deflection and boundary work, the most poignant cases that professionals talked about were those where the relationship between goods in pro bono work bubbled over and overflowed the field's boundaries. These were cases in which the relationship among goods was not problematized in professionals' discourse or even in interactions among advertising professionals, but where such problems became public in the broader public sphere. In other words, these were moments when the potential clash among goods became both actualized and, as the sociologist Jeff Alexander would put it, "societalized"—made visible for wider audiences who would not otherwise be privy to the internal workings of the advertising industry.[5] This goes back to another case that Tannenbaum mentioned—one that a few of our interviewees also raised as an egregious example of bad pro bono.

In 2016, Grey, one of the largest and most awarded agencies in the world, was forced to return a bronze Cannes Lion after public outcry. Grey Singapore, one of the multinational's dozen offices, had worked with a Maltese nonprofit focused on the plight of refugees from the Middle East and Africa. The project had yielded a web application that could—supposedly—scan the Mediterranean Sea in real time. The application would parcel the sea into manageable square areas, which could be streamed to any smartphone that had downloaded the app. In that way, people could combine their efforts, monitoring the Mediterranean from the comfort of their own couch and then letting the nonprofit know if they saw refugee boats in distress. The hope was to lower the horrendous death toll of those drowning en route to Europe. As the *Standard* put it in a laudatory article, "Spend your lunch break searching for migrants who might be in need of help."[6] The app was, fittingly, called I Sea.

The project was submitted to the Cannes Festival, where it won a bronze Lion for "activation and promo." But even as it did, questions began to emerge. On the very same day the application won its Lion, Apple removed it from the app store. Technology bloggers had been raising questions for a few weeks—there was something wrong with the

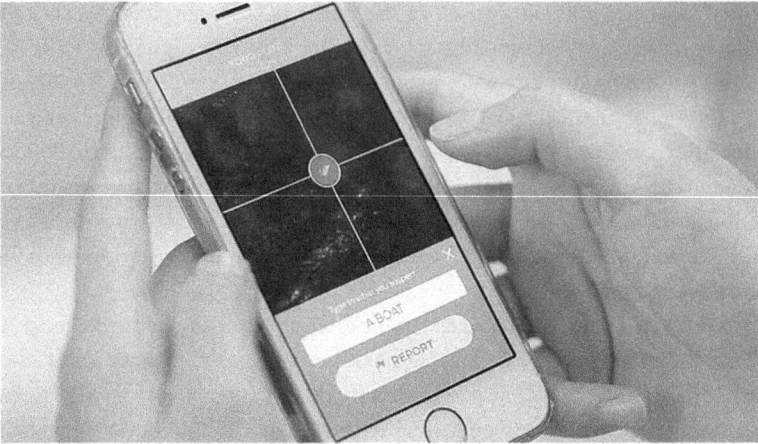

FIGURE 5. The I Sea app, made by Grey for Good of Grey Singapore, was conceived to stream live images of the Mediterranean Sea so users could report refugees and refugee vessels in distress. The app won a Cannes Lion in 2016 but the agency later returned it after critics pointed out it did not work.

application. The images didn't seem to change, even at night. It didn't feel right. Only a few days later, an *Adweek* writer explained, "the app supposedly provided satellite footage to users allowing them to 'flag' ships which could be distressed refugee boats in an attempt to prevent drownings at sea. Instead it showed the same image to all users, coupled with a weather report from Libya intended to give the impression that what they're watching is a live feed."[7] Grey began to backtrack—the app was real; it was just that it was still in its test phase. But this explanation came too late. For one, until these queries, nowhere had the agency disclosed that this was an incomplete test phase. The consensus was that someone at Grey had pushed an untested app forward as if it were operational so they could have a chance at the Cannes that year. As one marketer sharply commented: "What has winning a Cannes award become? When did the cost of winning and using this as a tool to reel in a new client come to this? Have we as an industry sunk so low that this becomes acceptable? …Let me reiterate, this award was won off the back of faking a solution to the refugee crisis."[8]

Grey gave back its Lion, although it admitted no wrongdoing. Instead, the agency noted that it won so many awards that it didn't need to undertake "scams," adding, "The saying 'no good deed goes unpunished' is apt in this case."[9] The app was never heard from again, with tech experts saying that, although it may have been technologically feasible, it was prohibitively expensive to be made operational.

What was going on here? Was the team at Grey truly so cynical that they knowingly submitted a fake campaign to win an award? In advancing their interests "off the backs" of drowning refugees, could it be that the moral good had played no role in their pro bono campaign and the award was the only thing that mattered? While we cannot be certain because Grey Singapore did not return our calls on that matter, we don't think so.

This is not to say that there weren't perhaps structural reasons this scandal occurred at Grey, as the agency was particularly explicit in tying pro bono work to awards. As one creative who worked at Grey told us:

So, if at any point in the year I'm like, [to the executive creative director], "Oh my God, I have this great idea, I think we should do X, Y, Z to prevent gun violence," I could go to him and pitch it. Specifically, what they do that's smart, I think, is they attach it to... So, Cannes is the big awards festival for ad agencies when you win a Lion and it's like one of the bigger awards in the industry. So, what they do here is, in order to give everybody a good shot at like having something to do to submit to Cannes at the end of the year, they'll have a council. And so, what happens is you come up with a bunch of ideas, could be for pro bono, it could be for clients we have, it could be for clients we don't have, it could be for your clients that you work on every day, whatever you want... And you say, "Hey, we just had this great idea for blank."

And you pitch it. So, first I would pitch it to my ECD [executive creative director], and he would either say yay or nay, "Yes, this is a great idea," or "No, this isn't a good idea." If it's a great idea, then it goes to the next level, which is the creative council, and the council is this international thing where all of the Grey offices worldwide [send] representatives, and they literally vote.... So, they will go through ideas from everybody across the world for these cool Cannes-worthy ideas, and I would say, a lot of them are pro bono because... you have a lot of flexibility there. And you'll pitch it and it gets a rating, like one to ten or something like that. And then ones, the ideas that get the highest rating, the agency will then support to help it try to get made.

This creative presented Grey's centralized procedure for grooming pro bono projects as a creative advantage. However, the impetus to conflate pro bono work and awards was not unique to Grey, nor does it necessarily mean that the proposed pro bono campaigns were not also selected for moral reasons. As this interviewee and another creative director at Grey narrated, they felt genuinely invested in the pro bono work they had done. At the time of the interviews, the agency was receiving media attention for producing a bold campaign promoting gun control in the United States.

In other words, we think it is fairly likely that the team working on I Sea was not so different from the people we spoke with. That the campaign was a daring idea that was likely to win an award was surely important, but it wasn't the only good. We suspect that the campaign had also been developed to serve an obvious moral purpose. The campaign had a simple and compelling moral template: crowdsourcing the safety of refugees and allowing a horrified global audience to actually do something tangible, to concretely help save a life. And so when the time came to send the campaign to Cannes, it was tempting to do so even if it wasn't fully operational—to punt the work of fully operationalizing the app to what the team probably hoped was an imminent future while ignoring some of its potential problems. Arguing, like the blogger above, that it was simply the cynicism of advertising run amok that constructs a Manichaean world of goods—a world in which there are people who work for moral reasons, while others do it only for fame and fortune. Yet this is simply not what we have found. Rather, advertising professionals and managers alike navigate multiple goods simultaneously, in situations that are usually more ambiguous and therefore more susceptible to missteps.

From the perspective of the people we interviewed, cases like I Sea— while uncomfortable—were also godsends. Moments that societalized the tension between goods afforded interviewees a means to understand themselves as relatively virtuous. They may not be saints, but the devil was always elsewhere.

The Ambiguities of Passion

Deflecting stigma was one important way that advertising professionals practically smoothed the relationship among goods. By pointing to egregious others, they could cleanse their moral motivations, even while openly admitting that pro bono work was both a moral ends and a means for existential satisfaction and advancing one's career. But this kind of boundary work was only one way to discursively navigate the relationship among goods; a very different way to navigate goods was interviewees' use of certain terms as semiotic bridging devices.

Reading through the interviews, we realized that managers and professionals alike consistently evoked the curious term *passion* when speaking about their work. They had a passion for pro bono campaigns, donated their passion to the nonprofit client, lost their passion, developed a passion, and engaged in passion projects. Systematically combing through the interviews with passion in mind, we found that the term appeared unprompted in more than half of the interviews.[10] In some interviews, it appeared on almost every page of the transcript. What was this passion, and what was it doing in these narratives?

At first glance, passion seemed to map neatly onto a moral grammar. In explaining how professionals approached pro bono work or how that work arrived at the agency, the language of passion was central. One creative explained that he tried to find "a bit of passion and purpose by doing more pro bono work and nonprofit work"; another said that he and his coworkers performed pro bono work on a climate change campaign because they were "very passionate about climate change and awareness toward it."

Passion as a marker of moral commitment was visible in the ways that advertising professionals talked about themselves, but also in the ways that managers talked about how they recruited specific people within the agency to perform specific pro bono projects. As we outlined earlier, managers not only talked about their own moral considerations; they also curated projects to match those of their employees. Passion was an important way that managers talked about these curatorial practices, such as talk of gauging "the passion" people in their agency had for different pro bono campaigns. Talking about a pro bono account that his team decided to take on, one middle manager in a planning department explained:

> There's a half a dozen of us on the planning team that are really passionate about that space, and we want to talk about it. We want to do work on it, and so there's a project that's coming down the pike, so we want to put the right people on it that feel interest in it.

Moreover, advertising professionals extended this passion to their pro bono clients, often depicted as being "passionate about what they do"—and sometimes even as having "more passion than skill." At certain moments, interviewees used the notion of passion to depict the target audience for the campaign, potential viewers who either should "have a passion" for the specific cause or whose passions could be awakened by the advertising campaign. It was passion all the way down: passionate advertising professionals passionately crafting a campaign for passionate clients to rekindle the target audiences' passions.

However, even when pro bono work was framed as a moral passion, listening carefully to our interviewees, we couldn't simply identify morality and passion. A partner in one small agency captured this when explaining why his agency put so much effort into its pro bono campaigns:

> We all take turns doing pro bono as it comes in the agency, because a lot of our pro bono work stems from employee interest, so obviously if you're passionate about something and it resonates on a personal level, that's where you get the best work.

Here, passion maps onto morality in a curious way. On the one hand, there is something intimately personal and untainted about passion. Coming from a place deep within, resonance, passion, and interests were used by interviewees interchangeably to depict an emotional connection to a project. At the same time, in talking about how employees felt passionate about something that "resonates on a personal level," the question of the good was defined not only in emotivist terms but also by personal investment. In the context of pro bono work, it may have been an investment in a moral good, but it was still a personal, individually held good. In other words, it was individual and variable. Some people could be invested in preventing the climate crisis, others in preventing bullying at school, and still others in gun control laws.

From Morality to Work

Precisely because they were etched so deeply into the individual, passions didn't need to be justified or explained: since passion was depicted in terms of personal investment, its relationship to the moral was not preordained. That is, although many interviewees talked about their passion for a specific pro bono cause or campaign in a moral register—not surprising in the context of an interview about their pro bono work—there were other uses of the language of passion, sometimes within the same interview. One art director, we were told, had "a passion for hand lettering"; another described how she worked on a fashion campaign for poverty alleviation out of not only a desire to help the poor but also a "personal passion around the fashion industry."

Indeed, in one interview, Shelly prodded a creative to elaborate a little more about what she meant by her passion for a pro bono cause. Hesitating a little, the interviewee swerved away from pro bono work altogether:

> I don't know... I mean, our Chase [bank] clients are pretty passionate too. I think it's just a function of [the fact that] this is their job, you know?

I think our Chase clients—it's weird…I think they're motivated by different things, so our Chase clients are motivated by moving cards, selling product, and our Y[MCA] clients are motivated by being able to keep doing the work they do and raising donations and making sure people know exactly how they help communities. They are equally passionate but in just kind of different ways.

As this creative explained, there were simply different passions at work here. One client was impassioned by making money and selling financial services, another by helping the poor. Although she interrupted herself to reflect that perhaps Chase's passion was "weird," these were nonetheless both passions, equally so. Who was she to doubt someone's passion? Even more crucially, what was common to these two images of passion was their intimate connection with a certain way of talking about work.

The lenses of both good work and the moral good helped make sense of the way other interviewees spoke about their different passions. For example, a small and relatively new agency's CEO relayed several "passion projects" his agency had taken on:

Right now we're working [in a pro bono capacity] with Big Brothers Big Sisters of New York [a nonprofit focused on mentoring underprivileged children] and helping them launch a new digital campaign to help recruit volunteers to spend time with their young clientele. We're [also] working on a new vodka that is coming to market via Hong Kong and Canada. And it's a premium—ultra-premium vodka that is quite interesting in terms of the positioning and the creative…

So, I think they're passion projects for different reasons. From an agency perspective, any time you get to work with essentially a blank sheet of paper, where you get to work with a brand that's new to the market or emerging—those are particularly enticing because you can often do more for the brand as opposed to inheriting something that's quite established. They also tend to be smaller, so they're not very profitable, and you're making a longer-term investment that you can help this brand grow and it can become more commercially viable. In the case of Big Brothers Big Sisters, that's a passion project because the heart and soul of that organization is charitable. And people love working on that because it makes them feel good.

Even though the CEO distinguished the passions of pro bono work from those of a vodka brand, the distinctions were secondary to both accounts' evident nature as "passion projects." Moreover, even the moment of differentiation between passions appeared in only some interviews. Like the CEO above, an executive creative director at another midsize agency explained that his agency had a passion for different projects, some of which happened to be pro bono and some of which were for paying clients. Talking about the difference between pro bono and paying clients, he noted:

> We treat them [the nonprofit Organize] as [a] real client, because we treat every single brief with the same amount of care, love, and passion. For us, there's no real difference between what we do for Netflix and what we do for Stella Artois and what we do for Organize [the nonprofit]. I think we just believe in the power of great ideas to solve problems and this is probably a very personal thing....
>
> We really care about the work, our just making it the best possible and putting [in] love and passion and commitment. We are very committed and like to engage. We like to work hard and take it to a place where we are all happy, including the client. It's hard because making something that is interesting is not easy. If you are an architect or a photographer, it requires work and passion and hours and craft and being considered and being smart on your decisions. We try to do it all the time. I didn't have this amount of gray hair three years ago.

What is so striking in this case is that passion was, first and foremost, an expected feature of work. If the agency treated pro bono work with passion, it wasn't because pro bono was so different from its usual line of work. It was just that the agency's passion was aimed at a different target.

Perhaps this should not come as a surprise; talk of passion, after all, did not take place in a vacuum. The question of passion and its relationship to work is both commonplace and has a rich history. Indeed, the vicissitudes of the notion of passion are some of the most interesting markers of our shifting cultural understandings of work. In the early days of the capitalist economy, passion was viewed suspiciously. For the economist and intellectual historian Albert Hirschman, capitalism emerged explicitly as a way to temper and tame "the destructive passions of men."[11] Economic interests provided structure and order, quieting unruly—and potentially darker—passions. In this reading of history, the iron cage of modern capitalism was not the accidental by-product of a Protestant ethic, as Max Weber famously argued. Rather, the iron cage was the point, at least in emotional terms.

Yet passion has struck back. The late-capitalist idea that workers need to have a passion for what they do expanded out of earlier notions of vocation.[12] The turn to passion both widened the scope of the vocation to any career and turned it into a highly individual, emotional attitude. Workers needed to realize something that was supposedly deep within themselves, and to then cultivate and exhibit their emotional commitment to their work.[13] In the influential career self-help book *What Color Is Your Parachute?*, which is often seen as heralding this change, Richard Bolles offers sage advice: "If you can, you'll do better to start with yourself and what *you* want, rather than with the job market and what's 'hot.' The difference is 'enthusiasm' and 'passion.' Yours. You're much more attractive to employers when you're *on fire*."[14]

This internal, individualistic fire is far from being an impediment that actors need to temper in order to further their career prospects. Rather, it has increasingly become a necessary component of the working self. As the quote reveals, workers should feel passion and exhibit it liberally. Career self-help books have increasingly stressed passion. Job interviewers use signs of passion in the decision and retroactive justification of who gets a job. Job seekers use passion as yet another way to transform economic necessity into virtue.[15] In short, passion has become a constitutive element of the new spirit of capitalism.[16]

It is in this context that passion emerged in the interviews. It was not some accident or fleeting fashion; talk of passion is widespread in the advertising industry. There are multiple agencies that have worked the word *passion* into their very name, including Passion and Poison, Passion Digital, and Passion for Creative. Online articles abound about the best way to fuel passions in advertising work, advising would-be advertising professionals that the key to a successful career lies in harnessing such passions. As one advertising professional commented in an interview for a trade article, "Other people will say it's only a job but I think you need to be committed and passionate about what you do and the minute you lose the passion for it is the minute you have to find something else to do."[17]

The Affordances of Ambiguous Passion

Passion was rooted, at least partially, in the place that work occupied in the new professional's soul. Still, as we showed earlier, this passion was also a moral passion. Indeed, as we tried to make sense of the notion of passion in the interviews, we came to realize that in many cases we simply didn't know how to code it. It was hard to tell whether the passion that interviewees spoke of was a moral passion or the professional passion of gratifying labor. In other words, the vocabulary of passion inserted ambiguity into discourses of the good.[18]

Passion afforded two modes of ambiguity. First, while we have shown that passion was used across interviews to depict different goods in the advertising world—that there was something like a social world-level ambiguity at play—there was also ambiguity within our interviewees' narratives. In that sense, passion could mediate and blur some of the possible tensions or even distinctions between goods. Second, in doing so, the ambiguity of passion allowed actors to slide from one good to the next in both their own narratives and the way that they described the coordination of collective action.

We start with the first ambiguity: how actors shifted seamlessly among different passions in their narratives. In an interview with a senior creative director at a midsize agency, he first mentioned passion when talking about how the agency's CEO would usually let them run with an idea if they felt passionately about it, then pivoted to talking about passion for the cause: "It's just like, 'Hey, go ahead do this as well. If you're passionate about it, go and do it.'" Then, only a few minutes later, when talking about how he organized pro bono work, he explained why he started working in small teams:

> The people that are number 19 or 20 [the nineteenth or twentieth person] that are involved in a project are maybe not as passionate about it because they're not at the foreground of the group. So, that's how we've been very successful.

Here, the passion was not only for the idea or the moral cause. It was also about the ability to perform satisfying labor and take ownership of the campaign. Still, from the standpoint of ambiguity, what is interesting is that it is not quite clear if the passion that the CEO approves of is for an idea or a cause. Nor is it clear if the passion that is hard to muster in a large team is a passion for the work (where the fewer people there are the more ownership they take over the project), for the creative idea (which may get diluted the more people work on it), or for the moral cause (because the advertising professional's ability to embody the good may be hampered).

Similarly moving among different goods, a manager in a large agency talked about his own work and how he saw his work for Donate Life, a nonprofit that focuses on encouraging organ donation in the United States:

The secret for me is [that] I can get as passionate about driving Geico's [the insurance company which was their client] roads as I can about driving registries for Donate Life. One is a much more personal passion and one is a business passion.... I think that's a big part of what will drive to a successful effort. Pro bono itself... the one piece that is different is generally you're not getting paid for it.

This manager seemed to distinguish between a "personal" and a "business" passion. The personal passion was already ambiguous—whether the personal was moral or simply about enjoying the work remained an open question—but the distinction was nevertheless there. Yet the very next sentence de-emphasized the difference between personal and business passions, blurring the boundary between the two goods. As passion was an important driver in the manager's ability to craft a successful campaign, it seemed that the difference between the two kinds of campaigns was reduced to the fact that pro bono work is unpaid.

In another instance of ambiguity, a creative repeatedly talked about her passion for pro bono work. She talked about the Ferguson riots and structural racism; about how she found herself reading writers Ta-Nehisi Coates and Jelani Cobb on what it means to live through American racism as a Black person. In other words, it was an interview where moral language was crucial. In this context, we asked the creative late in the interview to talk about what she found meaningful about the work:

The subject matter, obviously. And I feel like on a lot of these things, even advertising in general, what I like about it is that you are constantly immersing yourself in these like new worlds, so I just learned so much about the state of the planet working on that project and I also met a lot of people who were really passionate about it and were really optimistic about the future and that was really nice to be in that community for a little while.... But I sometimes feel that way on just random brands like even working on Chase [bank]. I'm like I'm pretty financially illiterate so working on it was kind of like "Oh, I'm suddenly engaged in this world that I should know a bit about." That's really nice because you can just keep doing that over and over for the rest of your life, basically. I forget what the original question was.

From talk of structural racism, this interviewee pivoted to talk about what it means to learn about a new topic, illustrating this with her experience working for a large bank. It is telling how the transition occurs, and that she ends her thought-process suddenly unsure of her footing or of the original question. This was the same interviewee who spoke earlier in the chapter about how Chase and the YMCA were both passionate about their projects, albeit in different ways. It is precisely in the context of these two clients, both with their own distinctive passions, that her narrative meandered when she spoke about what makes her work meaningful. This moment, when she forgot the original question, emerged from the discursive elision and ambiguity at the heart of passion. This ambiguity allowed advertising professionals to transition among goods and blur the distinction between them. And as we have seen, these transitions were not necessarily strategic or conscious.

So far, we have shown that ambiguity served as a narrative juncture where advertising professionals and managers alike could transition among goods or blur the distinctions between them. Last, however, this blurring of different grammars also sustained a second kind of ambiguity. This second ambiguity was one located at the heart of the collective act of negotiating different goods: how passion changed over time and how it shaped the way that managers, advertising professionals, and their clients worked together.

As a highly personal and emotional investment, passions fluctuated. Sometimes, of course, passions developed through the campaign. Advertising professionals often became more passionate about a project as they embodied its moral mission. Yet these fluctuations have another side. Much as advertising professionals could grow to have a passion for a cause, they could also grow out of it. As one CEO explained:

> There was a pro bono client that actually became very difficult to work with. And we just grew tired of it and we weren't making any progress. And I just had a frank conversation with the other party [the nonprofit] and said, "You know, I think we're done. We're not making any progress and that's not why we took this on, and I think you need an agency that is passionate and we've lost our passion for this." And so, we moved on.

At least as this CEO told the tale, passion did the work of justifying the agency's choice to back out of a project. Agency professionals' reduced passion seemed to have nothing to do with the cause's moral salience. Indeed, in this interview, the CEO never even told the interviewer what that specific nonprofit did. Instead, he talked about this case after saying that his agency took on pro bono projects that were workers' passion projects. When the work ceased to be satisfying as work, passion for the project evaporated.

Conclusions

This chapter has traced two ways that advertising professionals navigate potential tensions among different grammars of goods. They do so, first, through boundary work and stigma deflection. This occurred when they brought up dramatic cases when the tension between goods became societalized, and overflowed the confines of the professional sphere, as with the I Sea application. But such boundary work also appeared in more mundane, fleeting moments and references, such as when interviewees noted that they weren't like "the douchebags" in larger agencies, or like the vague and anonymous "others" who took on pro bono work just for the creative freedom or the awards. This way of navigating goods emerged as professionals talked of who they were not and what they would not do. Second, as important as it always is to consider how actors engage in constructing and maintaining boundaries, we also saw how actors navigate the goods as they talked about what they did do. In this context, the language of passion served a bridging function between different grammars. Returning to the metaphor of polytheism, passion was a general offering, a language that was modular enough that it allowed people to both blur the differences among goods and transition between them.

Yet even as they employed these narrative tropes, there was still something that was, at least at times, uncomfortable about pro bono work. As José Funegra, an executive creative director at Mother, concisely put it:

> To be honest, advertising is in a very weird place right now. There is this creative director who said something that I found super, super on point. Apparently, if I go to an award show, I may see all the efforts, all the pro bono efforts that agencies are doing, by this point we should have saved the world, right?

This rhetorical question is an existential reminder: a needling suspicion still left after pro bono campaigns came and went, after passion has been put to good use. If all pro bono campaigns are meant to make the world a better place, when will the world be saved? This points to questions of evidence and efficacy. It is to the measurement of such efficacy that we now turn.

7. Evaluating Goods: The Question of Measurement

Spend any time in an advertising agency, and you will hear a veritable alphabet soup of measurement: key performance indicators (KPIs) and returns on investment (ROIs), conversion rates and A / B testing. As a business, advertising is haunted by the question of measurement. Haunted, since measuring anything is far from obvious. How can advertising professionals know if their work had any effect on buying habits? Correlations between advertising campaigns and consumers' actions abound, but establishing a causal line has always been fraught. It was, once, mostly a matter of magical thinking and of hopefully squinting at correlations.

The advent of digital advertising has brought with it the ability to trace "clicks" from the first moment someone is exposed to an advertisement to the point at which that person makes a purchase—the elusive *point of conversion*. Even in this brave new world, however, measurement is expensive and uncertain; in an environment where people have multiple devices and are bombarded by advertising as they move through their surroundings, it is never easy to ascertain whether or to what extent a particular ad shapes behavior. Moreover, advertising agencies and clients alike often want to capture more abstract indicators like brand exposure, consumer habits, and changing attitudes and behavior. In short, measurement is a constant challenge in advertising, with different devices and tests that assign both a number and a value to advertising professionals' work. Such measuring devices, as the sociologist Emily Barman put it, "are a formal means by which actors can gauge the value of an entity or actor in a situation. They perform the act of calculation by assigning a value to a good."[1]

If advertising in general is haunted by this question of measurement, how does it affect the practice of pro bono work? Despite having no direct stake in measuring their pro bono campaigns' success, many of our interviewees—a full 60 percent—spoke unprompted about the question of measurement in their pro bono work. This opens up a slew of questions.

Is pro bono advertising effective? How, if at all, do advertising professionals *know* if it is? And how do different goods, as well as the complex ways they clash and blur, play into such measurement questions? As we show, there is more than one answer to these questions. In many cases, measurement was incredibly seductive. But without the absolute need to measure, quantifiable evidence of effectiveness was sometimes cast aside or treated in a cavalier fashion, with advertising professionals showing little interest in assessing whether and how well the project had worked.

To see how these questions of measurement played out, we begin with one case in which measurement featured prominently. This is an ideal case of sorts; measurement was successful, seductive, and aligned — perhaps even amplified — the goods that this book focuses on. The case is also a good entry point for clarifying some of the ways that measurement plays into pro bono advertising.

The World's Biggest Asshole: An Anatomy of Measurement

The World's Biggest Asshole was a campaign designed to register millennials, and especially millennial men, for organ donation. Although young people have historically been a small percentage of registered organ donors, the campaign succeeded; the number of registered donors spiked immediately after the campaign ran. The campaign also garnered awards — including the elusive Effie Award for effectiveness in advertising — and has been featured as an exemplar of successful marketing.[2] This campaign was led by the Martin Agency, also the agency of record for Geico, well known for the Geico gecko that is widely considered one of the most successful advertising campaigns in recent advertising history.

Like so many pro bono campaigns, the World's Biggest Asshole came about through both a personal connection and a sense of mission. Chris Mumford, then a director of account management and later the agency's president, had lost his brother, who had a heart attack and needed a heart transplant. While his brother did receive a transplant after a period of waiting, he died of complications after the operation. Following this harrowing experience, Mumford cemented a relationship with a pro bono organization called Donate Life America, whose CEO and president had heard about the tragedy. They asked if Mumford and the Martin Agency might be able to help them drive up organ donations. As Mumford related:

> He came to me and he said, "Will you consider working with us?" And I said, "I have no idea what we would do with you but, yes... there's an amazing need." And going through it, I realized just how complicated it

is and how hard it is to make a transplant happen and make it work. . . . And as I started learning more and more about Donate Life as an organization, I realized that we probably could find ways to help them. So that's really where it started. David [Fleming, CEO and president of Donate Life] found me through my brother and we became friends after that. . . . And it took a good full year and a half to figure out what we were going to do together.

After immersing himself in the problems facing organ donations and the organization itself, Mumford began to see a way forward. And, as one would expect by this point in the book, the way forward involved a tangle of different goods:

> A lot of the pro bono work we do as a company comes out of the passions of the people in our company. And we normally look for things where we can do something special and also, of course, do the kind of work that has never been done before and can get recognized. So, Donate Life fit into both of those categories, or all three of those categories. Obviously, it was a passion of mine, and so I pushed for it within the organization. David [Fleming] seemed like the kind of guy that wanted to do the kind of work that we wanted to do, so that was a plus. And the cause was not just a special cause, but it was something that I really thought we could make an impact on. There's other causes that if you're just trying to raise a bunch of money . . . you can't necessarily see the impact of what you do in an immediate way. And in this case, every person we could sign up to be an organ donor would ultimately make a difference and save a life. So, it was pretty exciting to look at it that way.

All three goods — morality, compelling labor, and recognition — aligned. As in so many of the cases we have detailed in the book, passion was here as well, taking the form of both a personal crusade and a moral cause. But another issue came to the fore early on: the campaign's possible effects. In Mumford's words, there was something "pretty exciting" about the campaign's goals. If the measure of success was the number of people signing up for organ donation, then each person who signed up could potentially save a life.

This was also an extremely targeted campaign. Rather than trying to promote organ donations in the abstract, the campaign targeted millennials, a generational category that at the time included people in their twenties and thirties. This age group, according to Donate Life, was underrepresented in organ donation registrations. And although any age

FIGURE 6. The World's Biggest Asshole campaign intended to increase organ donation among millennials. The 2016 video follows Sweeney, a contemptible person who does "asshole" things before dying and saving lives by being an organ donor. The campaign was created by the Martin Agency for Donate Life.

group is welcome to register, younger people tend to be healthier and are thus preferable organ donors. To get at that particular group, the Martin Agency's creative team zeroed in on the use of macabre humor. Inspired by previous advertising that used dark humor to talk about death, as well as by media personalities like Jon Stewart, their creative team came up with the World's Biggest Asshole. The two-minute spot, written by the Martin Agency and produced by Furlined, follows an "asshole" as he goes about his day. He throws a bottle of urine out of his car, shoots paintball bullets at a dog, gives a child a cigarette, and is generally "being an asshole." While arguing with a waitress about whether extra fries are included in a discount meal, he suffers an aneurysm and promptly dies. The waitress then finds something "completely unexpected": he had registered as an organ donor. In death, the asshole gets to play the role of hero. Viewers then follow his organ donations to different people who he saved by dying. As the advertisement ends, it underlines the point that "even an asshole can save a life." But the advertising accomplishment, of course, is the video itself, and the memorable, humorous portrayal of its asshole protagonist.

The spot, which apparently took some cajoling by Fleming to get through Donate Life's board of directors, was an immediate success. As Mumford related, it was picked up by online and television venues like Funny or Die, and the Martin Agency was also in touch with the satirical online newspaper *The Onion*. Like many of the other successful campaigns we outlined in the book, despite having no paid media behind it, the ad "went viral." But it did more than that too: when asked by a *Forbes* magazine writer about "the results of this film," Cori Kaylor from the Martin Agency's account management team noted:

> In addition to the video going viral with sixty million global views within two weeks, it's working and making a difference! Prior to launch, Donate Life received 149 registrations per day. Two weeks post-launch, they are now averaging 1,040 registrations [per day], an increase of 698 percent. The registry was 22 percent twenty- to thirty-four-year-olds prior to launch and saw a 236 percent increase. This group now comprises 52 percent of the total registry. But the most important statistic is that men twenty to thirty-four who were previously only 26 percent of the registry have registered and are now 56 percent of registrants, a 215 percent increase.[3]

There are a number of things to parse out in this litany of measurement. First is the usual suspect—the easiest of measures and the one that emerges first is social media views. On the one hand, this is the simplest measure to capture because social media outlets record views without the agency needing to put any money or much effort into measurement. As we return to later, the number of views also measures value—it indexes the campaign's viral reach and thus its quality.[4] In this case, however, the number of views was only the starting point. More crucial was the number of registrations and the percentages of different age groups in registrations.

That the Martin Agency could report the campaign's effects in such detail shows how well integrated they were with Donate Life. The nonprofit's national registry had been constructed the year before the campaign rolled out in order to cut across different state registries. Indeed, as Mumford narrated, the Martin Agency actually waited some time for Donate Life to get its national registry up and running before the campaign rolled out so that it could "do something in scale. [Since] it would be very difficult to do something state by state." This national registry created a new measurement opportunity, as well as a new and far more direct metric. While this was related to social media views, registration was a different measure, one that could help trace the effect of the engagement of viewers in social media. It was a measure of the intended ends, something that is often quite elusive in advertising. More than that, it was also an immediate measure. As Mumford described:

It's a major part of doing a project like this—you just want to be able to have an impact and measure it. And there's so many things out there where, you know... An agency will do a TV spot and run it, and you just won't even know what's real, what real impact it had. So, when you have a chance to literally track something on a daily basis to see what you've done, it's pretty exciting to watch.

As we return to later in this chapter, this immediacy is itself seductive and rare in the experience of advertising work. It is not simply that this campaign had an effect, but that the effect could be tracked in real time. The excitement of watching numbers change and to "literally track something on a daily basis" was visceral.

This was not only something that account or agency management spoke about. In our interview with Wade Alger, the creative director who led the campaign, measurement was again front and center. As Alger noted, shooting off the statistics during the interview:

The day after it launched, they went from getting 149 registrations a day to 1,022. So, I think that's like a 587 percent increase. So, not only did it work in the sense that it's hopefully a great piece of communication that we... that the agency is proud of, but also it also actually worked.

As with Mumford's narrative, the relationship between different goods came to the fore. The campaign was not simply work that he and the agency could be proud of in terms of the work or the awards it could garner—and garner awards it did—but it was also actually effective in that it achieved the nonprofit's goals.

Whereas for the account manager, the campaign's viral aspect was only one measure among many; from a creative standpoint, the fact that the video went viral with no paid media behind it held special importance. This was not simply a matter of getting a campaign out "on the cheap." Talking about David Fleming, the CEO and president of Donate Life, Alger's words are telling:

The fact that it actually worked for him and got our registrations up... that's really to me what really is rewarding, when you actually do work that *works*, you know? And it's easy when you have the Geicos of the world—millions and millions of dollars, of course it's gonna work. But when this has nothing behind it and it still works, that's a really great feeling.

The fact that Alger talked about *"our* registrations" is significant. As we noted, pro bono work often evidenced this kind of discursive blurring of protagonists that gave advertising professionals the chance to become moral agents. But more significant was that the campaign worked without "millions and millions of dollars." That the campaign caught on without the crutches of paid media was a pure index of its worth *as work*. Going viral, in other words, proved that the work's quality—rather than its media placements—was driving its success.

Of course, not all campaigns were as successful as the World's Biggest Asshole. What's more, in most cases, measuring success was a lot trickier. Yet we found some of these same themes across different cases: temporal immediacy, the question of "going viral," the relationship between measures and worth, and the way that measurement evokes different goods—sometimes blurring them, sometimes putting them on a collision course. Before we outline these ways in more detail, however, we need to say a word on measurement.

What Quantified Measurements Do

Our world is replete with measurement devices: from predictive algorithms to machine learning and big data, the practice of measurement has become ubiquitous. In this quantified existence, the importance of measurement instruments sometimes takes precedence over what they are designed to measure. This insight, of course, is not new. It was developed in Max Weber's classical notion of modernity's movement to a means-oriented rationality, where means are sanctified and come to replace ends.[5] But it was perhaps most importantly developed later, beginning with Foucault-inspired studies of governmentality and techniques of the self, as well as work from scholars like Ted Porter and Alain Desrosières that highlights the emergence of a new quantified world.[6] The resulting efflorescence of studies includes work on the rise of statistics and the construction of populations,[7] the increasing quantification of the self,[8] and the general "trust in numbers" that defines the modern (and to an even greater extent, the late modern) world. Throughout this literature, measures, numbers, and rankings change from being signifiers of something to take on a life of their own. For example, a host of studies in sociology and management have shown how rankings come to define an organization's mission, becoming an end unto themselves rather than focusing on what they were initially intended to measure.[9]

Advertising, in that regard, is a showcase for the rise of this measurement society. Of course, advertising has an economic purpose: to drive purchases. Measuring its effectiveness is thus important almost by definition. Economic transactions are a quantified endeavor, at least if we go beyond the most rudimentary forms of "truck, barter and exchange." What's more, measurement is embedded throughout the advertising campaign process. Consumer segmentation surveys are routinely done or ordered through other vendors; big data is increasingly crucial in the planning phase, with software analytics platforms such as Google Analytics, NetBase, Brandwatch, and others becoming essential tools for account planners and in-house analytics teams.[10] If we are to understand measurement in pro bono advertising, we need to remember that at least part of the reason for measurement's importance is that this is what advertising professionals constantly do. It has become an occupational habit.

There is yet another wrinkle in this complex landscape, one that is especially important for measuring pro bono advertising. While measurement assigns value to a good, it does not determine what kind of good something is. Is it a metric of success primarily capturing economic achievement, or does it index the quality of the creative work that led to that achievement? Especially if morality is defined in terms of its consequences, the question whether a given campaign succeeded in producing robust measurements becomes an index of moral achievement. Yet to understand how morality and other goods were intertwined with the practicalities of measurement, we must first understand what measurement "feels like" in pro bono work.

While measurement is often understood as a somber issue — part of the hard shell of modernity that we cannot cast off — it is equally important to think about the seductions of quantification. As the sociologist Georg Simmel noted long ago, the transformation of qualities into numbers has its own draws. For Simmel, the transformation of different qualities into the pure potential of numbers was one of the main accomplishments of the money economy and modernity.[11] It is precisely its abstract referent that makes money so compelling. Following this thread, in the world of online journalism, the communication scholar Caitlin Petre has shown how numbers and metrics can be enthralling. In her study, journalists at *Gawker*, an online magazine and blog, were mesmerized by their numbers going up and down. These analytics turned numbers into both a marker of journalistic value and an addictive game.[12] Numbers — whether the tally of likes and reposts on social media or unique visitors to a web page — became goods unto themselves. There are, in other words, seductions to measurement.[13] In this regard, pro bono work is an interesting case.

Seductions of Measurement: Magnitude and Rhythm

While some pro bono campaigns we followed were for massive organizations such as Save the Children, UNAIDS, and the Clinton Foundation, pro bono work was often performed for small nonprofits operating with shoestring budgets. This meant that advertising professionals' pro bono work often contrasted with more run-of-the-mill work with large corporations and brands. This difference affected the experience of measurement in a few ways. In ordinary commercial work, making a perceptible difference in a brand's sales is incredibly difficult. A 1 percent or 2 percent change in sales over a year is a huge achievement for any agency. In this world of slow, incremental change, working for a nonprofit was a distinct experience. Here, advertising professionals could make a big difference. Recall the numbers that the Martin Agency professionals rattled off: a 587 percent change within a few days, a 698 percent increase after two weeks. Their excitement about these numbers was palpable. That being said, these numbers were a product not only of the campaign's success but also of the nonprofit's size. It is simply easier to get a 698 percent increase when you start from a few hundred registrations.

The magnitude of these gains came up repeatedly when advertising professionals talked about measurement in the interviews. In many cases, this was where interviewees became most animated. Thus, for example, in talking about his work for a youth theater group, one creative related:

> Even in terms of ticket sales, they were [up] 200 or 300 percent just off the back of the work. All of a sudden, they just got way more press, they were more prominent. So, the rebrand really worked for them in a really powerful way.

In the world of youth theater, what 300 percent meant in practice was not explicitly defined. We presume that boosted sales did not amount to tens of thousands of ticket holders. Yet a 300 percent increase is incredible validation for both the advertising professionals working on the account and the nonprofit client. Thus, the measured effect was also reflected in the nonprofit's gratitude. Just before discussing the ticket sales increase, the creative talked of the theater's reaction to the "rebrand": "Oh, they loved it."

The relative magnitude of effects, then, offers its own seductions both in itself and in terms of the client relationship. But there is another theme that emerges in a careful reading of the excerpt above: the fact that the

increase in press coverage and ticket sales came "all of a sudden." This
theme appeared in many interviews, whether as a central theme or in
passing, as in the case of one of the creatives who led the Climate Name
Change campaign that we focused on earlier in the book:

> We actually had a petition [to change storm names to the names of pol-
> icy makers who deny climate change]. So, we figured 10,000 people or
> something are going to sign it. That number happened, like, overnight.

While magnitude mattered, it was also important that the effect was so
immediate — that it "happened, like, overnight." There was, it appeared,
something incredibly compelling about the temporality of effects. To
understand why this immediacy was so seductive, we need to put it
into context.

Much as the magnitude of effects that advertising professionals are
used to working with is different from that of many pro bono accounts,
the temporality is also quite different. Working for corporate clients, advertising professionals' work is often staggered in a variety of ways. First,
the work itself goes through many iterations, including multiple rounds
of back-and-forth with the client. Even after a campaign is approved, it
takes a long time to measure its success; rollout often takes time and the
advertising campaign's effects can often be ascertained only in the following fiscal year. The effect of advertising campaigns is rolled into the
future. In other words, while advertising is a world that is marked by a
frenetic pace or rhythm of work, it is also a world where the work's effects are often measured only once the advertising professionals working
on the campaign have long since moved on.

In comparison to such staggered rhythms, pro bono advertising was
quite different. A creative at Interbrand agency who had worked for
a nonprofit called Butterfly Home, which housed and supported children of incarcerated women affected by a 2015 earthquake in Nepal,
explained:

> [With regular corporate work, the creatives] become a little bit disinter-
> ested. And it's not because the work itself is dull, it's just such a meaty
> challenge. They can take six months, while something like the Butterfly
> Home — come in on a Friday and then you've gotta get it out by the Mon-
> day. And you're not second-guessing yourself and putting it up on the
> wall and refining it, refining it, refining it, over a three-month period.
> You're just blasting it. "Is it good? Is it bad? It's good. Let's do it! Let's

check in with the client. Yes. OK." This is in market. I can see a direct reaction to what I just created. In the case of Butterfly Home, it's like, "OK, we raised $250,000. How can we raise the next $250,000 in the next week?" And then you feel good about it.

The entire process was condensed. Rather than the usual back-and-forth, it was a short and simple process—if the idea was good, it went out. Goals were met not over months but in a matter of days. And it was this immediacy that explicitly allowed those crafting the pro bono campaign to "feel good about it."

In more general terms, the measurement of pro bono work recalibrates temporalities of work. It brings together rhythms that advertising professionals often experience as "offbeat"—those of crafting the campaign, sending it into the world, and assessing how and whether it has affected a brand. Pro bono work's quick turnaround and measurement of effects creates a eurythmic choir from a cacophony of processes.[14] Advertising professionals and the nonprofit alike can track in real time how a campaign is doing, sometimes down to a precise parsing out of demographics. Rather than a staggered temporality, advertising professionals experience how their work makes it into the world in a way that is all too rare in their everyday efforts. Referring to a different campaign, another creative at Interbrand said:

> Designers want to know that they have the power to change things and that their work means something. That sounds a little fluffy. I mean they want to win awards as well, but they want to see a reaction to their work that's instantaneous.

In an interesting twist, this creative tied the immediacy of measurement to the "fluffy" world of morality. Setting awards against measurement, then, the creative transubstantiated measurement into moral goods. At least in his narrative, the fulfillment that came from immediate results was a sign that recognition in the advertising field was not the only good that he was after in his pro bono work. It is to these intersections of measurement and the different grammars of goods that we now turn.

The Transformation of Measurement: Metrics as Indexes of Work and Morality

The magnitude and immediacy of pro bono campaigns' effects are crucial aspects of the seductions of measurement. Even without the interplay of different goods that this book highlights, such moments of measurement in pro bono campaigns can be important, understood against the backdrop of humdrum commercial work. But as the excerpt above attests to, measurement is also intertwined with different goods — and especially with morality and the value of work.

First is the matter of going viral. Much as in the World's Biggest Asshole campaign, most successful pro bono campaigns in this book were primarily — usually only — launched online. This was for obvious reasons. Online campaigns do not require as much money behind them. Buying television spots, magazine space, or billboard space is costly. And for nonprofits, a lack of funds was exactly why they needed pro bono advertising work in the first place. Without these resources, most pro bono campaigns produced online content and hoped the ad would go viral. In practice, it meant that to succeed, the campaign would have to be picked up without what marketing professionals call "paid media" — without the client paying to post the content. Instead, pro bono campaigns almost invariably relied on earned media — shares, views, and likes that emerge organically.

In the case of the First World Problems campaign presented at the start of this book, the campaign's viral spread seemed to prove its legitimacy in the eyes of the professionals who worked on it. As Frank, one of the creatives, put it:

> It was a lot. The YouTube [video] ended up [with] seven million [views], and this was 2012 and with no paid media behind it. So, that's legit numbers. And then, like I said, it was shared on Facebook and that got millions and millions of views.

It wasn't simply that the campaign was measured; Frank felt that he could trust the "legit numbers." Because the campaign was not being pushed down people's throats, social media and online measures that might otherwise be suspect became a mark of craftsmanship and a validation of his work.

Moreover, while viral spread was proof of work's intrinsic creative value, it was not the most important good that was measured. Rather, many interviewees presented measurement as a moral index. As one creative from Droga noted:

> On a pro bono client you actually care more about the effectiveness of the advertising because real things are at stake; not that the client's bottom line isn't a real thing, but it feels more urgent in some way.

As we have shown before, the advertising world is shadowed by cases in which a pro bono campaign appeared to be more a ploy to receive awards than a campaign with a cause. Advertising professionals used such campaigns as a foil to define themselves as moral. The egregious cynical other was a fun-house mirror through which the relative integrity of interviewees' intentions could be highlighted. While highlighting specific campaigns and exemplars was a strategy that loomed large, advertising professionals also often defined themselves as moral by emphasizing the importance of measurement. Much as measurement came to indicate good work, the very fact that interviewees took measurement seriously could be a sign that they were morally invested in the campaign regardless of personal gain. As a CEO of one small agency explained:

> I guess we wanted to treat a cause like a client, not as a hobby.... We need to see a path to effect. I just don't want "awareness" ... If a [paying] client came to us with their only goal being awareness, we would say, "That's ridiculous, your goal is not ... like, do you need to sell more stuff? What is the business implication of what it is you're trying to do and why is awareness your key proxy?" ... We want to look at "what does success look like?" and then "how can we reverse engineer that success?" It's not, like, [in a cynical tone] "we reached three million people" ... No, we got *this* to happen, we were able to put these many kids through a STEM program in high school.... We want real numbers behind it, not just to reach an "awareness" ... that is the main criteria that we have. I think it teaches the people that work here how to see things through and not just settle for, again, people hearing something or winning some award. I want them to see the people that we help.

In this case, a commitment to careful measurement was synonymous with commitment to the moral good. The CEO's argument problematizes the obvious metrics that many of our interviewees pointed toward: the number of views, likes, and shares of online content. As he put it, if a commercial client were to claim that all they wanted was "views" or "awareness," that would be a strange client indeed. Much as clients want to sell their products or increase their market share, nonprofits also need to have practical goals. These, in turn, need to be measured. The "real numbers" that define the campaign then demonstrate that the campaign served a moral end. Without such measures, he argued, it could be simply about "winning some award." In other words, what is important is not only that the agency can measure its effect but also the kind of thing that they measured.

This question of "the right measure" came up repeatedly in the interviews. Much like the magnitude of effects and temporal immediacy, part of the allure was the juxtaposition between the kinds of metrics that advertising professionals needed to think about in their corporate work and those that they thought about in pro bono campaigns. For Joydeep Dey, a senior planner at J. Walter Thompson (JWT), it was working on a campaign for Human Rights Watch that illustrated this stark contrast between commercial and pro bono metrics. The pro bono campaign in question aimed to apply international pressure on Burma to free political prisoners. As part of the campaign, JWT constructed an installation in New York City's Grand Central Station. The installation was a wall made up of small images of prisoners arranged in boxes that looked like barred jail cells. While the images of prisoners were two-dimensional photographs, the bars that they were behind were actually pens, positioned as if containing their captives. People watching the installation were encouraged to take these pens to sign the petition and thus to symbolically free a prisoner.

Talking about the campaign, Dey kept coming back to the language of metrics. He spoke about freeing prisoners as "the KPI" (the key performance indicator) and repeatedly returned to the question of evaluating success:

> While it was happening, we had Buddhist monks chanting prayers, so there was this serenity and this peace that was attracting everybody. Great, fantastic stuff, which then the magic of it was even though we only got two thousand signatures that day, which doesn't feel like a lot, but we took that, created a piece of content that then we used across digital media, across online advertising, to create a movement to get more petitions, which led to fifty-three thousand petitions.... [W]e won a Cannes Lion for it that year, which was great, and then submitted a Cannes Effectiveness Award, which is kind of the next step in the Cannes process. Once you win the Lion, you can submit an Effectiveness Award. And we didn't win that one, but it was a beautiful process of writing it, because usually you write a metric like, "This campaign led to $20 million in sales." "This led to a 10 percent lift..." And our metric was freed prisoners. We've, you know, we were able to free people, and I can't remember the exact number. It was, like, 137, or something very specific, people were freed. And so that was a very rewarding thing to work on.

As always, there are multiple registers operating simultaneously in this excerpt. First, as opposed to the last interviewee, awards and morality were not necessarily at odds. The project won the Cannes, something that Dey was quite proud of, and it was then submitted for yet another award—an Effectiveness Award within the Cannes Lions Festival. While JWT did not win the second award, the fact that the measured effect was freed prisoners in Burma rather than sales or market share made it particularly rewarding, a "beautiful process."

Yet this case should also give us pause. The metric that Dey is proud of is freed political prisoners—without doubt a noble cause but somewhat doubtful as a measure. International pressure is not easy to parse out. A total of 137 prisoners may have been freed, but was that more than those freed during any given year? What was the place of this particular Human Rights Watch campaign in the sum total of international pressure on Burma? Given the complex entanglements of international diplomacy, it is not surprising that the Effectiveness Award's jurors may have been skeptical. Once we move away from the phenomenology of measurement to the relationship between measures and the things they supposedly capture, some difficult questions arise.

Measurement without Accountability; or, Consequentialism without Consequences

A crucial difference between measurement in pro bono campaigns and in commercial advertising is this: Commercial clients routinely expected the corporation's marketing department and the advertising agency as a whole to expend a great deal of energy on measurement. Even if the measures were far from perfect, both clients and agencies spent a lot of time fitting measures to goals, thus turning measurable metrics into practices of accountability. That is, advertising professionals crafted measures as a way to show clients (and to prove to themselves) that the work they did had its intended effects, even if showing this was always difficult. In comparison, the measurement goals of pro bono advertising were often more vague. Nonprofits, large and small, did not always have a well-thought-out measurable goal in mind. This was for different reasons. For some, like the Human Rights Watch campaign, the goal was to change public opinion and engender awareness about a social ill—something that is inherently hard to quantify. Others didn't routinely need to quantify their interventions and were new to the game of measurement.

This means that there is often a gap between measurement and accountability in pro bono work. It isn't that there aren't any measures to use. In the case of online campaigns, for example, there are always the ready-to-hand views and shares. Rather, the dilemma is that the relationship between metrics and the nonprofit's goals is not clear. Of course, this is not always the case. When Iddo asked Lenny Stern at SS+K whether he had something to add at the end of the interview, Stern commented:

> You should really explore impact. And I don't mean social impact. I mean success. I think some people think pro bono is the thing you do to make yourselves feel good, to get a creative award and make your young people feel good. But increasingly, nonprofits, NGOs, mission-based organizations are becoming as metrics driven and as analytic as Proctor and Gamble [the consumer products behemoth]. Meaning, they know, "If I do this, what do I get out of it? Am I gonna drive new donors? Am I gonna drive fundraising? Am I gonna drive awareness? Am I gonna influence policy?"

Stern was right: we really did need to "explore impact." But perhaps as crucial is his argument about the shift in measurement culture. Whereas the nonprofits of old may have had a fuzzy notion of what they wanted to achieve, he argued that nonprofits increasingly came in knowing precisely what they wanted and which metrics they would use to measure these ends. They had become analytic. As in the case of Donate Life at the start of this chapter, measurement was baked into the campaign from the get-go. Without such measurable impact, Stern noted, creatives may get an award and "feel good," but they will probably not *do* good.

However, at least as far as we could tell, Stern was overstating the case: the majority of pro bono campaigns were not metrics driven. In cases where advertising professionals first came up with a campaign and only then looked for a nonprofit partner, any measure of impact was post hoc. In most other cases, nonprofits seemed less interested in metrics, or at least did not push the advertising agency to provide them. The role of the nonprofit in shaping measurement was thus crucial. While there were differences between agencies' level of commitment to measurement and the relationship between these measures and the nonprofit's goals, the investment in measurement was primarily driven by the nonprofit.

To illustrate this, we can return to the case of the JWT planner Joydeep Dey. Like many of our interviews, our conversation with Dey covered different pro bono projects that he had been involved with during his career. Before working on the Human Rights Watch campaign, Dey had worked with another nonprofit, the National Alliance on Mental Illness

(NAMI). When asked what he enjoyed most about the NAMI campaign, he answered:

> I think it was the fact that it was so easy to do. So, the way that it worked was you could change your profile picture to include the hashtag "I Will Listen," and you also received, if I remember correctly, a badge that went onto the things you "like" on social media. So, it became a way for you to identify yourself as somebody who would listen. And it just picked up like crazy, and people were so interested in doing it, and it was a very easy way for people to participate. And we don't know what conversations were had. We don't know what types of interactions that led to, other than the fact that people put their name out there and put their support out there. Just nice… nice to see that happen.

In this case, the gap between what was measured and the stated goals of the nonprofit seemed quite large. The campaign measured the number of badges and likes on social media. But such a measure says little—if anything—about how such badges were taken up in practice. Did people indeed listen to their friends' struggles with mental health more than they did before? Did the conversations this planner imagined materialize? Or was engaging on social media a gesture that was never translated into action? There was simply no way to know. Nevertheless, Dey went on to tell us that the badges became something that he both "feels good" about and can present as evidence of moral worth, "something that's nice to talk to people about." This, however, glosses over the gap between the measure and what it supposedly tells us about the world.

Whether or not advertising professionals glossed over the meaning of the measures they used was not primarily about any particular person or how that person may have seen his or her own work. While the Human Rights Watch campaign may not have deployed the most sophisticated methods of causal inference to determine the relationship between the campaign and its outcome, the claim about its efficacy became one of the most rewarding facets of the work. The possibility that he had a hand in freeing 137 political prisoners was an immensely gratifying metric, even if the underlying causal logic was flawed. Thus, the same people could feel extremely proud about the measures they used—and how those measures related to the specific nonprofit's goals—at one moment in the interview, then show a surprisingly cavalier attitude only moments later.

We saw this cavalier attitude in other cases where claims about measurement might have been less than rigorous. In one interview, a CEO talked about the agency's work on an antibullying campaign that rolled out in schools. The campaign involved an app in which students could record and upload instances of bullying:

> It's a remarkable piece of software. It's run by a remarkable group of people who have since become personal friends. And the amazing thing is that incidences of bullying have been reduced almost 70 percent immediately upon installing this system in a school.

While we did not check the veracity of this statement, arguing that a video-based antibullying application immediately reduced bullying by 70 percent is a tall order. But the point is not that this interviewee might have been less than truthful. Rather, he uncritically channeled impressionistic measures from the nonprofit, which in turn may have been channeling these measures from a school. What measurement was — and what it wasn't — was defined elsewhere.

Last, it is important to note that this relationship to measurement did not operate in a vacuum. Advertising professionals act as cultural intermediaries.[15] Planners and creatives alike see themselves as cultural experts — as analysts and producers of "culture," however vaguely defined. As we have seen, focusing on images, narratives, ideas, punchlines, and cultural tensions led many advertising professionals to define their profession as one that straddles "art and science."[16] In that space between art and science, the place of measurement was somewhat suspect. As one creative said:

> The best part about it is when people who don't work in advertising have seen the spot and were talking to me about the organization. Because that makes me feel like it's working. You know, I think when we're in our industry, the end result is sort of squishy sometimes for us. . . . [The nonprofit was] not looking for big mega-donations; they're looking just to get on the map. So, I think [it] was obviously the more holistic kind of win. But I also think sitting in an edit with all of the pieces and being like, "Wow, we were able to get all these partners on board — all these celebrities, all this talent, for nothing, to do this."

Once again, part of what shapes this discussion of measurement is that the pro bono was "looking just to get on the map" and create awareness of both the organization and its cause. The result was a more "holistic" success — that is, one whose constituent effects cannot quite be pinpointed. Equally important was this general "squishiness" that the interviewee attributed to advertising. In a world of squishy end results, meaningful measures are feel-good impressions; people talking about the campaign or celebrities willing to donate their time and talent to the cause.

Taking the side of art to the extreme, some interviewees — all of them creatives — seemed to militantly oppose the very idea of quantifying what is primarily a cultural intervention. In such cases, they argued, their work "created conversation" or "moved the needle." Metrics were beside the point. As one art director said when asked what he liked best about working on a particular pro bono account:

> You look at certain brands that just shape culture and shape conversation. [For example,] the fact that there is now a statue of a little girl down here [on Wall Street, in New York City] staring down the bull [statue]. There are just thousands of photos of people tweeting about that today, and that's changing the conversation. You know, trying to be a part of something that influences. Culture influences a certain segment of an audience, whether it's above the line of something that everyone is going to see or if it's below the line and not everyone is going to be paying attention to . . . but you know that you were part of something that actually made an impact.

In previous chapters we showed how advertising professionals oscillated between two ways of treating their pro bono campaigns as moral: based on the authenticity of their moral convictions as ends unto themselves, and based on the consequences of their actions. Yet consequentialism, it seems, did not always require professionals to carefully parse out what these consequences were. In other words, it did not force professionals to think through the relationship between the available measures they were afforded, and the goals of the campaign. When the relationship between these measures and the campaign's goals were underdefined — that is, the nonprofit did not attempt to or succeed in linking measures and effects — advertising professionals were left with a facile consequentialism free of consequences. Pro bono work was morally compelling because it made a positive effect on the world, but that change was presumed more than it was observed.

Conclusions

We began this chapter with Barman's definition of measurement as "assigning a value to a good." Yet if measurement entered into this book's story of different goods, it was through a double transubstantiation. It was not only that measurement transformed a good into a (numerical) value; the numerical value was transformed into an index of a good—whether moral or creative—that could not quite be measured.

As in other fields, there is nothing automatic about the way measurement indicates goods. Rather, it is more useful to think about measurement as a set of affordances, providing particular resources and shaping some of the narratives that advertising professionals can tell to themselves and to others about goods in pro bono work. For most of our interviewees—or at least for most of the interviewees who spoke about measurement—metrics were seductive. As with the differences between pro bono and paid work more generally, it was not only that measurement allowed advertising professionals to experience their pro bono work in a certain way but also that it allowed them to experience their labor in ways that they often craved in their regular campaigns for paying clients.

While some advertising professionals and agencies said that they proactively looked for nonprofits and projects that took measurement seriously, most of our interviewees didn't use this as a selection criterion. As opposed to managers' careful curation of goods described in chapter 5—where projects were vetted to be organizationally viable and to offer employees interesting work, a high likelihood of recognition, and a feeling of moral investment—the question of measurement almost never came up when managers talked explicitly about curating their pro bono projects.

Some measures were always available. As pro bono work was almost invariably digital, online likes, shares, and views were ready-to-hand. The relationship between these measures and the supposed ends of the campaign, however, was often "squishy," in the words of one creative. Where careful calibration of measurement to the campaigns' goals either left something to be desired or was almost completely absent, advertising professionals still spoke enthusiastically of the effects of their work to further a moral cause. But these were amorphous outcomes—a consequentialism without consequences.

8. Tangled Goods

"Brands are allowed to have a social conscience," says Rich Silverstein, cofounder of the agency Goodby, Silverstein & Partners (GS&P), as the camera focuses on a plentiful mass of Doritos chips falling gently off a conveyor belt. Flashing past in a pleasing slow-motion shot, this mass of triangular snacks is familiar. But against the backdrop of xylophone accompaniment, we notice that these chips are unusual. They are brightly colored: a cornucopia of rainbow hues. Silverstein explains, "With Doritos we did rainbow chips for a gay pride parade. And I think that's what's changed in advertising. You're allowed to bring the social commentary into the brand. That's a big deal."[1]

The "social commentary" Silverstein refers to has become part and parcel of advertising for contemporary brands, so much so that GS&P's website has a tab dedicated to doing good. The tab, branded "DoGood," is headed by text declaring, "Sometimes it's possible to do good while doing well." The snack corporation Frito-Lay (owned by PepsiCo) can today do well by appealing to chip consumers who support gay pride and LGBTQ causes, while GS&P's advertising does good by advancing the cause of LGBTQ visibility and acceptance, performing the kind of second-order CSR work that we described in an earlier chapter.

While not a pro bono account, the kind of work GS&P did to align the Doritos brand with gay pride represents a broader shift in the advertising industry. As we have described throughout the book, advertising has played a prominent role both in making visible the CSR work that corporate clients initiate—visibility, after all, is what these CSR efforts are often after—as well as its own CSR efforts in the shape of pro bono work for a variety of nonprofits. But as the Doritos example shows, these CSR efforts are more than a reaction to critique that gave it its important historical push. As so often happens with critiques of capitalism, CSR has been co-opted and turned inwards.[2] "Advertising for good" is not something that firms reluctantly do, but that they find meaningful and believe actually helps their bottom line in a variety of ways. "Doing well by doing good," as the mantra goes.

What "the good" means, however, is not straightforward—and tracing this tangle of meanings has been the empirical crux of this book. The good in pro bono work is the literal translation of the *bono* of *pro bono publico*, while also representing a collection of other notions of what it means to be good and do good. These include the existential good that is inherent in "good work"—itself an amalgam of creative freedom, control over the labor process, and gift relationships with the nonprofit client and the recipients of its mission. It includes the consecration of both the actors and the work in the field, and the recognition and careers that such consecration affords. For managers, it includes organizational goods—helping them to recruit and retain talent, as well as providing a safe training ground where advertising professionals in the agency can cut their teeth.

The relationship among these different goods gives rise to different patterns of navigation for both managers and professionals. Managers, as we have shown, perform crucial practices of curation. Beyond attending to organizational economic goods, they also need to forecast reactions of the advertising professionals in their firms. Attending to these potential tensions, they let in only those pro bono campaigns for which they believe different goods will smoothly align. Such work, while crucial, does not resolve all potential tensions among goods. In our interviews, advertising professionals relied on a series of different narrative techniques to make the tangle of goods tension-free. They did so through boundary work, pointing at cynical others such as agencies and campaigns in which the goods sharply contrasted. They also did so more implicitly by relying on the language of "passion" to pivot among goods. A passion, as we have shown, was the ultimate floating signifier, enabling advertising professionals to transition seamlessly among different grammars of goods.

Last, we have shown how the question of the campaign's effectiveness percolates into the question of goods. Part of the seduction of pro bono work is precisely that of measurement. Both in terms of its immediate temporality and in terms of the size of its effects, pro bono work offers professionals a more tangible experience of "effectiveness" than does much of their work for large corporate clients. At the same time, however, the relationship between measurements and campaign consequences on the ground is often unclear—a consequentialism with vague consequences at best. The good and the effective, like the different goods of pro bono more generally, tangle and untangle in patterned ways.

Pro bono advertising, we argue, cuts to the heart of inquiry about the profusion of goods and patterned tangling and untangling of grammars. In that sense, we have attempted to think about how we can productively conceptualize and study multiple grammars. But attending to these entanglements also provides a glimpse into the practical workings of CSR more broadly. Activity "in the public good" now appears comfortably installed in the activities of corporations located at the heart of capitalism — from multinational energy corporations to large banks, from advertising agencies to pharmaceutical companies. But how does such work make sense to those who perform these projects? Finally, understanding the relationship among goods in pro bono work helps us see what happens when such projects are taken up and brought to public attention, and how notions of the good shift as they move into the public eye.

By taking stock of what we have learned, and opening up some new comparative and analytical questions, this chapter outlines some of the ways that pro bono advertising can make us look anew at these questions.

Grammars of Goods, Relevance Structures, and Levels of Analysis

Throughout the course of this book we have developed a new understanding of the ways that different grammars of goods tangle and untangle within a particular social world. At the end of our journey, we would like to revisit our starting point and specify how the theorization we have developed allows us to see new things in our data and how it opens us to see new questions in other cases.

Our starting point is that it is useful to think about the different goods that we outline not so much as elements of a cultural repertoire but as available grammars. Here, we join in a simple insight with a wide movement in the sociology of culture: meanings come in packages. There is an implicit entailment among elements. To take one example, *if* we use moral language, *then* we also need to manage, or somehow account for, the fact that pro bono work also moves careers along. This is both because of the narrative structure of goods and because these goods, as Friedland, Thévenot, and others remind us, are embedded and embodied in particular organizational and institutional structures. Grammars, in this regard, can be thought of as distributed — they inhere in actors but also in institutions, organizations, and even the material affordances that media advertising professionals work with (e.g., the ability to see shares and likes on social media).

This does not mean that managing different grammars needs to be particularly hard or that goods are somehow "incommensurable" or at odds. This, we think, reproduces a kind of abstract academic purism that has little purchase in our data. After all, as we have shown, morality and awards can coexist quite nicely when advertising professionals shift their moral discourse to talk in consequentialist terms. What it does mean, however, is that we need to think about meaning as loosely organized bundles. As people inhabit a world of different goods, they reach out for different available grammars and work either to tangle or to untangle them in different situations.

Such tangling and untangling, purifying and blurring, are practical achievements. It is precisely because we begin with practical action that we cannot assume that goods necessarily compete. To return to our data, we showed how in some situations it may be difficult to parse out good work (in terms of professionals' existential relationship to their labor) and the recognition of that work in awards and in the field. After all, if the work is good, shouldn't it win an award? Similarly, in some situations, the moral good and good work become almost synonymous. But this too is not preordained. In other situations, good work and moral work are perceived as at odds with each other; at certain junctures, the kind of flashy work that tends to win awards was considered as a mark of bad work and an index of moral defilement. Both as a methodological stance and as a theoretical one, we think that the sociology of culture needs to be agnostic about the "natural state" of different goods.

As we laid out in the introduction, and alongside Roger Friedland's later work, we must push further Weber's metaphor of polytheism of values.[3] In Weber's usage of the metaphor, the polytheism of values entails the need to choose which of the gods we follow. As Weber put it, the gods "strive to gain power over our lives and again they resume their eternal struggle with one another."[4] Here, we think, Weber muddled his own metaphor.[5] For, as Weber himself saw well in his study of religion, the idea of eternal struggle is not quite polytheistic. Polytheism assumes that gods inhere in different domains. They clash sometimes, they work seamlessly in others, they fall in love and produce little godlings. But in almost no case do they inherently clash. The Manichaean undertone of eternal struggle is a precursor to monotheism rather than a defining feature of polytheism.

Rather than assuming struggle, taking the metaphor of polytheism seriously means that we think about the relationship among gods more openly. This is for a few reasons. First, this is because each one of these grammars is far from unified or simple. As Gabriel Abend has shown (and as any philosopher working on metaethics knows all too well), "the moral good" can mean a host of different things. There are many different ways to define the good, and each has its own logic of entailment. While these are all "moral" in the minimalist sense that we use in this book—as defining actors' selves across situations in salient and emotionally loaded ways—they make different background assumptions. The narratives that we have heard include elements of different conceptions of the moral good. To return to the metaphor of polytheism, gods often have more than one facet. As one depiction clashes with other goods, another may not. It is in this sense that grammars are "loose." In contrast to both logics and regimes of worth, in any grammar there is simply a lot of internal complexity.

A second reason to think about the relationship among goods in a more open way is that any "move" may be highly ambiguous. Think of our discussion of the language of passion as the ultimate ambiguous offering. The same narrative move can be equally effective across different goods, blurring the distinctions between them. It is also the case that, much as in polytheistic mythologies, the domains of different gods may overlap. While we identify different grammars, some situations tangle grammars such that it is hard for actors to parse them out, while other situations put them on clashing trajectories. There is no pure logic of grammars, only situational, practical, tangling and untangling.

Thinking in terms of such a situational entailment of grammars propels us to think more carefully about what the notion of a situation entails. The situation is an important part of the interactionist banner, but it is something that sociology has not thought about nearly hard enough. In originally focusing on the situation, interactionists made two important points, still neglected after more than half a century: (1) there is a radical creative potential in interaction that cannot be completely accounted for by actors' pasts and structural context, and (2) a good portion of what occurs in the social world is not carried around in actors' heads but is a result of patterned creative practical solutions to problems they encounter.

These points were crucial in going beyond the platitude that all action happens in a particular situation. Still, interactionists have not theorized the structure of the situation as such—treating it as a self-evident moment in which action takes place. This, we think, hinders some of our ability to think about the patterned way in which goods are interrelated. While many sociologists of culture pay homage to the practical situation in which goods are invoked and deployed, they treat the situation in something of a one-dimensional way, a practical point in time and space.

Yet situations are structurally complex. As the chapters of this book show, the same situation can be seen through different prisms. Working on a pro bono account is practical labor, but it is also something that defines the self beyond the present; it stretches into the professional future—shaping careers and recognition in the field; it also makes the work within the advertising agency more or less tolerable, more or less glorious. We can think about these different facets as different layers of the situation. Or, to be more theoretically precise, as overlapping structures of relevance that have the situation as their nexus.

Here, we draw on the work of the founder of phenomenological sociology, Alfred Schutz, who saw relevance structures as the basic ways through which we understand situations, objects, and other people as particular kinds—what he called "typification."[6] Relevance structures are both culturally given and situationally emergent in practical action. We see things in particular ways because we have learned to treat certain aspects as relevant. Think, for example, about the immediate relation we construct between how someone dresses and their social class, as opposed to height and social class. But we also see things differently depending on our practical projects. Drawing from pragmatist thought and Weber's sociology, Schutz saw that typifications depend not only on what he called the "sedimentation" of other situations in the structure of our experience but also on the particular project actors are engaged in—what we are trying to do and whether the environment we are embedded in smooths over our projects or resists them.

Our point is that situations often entail multiple relevance structures simultaneously. While in some situations we may attend to certain relevance structures rather than others, in many situations these are co-relevant. Even as advertising professionals attend to the moral dimension of the pro bono work, their careers are also relevant, as is the joy they take (or not) and the meaning that they find (or not) in their work. As with everything else we described, the question of how many relevance structures are experienced in a particular moment and whether one relevance structure is more central in a given moment is empirical—it cannot be predetermined theoretically.

Once we jettison the unidimensional structure of situations to think in terms of a nexus of multiple relevance structures, the relationship between goods becomes theoretically clearer, and is also empirically more productive. This allows us to see how situations carry both embedded pasts and multiple possible futures. Different relevance structures extend differently in time and rope in different aspects of an actor's life. Moral discourse, for example, reaches outside the work to define the actor across situations. But this is more than an abstract extension, as advertising professionals often explicitly imagine what they would be able to tell their friends or their spouses. Similarly, striving for recognition and awards is the stuff of applause and time spent on the French Riviera, but also the extension of that consecration into future careers and salaries. Different relevance structures not only point in different directions; they point to different timelines and other moments in actors' lives.[7]

These relevance structures and temporalities, again, may overlap. First, there are some boundary concepts that reach toward different goods. The existential relationship to labor, for example, is primarily located in a professional domain, as it defines the professional as a particular kind of craftsperson. But finding meaning in one's work has also become moralized—that is, something that defines the person across situations. Increasingly, while we may be agnostic about what kind of meaning people find in their work, we expect them to find some sort of meaning there, and we see their failure to do so as a broader, intersituational failure. That is, in our terms, we see it as a moral failure. Finding meaning, then, is at the interstices of a good located within work, and one that is located beyond it.

More importantly for our purposes, it is also the case in a more practical, mundane way. In many moments, we would be hard pressed to separate the relevance structures of our actions. In that regard, we can move away from the specific case of pro bono advertising. It has become a truism that many of our actions (if not most of them) are overdetermined—they are the (always provisional) end point of multiple processes and considerations. Is writing a book such as this current one a move in a career? It will look good on the authors' CVs—perhaps leading to a promotion or helping them find an elusive tenure-track job. But it may also be the very thing that gives the authors' job meaning. In the second regard, it is not about recognition but about meaningful work. Then again, there are moments when making a career move (perhaps by citing particular influential authors in the vague hope of currying favor, making alliances, or joining the "right" club) can be experienced as being in tension with crafting good work. Many other examples are more complicated still. Was participation in the Arab Spring demonstrations about democracy in Egypt or about seeing oneself as a new global and "Western" citizen? Or was it about the camaraderie of camping and chanting together in Tahrir Square? Each action propels us in multiple directions. In many cases, the kinds of background assumptions about the good that each invokes, to return to Gabriel Abend's felicitous phrasing, may be quite different.

The point is not, however, to note that life is complicated and every action overdetermined. This is true, of course, but it is not theoretically surprising.[8] The point is that to understand the social phenomena that we find important—a particular form of CSR in our example—we need to outline the patterned relationship between goods. Since the analysis of the relationship between grammars of the good is inherently also an analysis of overlapping structures of relevance within a situation, we need to pay attention to the patterning of situations and their structure.

Here, we need to think more carefully about the relationship between a cognitivist version of "culture," understood as the kinds of meanings people carry with them wherever they go, and a more distributed version of the notion of culture. A way to think about it is to wonder whether the grammars of goods that we describe in this book predate the situation of working pro bono, or whether they follow from it, analytically and temporally. In one sense, we believe, the grammars we describe predate the situation. In order to evoke something, there needs to first be something to evoke. Vocabularies of meaningful work, of the morality of aiding distant suffering, and of "making it in a career" are historically emergent grammars that are recognizable well beyond the advertising world we describe. They are not constructed ex nihilo.

But this is too facile. It is not that people in the advertising industry, as far as we can tell, were looking for a pro bono opportunity before the rising popularity of CSR in the 1990s. The Ad Council notwithstanding, there is simply no evidence that advertising professionals were actively looking for such opportunities. But once CSR took over, and pro bono work emerged, it found the grammars or good "waiting for it." In that sense, grammars of goods are available at particular junctures, and they are more or less likely to be invoked. They are, to use J. J. Gibson's term, "affordances" shaping possible understandings and actions.[9] The crucial theoretical nexus is the interaction between possible grammars and the structured exigencies of situations. It is in this sense that the situation is not simply an added-on feature and that the grammars of the goods are, also, situationally located grammars.[10]

The situation of pro bono work, then, evokes different grammars that were existent only *in potentia*. Yet it does much more than that. The challenges of the situation, and the grammars it evokes, set up the choreography of tangling and untangling that we depict in this book. The challenges also push advertising professionals and managers alike to particular "solutions"—ways of navigating goods that are themselves patterned. This is why the ways of preempting potential tensions through managerial curation, the language of passion, and the shifts to a conse-quentialist moral vocabulary are so significant. These do not constitute a shared know-how, spreading through communication networks or idiocultural diffusion among advertising professionals;[11] they are recurring creative solutions to recurring practical problems. Situations, then, both summon culturally available grammars of good, position them in relation to one another, and nudge actors toward patterned routes that they use to navigate them.[12]

At last, we can say something about what we see as the *fit* between the advertising field and pro bono work as one kind of CSR practice. This fit can be thought about in two ways. First, it is all very personal. In an era when work needs to have meaning, pro bono work supplies that meaning in abundance; in a job in which people intermittently feel uneasy about the kinds of effects they have (or don't have) on the world, pro bono work allows them a different kind of moral selfhood. For those yearning for recognition, pro bono work provides new avenues to become consecrated and known. This is the *existential fit* between pro bono work and the advertising field.

This existential fit, however, is only one side of the coin. It is predicated upon, and it recursively constitutes a *structural fit* that itself operates at multiple levels of analysis. Organizationally, it is made possible because this work—while still drawing resources—allows managers to recruit and retain talent, and to train employees in a safe sandbox of sorts; in terms of professional structure, it allows people to challenge jurisdictional boundaries that they find frustrating in their everyday work for corporate clients; on the field level, it provides avenues for consecration and possibilities to move within and among agencies. While there are other ways to produce CSR work in advertising in this era, this kind of fit means that it becomes an "obvious" way of participating in the world of contemporary capitalism.

Thinking about the fit between CSR work, different goods, and the patterning of the advertising world also has empirical echoes beyond the situations of work that we focused on and beyond the social life of advertising. First, if pro bono work is defined by the tangle of different goods that we describe, what happens when the work moves from the agency to the wider public? That is, what is the relationship between the tangle of goods that defines the work and how that work then appears in the public sphere—something that we touched upon briefly but could not develop, since the bulk of our data centered on the work. Second, if the tangle of goods we describe is a property of situations rather than of particular people, how do patterns of navigating CSR look in other fields that have institutionalized pro bono work in a somewhat similar way, such as law? What kinds of family resemblances and differences might we expect to find in other cases of CSR work?

Morality, Grammars, and the Public Sphere

Advertising, in structural terms, has always been in the business of taking brands from corporate backrooms and into the public eye. While there has been a recent movement toward more "surgical" advertising that targets particular micropopulations — or even individuals — advertising is still rooted in its ability to command the attention of people as they go about their lives. Think, for example, of the installation at Grand Central Station on political prisoners in Burma, which commuters encountered as they tried to get from one place to another. Even as we may be increasingly exposed to online advertising, as we surf the web or look through our social media, the movement is still toward a more or less diffuse public. Indeed, even as it does so in very different ways, and to very different ends, it is similar to journalism in that regard: depending on its ability to direct the flow of public awareness.

How should we think about this move to public awareness? Here we find the interaction between two strands of thought about the public sphere productive. On the one hand, Ari Adut argues that the ability to direct conversation in the public sphere is premised on the power to create spectacle.[13] Being in public is not so much about reasoned discourse, as it is about attention-grabbing and dramatic performance. In that regard, the public sphere — and particularly the politics of being in public — is a far cry from the Habermasian communicative utopia. Being in public is being seen, and the politics and aesthetics of such visibility are crucial for any theory of the public sphere. Yet as other students of the public sphere have stressed, this is also a moralized domain. The public sphere is "saturated with discursive moral 'stuff': speech acts, narratives, accounts, claims."[14]

The relation between visibility and moralization is a crucial one. While not all "publicness" is moralized, much of it is. The movement of elements from the particular world they originated in into "the public" is, as Jeffrey Alexander has shown, a *moral* transformation. The public sphere is, at its heart, a moral sphere and the process of becoming widely available — of being "societalized," as Alexander calls it — is a morally imbued one.[15]

Whether or not the public sphere is necessarily moralized, our case hints at the transformations that occur as goods move into the public eye. When they were interviewed in the press, and when the campaign got enough recognition to be written about and highlighted in the media, the moral grammar was purified. Pro bono work, then, sheds the tangled grammars of goods we have described; even moral discourse loses its consequentialist trappings to return to a kind of Kantian realm of pure ends. In other words, while the world of goods we described in this book is a polytheistic one, the mundane societalization that occurred as it came into public focus was accompanied by a monotheistic transformation. While the campaigns were depicted as good work, in the sense of creative and aesthetic objects, the creativity of good labor disappears as a grammar.

This transformation of pro bono work as it moves to the public sphere is important in two seemingly opposite ways. First, through these lenses, we can think more clearly about the relationship between spectacle and grammars of goods. One of the upshots of the purification of goods and the distillation of the moral as the only relevant grammar of good as it moves to the public sphere is that—if we forget the pasts of this transformation—we lose our ability to understand failure. Thus, the example of Grey's I Sea campaign—the refugee-saving mobile application that wasn't—is instructive. If we do not understand how projects tangle different goods, the only way to understand the release of the test application before it was ready, and submitting it to the Cannes festival, is by assigning it to the realm of the demonic. When all that is left is the moral, then the failure must be a purely moral failure.

Taking the work of pro bono seriously thus allows us to think of the role of different grammars of goods in the public sphere, even as these are elided. The point is not that the moral appears only when the campaign becomes societalized. As we have shown, that is far from the case. Yet the moral is stripped away from the tangle of grammars that made pro bono work so compelling in the first place and that was the precondition of its emergence into the public sphere. To really understand this, of course, we need to follow the process of societalization more than we have in this book. But we believe that our findings open some questions that students of the public sphere can find productive: about the process of purification and about the echoes of other goods that the object carries from its past.

Last, if situations include their potential futures, as we have argued, then the inverse is also true. The potential purification of the disparate grammars of goods within the public sphere is already relevant in the process of pro bono work. In terms that phenomenological philosophers gravitate toward, the move into the public sphere is always-already present as a potential. How this matters is something that we can only speculate about because our data, again, do not adequately trace how advertising professionals interact about their pro bono work beyond the agency. Still, we can see some glimpses of these other situations when professionals told us that they often talked about the work they did with their friends, their parents, or their spouses. In these moments, the moral dimension was salient. The point is not that advertising professionals obscured other goods, although they may have. The point is that being in public meant that the work was moralized and purified of other grammars. For professionals who are often criticized as amoral, and even stigmatized, this is a moral privilege.[16]

Beyond Advertising: CSR and Goods in Comparative Perspective

Focusing on the variation in situations — and the patterned way goods are tangled and untangled within them — allows us to better understand what happens when pro bono work moves into the public sphere, when the situation radically changes. There is, however, another form of variation that may prove generative: variation among fields. Pro bono advertising is but one instantiation of CSR in the wider world of contemporary capitalism. If the patterns that we find emerge at the interstices of situations, affordances, and organizational dynamics, how do these vary across fields?

To get at such variation, we need to return to two pillars underlying our analysis in this book. First, we approached CSR as practical work, focusing on the actual people who need to both assign and enact pro bono work, and the challenges and draws of that work. This allowed us to understand something about the existential and structural fit between the advertising field and pro bono work. How, then, might our approach be transposed to other fields? Is there a variation in terms of fit? Are some places "a better fit" for CSR than are others? Do these fields give rise to a different tangle of goods? The short answer, of course, is that in most cases we don't know. While there is an explosion of work about CSR, these studies have not focused on the perspectives of the actors performing CSR, but on larger macro-determinants, on history, or on the personal moral values of managers and workers who perform the work.

A partial exception to this dearth of literature comes from law, the field that is perhaps the closest to advertising in terms of its CSR practices. The term pro bono arose in the world of law and is perhaps even more salient in that field.[17] Indeed, pro bono is deeply institutionalized in law. The New York Bar Association defines pro bono as public service for a governmental entity or work that

(1) assists in the provision of legal services without charge for
    (i) persons of limited means;
    (ii) not-for-profit organizations; or

>(iii) individuals, groups or organizations seeking to secure or promote access to justice, including, but not limited to, the protection of civil rights, civil liberties or public rights.[18]

Indeed, pro bono is so deeply institutionalized in law that, in New York State, pro bono has become mandatory. In fact, since 2015, to receive admission to the state bar in New York State, lawyers need to show that they first conducted a minimum of fifty hours of pro bono work.[19] Eight other states have yearly mandatory reporting of pro bono work, explicitly designed to encourage such work.

The establishment of the pro bono mandate revealed some of the underlying assumptions about such work in the world of law. Pro bono work, here, is moralized, and even some objections to the mandate were couched in moral language, claiming that it may induce cynicism toward pro bono work instead of following lawyers' purer moral motives.[20] But even in such documents, there are hints of other goods.

First, there are organizational goods to be had. The confluence of "doing well by doing good" is unsurprisingly visible throughout the literature on pro bono in law. Much as in the chapter on curatorial practices in this book, pro bono work, though a drain on resources, is made less onerous, and even beneficial, for the organization. Pro bono work becomes a recruitment and retention tool that senior partners dangle in front of potential recruits, and the work provides "practical training" for junior lawyers in the firm.[21]

Other findings by legal scholars studying pro bono work also bear some uncanny resemblance to our own. The legal scholars Cummings and Rhode note that "although firms receive potential opportunities from nonprofit organizations based on client need, our survey data suggest that key considerations in selecting matters are whether a case is likely to appeal to firm associates and provide good training... 'what people [i.e. lawyers] are interested in and match that with what is happening on the ground.'"[22] As in the advertising world, managers (or senior partners) need to anticipate the kinds of moral commitments and goods that those who will actually perform the work would be excited about.

Moreover, much as in the world of advertising, it isn't only a matter of balancing the moral "good" with the organizational requirement to do "well." Pro bono work itself, as labor, is also important. The actual work with pro bono clients is often experienced as quite different from the work they do at the firm, in terms of subject matter and involvement. As one sociologist of law noted in reference to survey data: "The finding that large law firm attorneys derive more benefit from pro bono in the areas of interviewing and people-related skills may be indicative of the tendency among large-firm attorneys to have little direct contact with clients.... In most cases, these lawyers may have very little opportunity to see a case through from beginning to end, since much of the work within large law firms amounts to working on fragments of cases."[23]

Thus, while law is professionally less fragmented than advertising—in the sense that all lawyers have to pass a relatively similar bar exam across states—lawyers often work on aspects of a case rather than taking ownership over the process in its entirety. Pro bono work may thus be professionally compelling for a somewhat similar reason as in advertising: the ability to take ownership over the entire work process and to follow a case from inception to conclusion. This ends up, as other researchers put it, "providing aspirants to partnership with interesting and satisfying work that compensates for some of the many unsatisfying aspects of large law firm practice."[24]

Reminiscent of advertising, pro bono work can become a vehicle of recognition for individual lawyers and law firms. Lawyers increasingly put the pro bono cases they worked for on their résumés, showcasing their capabilities. Moreover, the institutionalization of pro bono also gave rise to the creation of a position of pro bono counsel, who organizes and allocates pro bono efforts within large firms. Thus, the position itself becomes an avenue for career mobility, a new area of specialization that lawyers can work their way into.[25] On the level of the firm, researchers have noted how pro bono efforts become a vehicle of distinction—a way to denote the elite status of a law firm.[26] A form of organizational conspicuous consumption, it showcases the values of the firm while also signaling that it can afford to spend its time on projects that don't make immediate sense in economic terms.

In short, then, the tangle of goods in the current world of law in the United States bears some striking similarities to that in advertising. Listening carefully to what lawyers say, we can hear a moral grammar intersecting with narratives of meaningful work; grammars of recognition and careers tangled with organizational goals.

But the point is not simply that "it also happens elsewhere." It inevitably does. Rather, the approach we have developed can be used as a yardstick for thinking about other cases comparatively. What is the role of institutionalization in the different shapes that pro bono takes? How does the codification of what pro bono even means affect the way these goods are tangled? How do different professional structures—with different jurisdictional lines—matter? Does it matter that law is not organized around awards? While we can glimpse a tangle of goods in both worlds, thinking about law can turn some of the coordinates of our case into variables rather than constitutive elements.

Going further afield, from pro bono work to other sites in which CSR is common, the empirical pickings are slimmer. There are, to the best of our knowledge, no studies of the actual work of corporate CSR as it is practiced and made meaningful. While there are calls to focus on the narratives and practices of CSR, these have been rather more aspirational declarations of intent than sustained empirical projects.[27] Still we can find hints of the tangle of goods and of some relevant axes of variation in snippets of publicly available data in other fields.

One place where we can get oblique glimpses of other goods is in pharmaceutical corporations and their CSR projects. Such projects are often done to increase access to health in poorer and underserved areas, and interviews conducted with managers overseeing these efforts are telling. Thus, in an interview with a Merck executive, he related a CSR project called Project Sambhav:

> There was a need in India to treat nearly 15 million people infected with the Hepatitis C Virus (HCV), 70 percent of whom lived in rural settings. The problem was cash flow issues prohibiting patients from managing the cost of treatment. Project Sambhav provided access to Pegintron (one of Merck's Hep C medications) for patients with limited or no insurance coverage. Through an innovative micro-financing program, patients were given zero-interest, no-collateral loans to pay for their medicine over an extended period of time. . . . The micro-financing piece enabled them [patients] to access medicine at a cost they could afford over an extended period of time. Project Sambhav addressed an important social need, while at the same time, allowed Merck to create a market in a place where it previously did not have one.[28]

As this interview excerpt makes clear, this is a moral mission—getting medicine to those who need it. Still, this mission is complemented by another: the project also "created a market" for Merck to expand into. Again, doing well by doing good. How, though, do the people actually working on this project see it? Is it also a way for them to show their problem-solving skills and advance in the company? Is the work of creating new markets a professionally interesting one?

To take another interview example, a Pfizer executive talked about the company's CSR efforts in sub-Saharan Africa: "The fact that we still have neglected tropical diseases is a real issue and a real problem. We're making inroads, but collectively we can all do a better job."[29] In an era of zoonotic diseases such as Ebola and COVID-19, do people who do this work see themselves as working on important areas and problems—not only in moral terms but also in professional terms?

In another field, big oil, CSR often takes the shape of protecting nature and investing in "clean" energy. The same corporations that drive some of the worst elements of climate change develop renewable projects—harnessing the power of gravity for small-scale energy consumption in an African village, or saving a tract of forest even as they explore the deep sea for oil. What are these people thinking? In informal conversations with some workers who did CSR work for a big oil corporation, Sonia found that the role of science—of a green future, which energy companies realize may be coming even as they obstruct and delay it—played an important part. CSR work, in this regard, was also working at the corporation's new frontier.

CSR in pharmaceutical corporations and big oil, hazy as they are without better data, opens up comparative vistas. What is the role of the imagined future of the industry in decisions to take on CSR work? In light of pandemic experiences, paying more attention to tropical diseases suddenly seems important; with the world slowly transitioning to renewable energy, CSR work may also be simultaneously understood as inhabiting the future of energy business. As opposed to the work of advertising, the CSR work of other industries may have the temporality of a changing world as a crucial question. Moreover, is there a sense in which CSR, in fields where such work is further away from the everyday work of the profession, becomes less tangled? Could it be that in these cases CSR is less appealing precisely because it cannot afford the kind of tangle of goods that we have described in this book?

While here we can supply more questions that we can answers, our approach in this book opens up a way of thinking and studying the world of CSR—a world of practical activity, where the tangling and untangling of goods plays a crucial role.

Navigating Goods and the Practical Life of CSR

What does this all mean for the study of goods? Our work has a few upshots. First, theoretically, we argue that the kind of research we have crafted makes a case for why it is useful to think in terms of grammars. To understand the tensions, challenges, and navigations outlined in this book, we need to think in terms of entailment rather than the strategic use of particular cultural elements. The relationship between these grammars of goods is, however, not set in advance. As situations are layered, goods tangle and untangle in different ways and as practical accomplishments. Thus, we call for a deepening of our engagement with the notion of the situation, with its relevance structures, layers, and temporalities, as well as for a more empirical sociology, one that makes fewer assumptions than those that sociologists studying the good are prone to make.

Practically, such an approach also means that we must move between different levels of analysis — from the profession to the organizational, from field analysis to the intersituational reverberations of morality. If we are to understand the ways different goods are afforded and lived through, we must allow actors' multiple and layered ways of being embedded in the world to guide our analysis. Doing so also allows us to see the patterned ways actors tangle and untangle goods as they navigate different grammars.

These patterned navigations are, at last, an important part of how CSR efforts are sustained on the ground. Without describing the practical work CSR takes, we leave a black box unopened. People need to perform this work, and — as we have shown in the case of advertising — the work can often be compelling. Without understanding these practicalities, tensions, and seductions, it would be hard to account for how particular kinds of CSR work end up inhabiting particular fields.

Focusing on the practical life of CSR allows us to also show some of the limitations and opportunities within the current structure of pro bono in the advertising field. The people we interviewed were, by and large, morally invested in their work. They often worked nights and weekends on their pro bono campaigns; they took pride in their ability to use their professional skills for causes they cared about. They wanted to do interesting work, they enjoyed elements of the labor, and they wanted their careers to take off, but the moral grammar was a crucial one. While on a systemic level CSR emerged, as our interviewees would say, to "put lipstick on a pig," pro bono works so well in the advertising industry precisely because of how it fits with advertising professionals' existential challenges and yearnings. In a limited way, pro bono also does *do* good. While the question of measurement is often fraught, these campaigns bring particular problems to the public sphere, and at least for a time, they can result in an outpouring of resources and action from the people whose attention they managed to snare.

With that said, the causes are often those that professionals are idiosyncratically invested in, or even those that some professionals believe are "hot" at the moment and will garner attention. As such, from a broader structural point of view, pro bono is not a viable way to tackle the world's ills. But this, perhaps, is not the point. It would be undoubtedly good to invest more money in organizations such as the Ad Council, and to take advantage of the kinds of entanglements of goods we have described. But our book does not pretend to provide solutions it is ill equipped to give.

What we can say is that if we are to understand this era of CSR in contemporary capitalism, then we need to understand how professionals enact it on the ground. This entails an appreciation of how they experience moments of boredom and of rapture, how they navigate multiple grammars of goods and relevance structures, how the moral is entangled with multiple other grammars of goods. In short, and without reverting to easy cynicism, it requires that we carefully trace how the possibility of moral action depends on such entanglements and navigations.

Acknowledgments

We would like to thank the interviewees who participated in this study. Advertising professionals are overworked, and spread thin. They all took time to sit with us, answer our unending string of questions, and walk us through their work. Thank you!

Otherwise, this book took almost four years to write, and many debts accrue over such a time.

Three people were particularly crucial for the book: Roger Friedland and Nina Eliasoph provided some of the early, and most formative, comments on the emerging framework of the book. Nina raised the question of the navigation of goods; Roger the polytheistic impetus (although we might have taken the idea in directions that are not quite his); Paul DiMaggio probably realized that having Iddo as an office neighbor had its downsides after the nth time Iddo bounced into his office to discuss the latest data excerpt he was enamored of, and to talk organizations and culture.

We would also like to thank the following institutions, workshops, and colloquia where we presented our work: the University of Melbourne, which housed Iddo during a sabbatical when we started writing (with special thanks to Max Holleran), the École des Hautes Études en Sciences Sociales in Paris, where we presented some of our early ideas, as well as colleagues at the University of Amsterdam, Harvard, NYU Steinhardt, the Hebrew University, the University of Haifa, Yale, and NYU's Sociology of Culture Workshop.

At these talks, or over coffee, colleagues have been incredibly generous with both their critiques and their friendship. We would like to thank Jeff Alexander, Gianpaolo Baiocchi, Beth Bechky, Mathieu Berger, Daniel Cefaï, Kobe De Keere, Yuval Feinstein, Gillian Gualtieri, Jeff Guhin, Eva Illouz, Colin Jerolmack, Nahoko Kameo, Eric Klinenberg, Carly Knight, Monika Krause, Michele Lamont, Steven Lukes, Pamela Pricket, Leah

Reisman, Gisèle Sapiro, Anna Skarpelis, Stefan Timmermans, Vered Vinitzky-Serousi, Robin Wagner-Pacifici, and Viviana Zelizer who all provided important comments at different junctures.

Shelly would like to thank Paula England for persuading her to take Iddo up on the offer to collaborate on this project and for diverting some research funds to make it possible.

Sonia would like to thank Guillermina Altomonte, Jana Glaese, Eliza Brown, and most of all, Sam Dinger for the invaluable feedback and support they offered her during the course of producing this book.

We also thank Marina Theophanopoulou for her work on the history of pro bono in the advertising world and for digging up articles and press releases that helped us contextualize our interview data, Abigail Westberry for help with proof reading, and Claire Sieffert for wonderful editing of this manuscript! Claire saved us not only from grammatical monstrosities but also from many places where our arguments weren't as clear as they should have been.

At the University of Chicago Press, we would like to thank Katherine Faydash for her careful copyediting as well as Michael Koplow and Mollie McFee for ushering the manuscript along. This book went through the hands of two wonderful editors. The late Doug Mitchell took on the project in its early "advance contract" phase, secured incredible readers, and was his usual warm, hilarious, and incisive self. After his death, Elizabeth Branch Dyson took on the project. She was patient with a book that took too long, and a wonderful reader and incisive commenter. We couldn't have hoped for better editors.

Appendix: Notes on Method

This project began when Iddo, conducting an ethnography of planning and strategy at Deutsch, a medium-sized advertising agency in New York, started to see pro bono projects everywhere he went. Talking to his colleagues in the agency and looking through trade journals and personal portfolios of advertising professionals, he realized that this was the general state of the field. Surprised, and feeling like there was an interesting empirical and theoretical story afoot, he proposed to Sonia and Shelly they form a joint project. Sonia was conducting interviews about economy and worth with small businessmen and businesswomen in Argentina, and was enmeshed in the literature on grammars of worth; Shelly was conducting ethnographic work and interviews with sex-toy designers, also thinking and writing about the relationship between different notions of "the good."

While this is partly a matter of the biography of the project, there are a few important methodological upshots to the way it came about. First, while we describe our main source of data in detail, we also had other points of data. Iddo was present as advertising professionals talked to one another about pro bono work and could identify the way they talked in interviews with the way they talked with one another at work. While we draw from the ethnography sparingly, this makes us more confident that the narratives we heard were not made for the benefit of "outsiders." Iddo also drew on thirty-five additional interviews he conducted in order to compare pro bono work with the work advertising professionals do for paying clients. Similarly, Shelly had previously interviewed advertising professionals and designers about the relationship between different forms of work and goods, and she compared her findings to those she had in this other project.

Still, the book is based primarily on semistructured interviews with seventy-three managers and advertising professionals in the New York area — from copywriters and art directors who craft the textual and visual language of the campaigns, through account planners and account management personnel, to middle managers and CEOs. To follow pro bono accounts across different positions in the agency, we interviewed eighteen upper-level managers, twenty-four middle managers, and thirty-one lower-level advertising professionals. The interviewees were sampled from thirty-four agencies and yield detailed narratives about 108 distinct pro bono campaigns.

To construct our sample, we identified all the large agencies in New York and then added all agencies in various "top 100 agency" lists in advertising trade publications. This provided us with a list of successful agencies that we then organized on the basis of size, assuming that different kinds of organizations perform pro bono work slightly differently. As the table demonstrates, we ended up dividing the sample into boutique agencies that employed 11-50 employees, small agencies with 51-200 employees, medium-sized agencies with 201-1,000 employees, large agencies with 1,001-10,000 employees, and huge multinational agencies with 10,000 or more employees.

We used a variety of recruitment strategies for each agency we contacted. We began by emailing the CEO's assistants and, in large agencies, the agency's public relations officer. Because these strategies yielded few responses, we then identified pro bono campaigns through agency websites and looked for the names of the professionals who worked on them. We then reached out to them directly through LinkedIn, a career-oriented social networking platform used by nearly everyone in the industry. Although sending LinkedIn messages directly to advertising professionals yielded a far higher response rate than cold calls and emails to assistants and public relations officers, we still initially struggled to recruit participants. Perhaps even more frustrating was that after potential interviewees agreed to participate in an interview, they often either canceled or neglected to follow up when we tried to pin down a time. We had to develop a thick skin as interviewees canceled or failed to show up.

Drawing on her ethnographic experience with designers, Shelly began gently nudging advertising professionals who had initially agreed to participate but then "ghosted" us; she sent a follow-up email that started by saying something like, "Just circling back to you to bring this up in your inbox." These polite reminders, in the lingua franca of corporate knowledge workers, acknowledged that advertising professionals are notoriously overworked and always juggling more responsibilities than they can handle. To our delight, we found that this strategy worked in an overwhelming majority of cases. Those who ultimately resurfaced often apologized for not getting back to us earlier, suggesting that they were closely monitoring the content of their inbox even when they ignored our emails. We used this same strategy to resolve similar recruitment struggles when we conducted limited snowball sampling for some specific pro bono campaigns, as we tried to interview multiple people who worked on the same project to triangulate different narratives.

We therefore found—in line with interview studies conducted with elite personnel in investment banking and venture capital[1]—that getting access to the field obligated us to embody the professional know-how of our respondents and to strike a fine balance between acknowledging how valuable and in demand their time was and continuously reminding them of the importance of their commitment to participate in our study. Despite these challenges, when we did end up sitting with advertising professionals, we found that they were excited to talk about their pro bono work, and they often went far beyond the time allotted to us for the interview, even pushing back other meetings they had lined up, to show us campaign videos and materials and to go into detail about the work and what it meant to them.

While we talked to whomever would answer our emails, we aligned our sample with what we knew of the structure of the advertising world. The interview sample of managers skews heavily male—with thirteen male upper managers to five females, and only three female middle managers of the twenty-four managers. Of the thirty-one nonmanagerial advertising professionals we interviewed, seventeen were men and fourteen women. This largely mirrors the advertising industry more generally, where women account for only about 28 percent of creatives in advertising agencies in the United States and an even lower percentage of managers.[2] The sample is also overwhelmingly white, with only a few exceptions, again reflecting the percentages of creatives and managers in what is still a predominantly white industry.[3] However, gender and race, while important, did not prove important as a source of variation in the study, except in that, comparatively, women tended to talk more about feminist causes such as wage equality and reproductive rights. The same was true of gay respondents, who more frequently took on LGBTQ+ causes.

As we note in this book, pro bono projects arrived through multiple avenues to these agencies. Rank-and-file professionals often initiated the projects by bringing causes that they cared about to the attention of management and then looking for a nonprofit to work with (n = 11). Sometimes, professionals brought the work to the agency through preexisting personal networks or connections with specific nonprofits (n = 17). In still

AGENCY SIZE AND INTERVIEWEE OCCUPATION

Agency size (employees) (n = 34)	Upper management CEO / founder / partner	Middle management	Professionals (creatives, planners, and account managers)
Boutique 11–50 (n = 8)	9	1	4
Small 51–200 (n = 8)	5	4	7
Medium 201– 1,000 (n = 10)	3	9	13
Large 1,001– 10,000 (n = 4)	NA	6	4
Very large 10,001+ (n = 4)	1	4	3
Total	18	24	31

Note: Given the size of the agencies, the CEOs in boutique agencies are often also partners and founders, and are intimately engaged in the creative work. Boutique agencies also rarely have middle management. As a result, given direct involvement of managers in the work process, we undersampled workers in nonmanagerial positions.

other instances, advertising professionals took a more entrepreneurial approach by generating a campaign idea first and then pitching it to a nonprofit that they thought was a good fit (*n* = 12). Yet an equally significant number of pro bono project opportunities came from the top down: either through the Ad Council (*n* = 12), through managers' personal or professional networks (*n* = 20), or from a nonprofit requesting pro bono creative services through ordinary channels for new clients (*n* = 9). While we sought to identify patterns in how these pro bono projects arrived at different agencies, we found none, especially because for a quarter of the projects (*n* = 27), respondents did not actually know how the pro bono campaign they worked on had gotten there.

Our sample is also differentiated in terms of the actual work that advertising professionals did. Advertising, as we noted in the introduction, has fractured into several different positions. We tried to talk with an equal number of lower-ranked advertising professionals and higher-ranked managers. Within each category, we attempted to talk with a sample of creatives, planners, and, to a lesser degree, account managers. This was because, in general, we found that account managers were less likely to be assigned pro bono work. Given that the account manager's role is to represent the client's interests in the agency, and that pro bono work is a gift of sorts (as we developed in chapter 3), they were less involved in the work and thus less represented in our sample.

The data for this book are largely narrative driven, which raises both the possibility of desirability bias in interviews and questions about our ability to get at situational shifts in a single interview context.[4] The fact that we can rely on some ethnographic observations (while nice) does not absolve us of the challenges of narrative-based inference. While these remain difficult problems for any interview-based research, we considered these challenges in how we designed the interview questions and in our analysis and writing. For one, in most cases we had more than one interviewee within each agency, and we triangulated the narratives of top-tier managers with the narratives provided by middle managers or advertising professionals in nonmanagerial positions. More important, though, this book is about how actors negotiate different grammars of goods, a negotiation that occurs through talk. This strengthened our warrant for an interview design and lessens the risk of our analysis being weakened by its narrative form. As we infer from one context of talk to another, we are less worried about whether situational pressures would completely change the story we are telling. As Richard LaPiere noted almost a century ago, when we ask about symbolic moments (e.g., voting), the correlation between interviews and real-life situations tends to be better than it otherwise might be.[5]

In terms of interview design, in each case, after initial demographic questions, we asked the interviewees about their work in the agency generally. We then asked them to select one or more pro bono accounts that they were closely engaged with. In each case, interviewees were asked about the pragmatics of the pro bono work: how the account arrived at the agency, how they delegated the work, what their role in the work was, and the work process in detail. We also asked whether interviewees had ever declined pro bono accounts and how they assessed different pro bono opportunities. In closing, we asked why they thought pro bono work had such a prominent position in the advertising industry. Using a mode of ethnographic interviews, we distinguished broadly between two kinds of responses. One was a "how" and the other a "why" response. Alternating between both types of questions,[6] we did not assume a perfect correspondence between narratives and behavior, but we did assume that this style of interviewing was good enough to uncover patterns of action and symbolic investments. For example, in chapter 5, dealing with the managerial role and the curation of pro bono work, we do assume that the managers we talked to answered to the best of their recollection about how work was assigned to professionals in the agency. Here the triangulation of interviews was crucial. Given our methods, the interviewees' constant referencing of different goods—their own shifts from how they did their work to why they found it compelling—was especially noteworthy.

In most of our chapters, however, this was not the only, or even the central, mode of inference. For example, chapter 6—especially when we delve into the way "passion" operates discursively—does not assume that people "really" have a passion for whatever they do. What we do assume, is that the language of passion appears in other situations beyond the interview. That is, much as the term *passion* operates to move from one grammar to another in interviews, it was used to do so in other situations. This, we want to emphasize, is a different mode of inference: it is inference from talk to talk rather than from talk to action. In that regard, the important thing is not triangulation of accounts, but our evidence— through looking at trade journals and mission statements, as well as through Iddo's ethnographic work—that the discursive structures and grammars we heard in the interviews were common ways to talk in the advertising world. The grammars we describe, after all, are ways of making sense of different goods and ways of making sense of one another's actions. In that regard, what we find important is that people talk about their pro bono work in the ways we outline in the book.

That said, we should highlight some aspects of our sample that limit the results. First, all agencies are based in New York City. Although many of the larger ones are global agencies, and managers and professionals often told us about projects they did before arriving in New York (whether in other places in the United States or in Europe), there might be a New York City bias in terms of the relatively liberal political slant of the campaigns, and possibly in the specific ways grammars intersected. Second, because we sampled high-profile agencies, it might well be that less distinguished agencies mobilize pro bono work in other ways— for example, as a way to attract clientele by breaking into new brand categories, something that a few of the smaller agencies in our sample suggested. Third, because we sampled managers and professionals who performed pro bono work, the sample skews toward success stories in that we do not have the voices of those who consistently avoided such work. While we raise the first two issues as limitations, we note two considerations that justify sampling on success: the research question we ask in this book is about how pro bono work is managed. Thus, cases in which it is consistently avoided are of limited analytic value; we also asked in each interview about cases in which the agency declined specific pro bono accounts, and given that almost all managers could tell of such cases, we can analytically leverage the internal variation among projects within interviews.

All interviews were recorded and transcribed. Interviews lasted between forty-five minutes and two hours. The vast majority of interviews took place in advertising agency offices. After transcription, all interviews were then read and coded for emerging themes by the authors. The authors then iteratively coded the data, constructing separate codes for different grammars, and then recoded the data to focus on moments in which two grammars intersected, mapping the moments in the interviews in which they were tangled, and when they clashed. Throughout, we focused special attention on moments of empirical and theoretical surprise, and we iteratively read the literature and returned to the data to make sense of such surprises.[7] While many of our interviewees were happy to use their real names and the projects they worked on, some asked to remain anonymous. In these cases, we use pseudonyms, and—in some cases—also masked the projects they worked on. We did not, however, create "composite characters" or "composite projects."

Notes

CHAPTER 1

1. Hauptman 2019.
2. For a detailed account of the study's design, methods and limitations—including details on both participants and projects—see the appendix.
3. Schwartz 2012.
4. Guttmann 2019a. We note that this estimate includes revenue from public relations agencies and related services.
5. Guttmann 2019b.
6. Bithel n.d.
7. WPP n.d.; Omnicom Group n.d.; Publicis Groupe n.d.; Interpublic Group 2019. For WPP and Publicis, revenue was converted using an average exchange rate for 2019.
8. New York City Comptroller's Office 2019.
9. Navon 2017, 144.
10. Navon 2017, 144.
11. Kennedy 1968.
12. Schudson 1984, 7.
13. Jones and Nisbet 2011; Shamir 2004, 2008; Soule 2009.
14. Rayman-Bacchus 2004, 22.
15. Barman 2016.
16. Brammer et al. 2012: 20. See also Kaplan and Kinderman 2019; Kinderman 2012.
17. See Carroll 1999.
18. For National Context, see Gjølberg 2009. For the effects of firm size, see Koos 2011. For regulation regimes, see Campbell 2007. For state structure, see Matten and Moon 2008. For global pressures, see Lim and Tsutsui 2012.
19. For value systems and CSR, see, e.g., Hemingway 2005; Witt and Redding 2011. For sense-making attempts of individual actors, see Basu and Palazzo 2008.
20. Here, the pickings are slimmer. However, for narratives of CSR, see Haack et al. 2012; Windell 2007. For the practical patterning of CSR, see den Hond, de Bakker, and Neergaard 2007.
21. See, e.g., Carroll 1999.
22. Steimel 2018, 133–34.
23. BipiZ 2016.
24. Waller 2010; Waller and Lanis 2009.
25. Omnicom 2016; Interpublic Group 2014.

26. Certain positions, such as digital planner and account planner, which were kept distinct in larger agencies, seemed less so in smaller ones.
27. Shaban 2019.
28. Malefyt and Morais 2012; Moeran 1996.
29. For the notion of jurisdiction as a way to understand the relationship among professions, see Abbott 1988.
30. For a fuller depiction of agency size in our study, see the appendix.
31. Taylor 1989.
32. Weber 1994, 78–79. See also Friedland 2014.
33. For research on valuation in art, see, e.g., Velthuis 2013; Gerber 2017. For work emerging at the interstices of actor-network theory and the sociology of valuation, see, e.g., Latour 2013; see also Muniesa 2011.
34. Boltanski and Thévenot, 2006.
35. See Boltanski and Chiapello 2005.
36. Friedland and Alford 1991, 248.
37. See Thornton et al. 2012. For a brilliant critical essay, see Haveman and Gualtieri 2017.
38. Thus, it brings this tradition into closer connection both with March and Olson's (1976) classic emphasis on the negotiations of goods that cannot be rank ordered and with studies of "institutional work," with their focus on creative actors' negotiation of goods. See, e.g., Zilber 2002. For a closer dialogue, see Thévenot and Friedland's (2016) attempt to clarify the similarities and some of the areas of disagreement between the approaches.
39. For the notion of blending logics, see Pache and Santos 2010; Thornton et al. 2012. For the language of aligning logics, see Besharov and Smith 2014, 367. See also Battilana and Dorado 2010; Binder 2007; Heimer 1999; McPherson and Sauder 2013; Smets et al. 2017.
40. Skelcher and Smith 2015.
41. Abend 2014.
42. For important American repertoire theorists, see Lamont 1992; Swidler 1986, 2001. Although our work is couched in grammars and discursive structures, it owes much to repertoire theory's pragmatist bent. We also note that the notion of cultural grammars precedes both the logics and the "regimes of worth" literatures, going back (at the very least) to Kenneth Burke's 1945 work. To an extent, a similar tension between grammars and repertoires could be seen in the 1940s—between Burke's grammars of motive and C. Wright Mills's (1940) vocabularies of motive.
43. We draw the notion of affordances from Gibson (1979). For a call for a sociology of "enabling conditions," see Abend 2020.
44. Moreover, such a view also implicitly associates compromise with a dilution of moral purity: a compromise necessarily means that actors cannot affirm the moral value of what they are doing according to the relevant grammar of worth.
45. In one of the most insightful studies within this vein, the sociologist David Stark takes up the question of what the relationship is between potentially incommensurable orders of worth by arguing that modern corporations actively seek to foster ambiguity. Corporations in the information age deliberately bring together diverse forms of knowledge and expertise in such a way that employees must constantly grapple with several competing "conceptions of what is valuable, what is worthy, what counts" (Stark 2011, 5). Indeed, for Stark, it is the interplay between competing evaluative principles that generates the primary source of value within the corporation: innovation.
46. See, e.g., Zelizer 1997. We note here, however, that our pragmatism also extends to

Zelizer's work. At certain junctures goods are inseparably tangled. But in other situations, they are sharply delimited from each other. Neither state (purified *or* tangled) is the natural state of things. In the social world of goods, no such natural state exists.

47. In this section, and throughout the book, we are deeply indebted to Roger Friedland's (2016) insights and his emerging work on the "religious sociology" of institutional logics.

48. See Lainer-Vos 2013.

49. Battilana and Dorado 2010.

50. For career stage, see Pache and Santos 2015. For an underdeveloped, yet intriguing, note about the importance of situations, see Galaskiewicz and Barringer 2012, 60-62.

51. For the metaphor of navigation in the context of institutional logics, see Eliasoph et al. 2019.

52. For a sustained theoretical account of how pasts, and possible futures, work their way into the situation, see Tavory 2018; Fine and Tavory 2019.

53. The writings of Tim Hallett and his colleagues and of Nina Eliasoph and her colleagues are especially important in this context. See Eliasoph 2013; Eliasoph et al. 2019; Hallett and Hawbaker 2020; Hallett and Ventresca 2006; Lichterman and Eliasoph 2014.

54. Mauss (1923-1924) 1990.

CHAPTER 2

1. For an insightful analysis of descriptive relativism in sociology, as well as its pitfalls, see Lukes 2008.

2. For a more elaborated sociological treatment of the definition that we employ in this chapter, see Tavory 2010.

3. In popular imagination, this is actually quite often thought to be the case. Advertising is unflatteringly typecast as an industry run by cynical, ruthless men, clinking champagne glasses on rooftops in Paris to celebrate a new chance to topple their rivals with little thought to their work's often terrible effects (see, e.g., Steel 2015). The industry has long been understood as cutthroat and callous, propelling people toward excessive consumerism or manipulating consumers in order to make money. Women were partially entreated to smoke through the association of cigarettes and feminism. The Marlboro man, designed by Leo Burnett's advertising agency, became a cultural icon, even as evidence of smoking's dangers were increasingly obvious. Doing moral work, then, was also a way to contend with this image. See Cohen and Dromi 2018.

4. Boltanski and Chiapello 2005; Kuhn et al. 2008.

5. Cohen and Dromi 2018.

6. See chapter 7.

7. See, e.g., Packard 1957; Wu 2017.

8. Schudson 1984.

9. Hochschild 1983.

10. Advertising professionals do, of course, constantly complain about clients. See, e.g., Malefyt and Morais 2012; Moeran 1996. Yet they mostly complain about them as clients rather than in terms of their moral standing.

11. Tavory n.d.

12. To a certain extent, people are always active agents whether or not they feel constrained. For a useful definition of the feeling of agency, see Hitlin and Elder 2007. See also Emirbayer and Mische 1998.

13. Lytton 2013.
14. As we return to in chapter 4, this relationship between means and ends is a complicated one. On the one hand, taking the moral good as an end unto itself is precisely the mark of a Kantian vision of the moral. On the other hand, advertising professionals' ability to exercise their craft and perhaps even win awards for their work makes a vision of moral work as pure end untenable.
15. Following the interviewee's request, this is a pseudonym and the agency is not identified.
16. Sennett and Cobb 1972.
17. Moreover, nonprofits often paid some reduced rate to the agency, making interviewees uncertain about just how pro bono the pro bono campaign was.
18. We emphasize that we do not infer from these answers what advertising professionals would actually do in such a case but are interested in the fact that these subjunctive questions elicit moral narratives instead of other possible narratives. See Jerolmack and Khan 2014; Lamont and Swidler 2014; Tavory 2020. See also the appendix.

CHAPTER 3

1. That said, requesting a simple execution of a predetermined idea may have curtailed advertising professionals' abilities to take moral ownership of the project as well. However, as the excerpt makes clear, the "easy no" was not about a moral calculation.
2. Bourdieu 1977; Mauss (1923-1924) 1990. See also Silber 2009.
3. Homans 1958.
4. See, e.g., Burke 2014. As Burke notes, the Latin term *fecit*, "to make," in the context of artwork was used in the Middle Ages and during the Renaissance to refer not only to the work of the artist but also to that of the patron who commissioned the piece.
5. Ronen n.d.
6. Abbott 1988.
7. Hyperakt n.d.
8. See Sivulka 1997. Of course, the attempt to influence consumers' emotions did not emerge in the 1960s, but the "creative revolution" of that period solidified the place of emotion in the field.
9. On unalienated labor, Marx notes that man supersedes merely animalistic production. As he writes, "The animal only fashions things according to the standards and needs of the species it belongs to, whereas man knows how to produce according to the measure of every species, and knows everywhere how to apply the inherent standard to the object; thus man also fashions things according to the laws of beauty" ([1884] 2000, 90-91).
10. See Smith (1776) 1999.
11. Sivulka 1997.
12. See Tavory n.d.
13. We also note that, for at least some interviewees, engaging in the process of production helped bring distant suffering closer. In other words, engaging in such work gave shape to the distant recipients of the philanthropic "pure gift." However, this was relatively rare in the interviews, since even production seldom involved these recipients.
14. Godbout and Caillé 1998, 7. We note also that this is where the uncertainty linked to the gift's extended temporality becomes important. Gifts do not simply occur in the moment of exchange but gain some of their most indicative features as actors continue or discontinue the gift relation over time.
15. See, e.g., Darr 2003.

16. While thinking in terms of exchange already locates it within a market economy (see Graeber 2011; see also Elder-Vass 2015), in this case such constraints are apt. The gift lives precisely within an economy of exchange. Of course, one can stretch the metaphor of the gift even further. The very possibility of working on a moral cause is a gift of sorts—the gift of meaning or of redemption, as we outlined in the previous chapter. But this is a distanced gift, where the nonprofit is but the intermediary between the pro bono campaign and more or less distant suffering. In comparison, the immediate exchange between the nonprofit and the professionals working on the campaign has to do with the work itself.

CHAPTER 4

1. Neff and Schultz 2017.
2. Neff and Schultz 2017.
3. Neff and Schultz 2017.
4. Cannes Lions n.d.
5. For the general field-level analysis that we employ in this chapter, see Bourdieu 1985.
6. Art Directors Club n.d.
7. *New York Times* 1921.
8. On the embodied practice of "walking through a gallery" as social accomplishment, see Bourdieu 1993; Bourdieu and Darbel 1991. For an ethnomethodologically inspired analysis of the accomplishment of "doing-being" in a museum, see Jansen 2008.
9. Most senior managers of advertising agencies have spent their careers in the advertising world. Thus, CEOs are considered "internal" to the field of advertising as a creative endeavor. Data for this assertion are based on the CVs of jurors in Cannes Lions and Clio Awards collected and analyzed by the authors.
10. Clio Awards n.d.
11. Cannes Lions n.d.
12. For work on this paradoxical consecration of the Man Booker Prize, see Anand and Jones 2008; English 2002, 2005. For an analysis of art literary awards rooted in Bourdieu's sociology see Heinich 1999.
13. See, e.g., Fox 1984.
14. Even in the case of the Effie Awards, the jury mostly comprises industry insiders.
15. Calkins and Holden 1905, 6.
16. Calkins and Holden 1905, 12.
17. Packard 1957.
18. Schudson 1984.
19. Polonsky and Waller 1995, 26. Although agencies may hope that clients see performance in this way, Polonsky and Waller's data from Australia suggest that clients did not in fact care much about awards.
20. Hester 1988, 32. See also chapter 5.
21. Helgesen 1994; Hester 1988.
22. One notable exception is "young talent" awards, which are given to individual creatives as an explicit boost to their budding careers.
23. Interestingly, at least in our interviews, this expectation seemed more prominent in interviews with managers of smaller, upstart agencies. Awards, as interviewees noted, helped put small agencies "on the map." Meanwhile, managers of larger and more established agencies rarely talked about awards as if they directly secured clients. These managers, too, noted that awards were good for business but conceptualized the rela-

tionship in a more roundabout way—again, through the potential employees that the awards attracted. As many CEOs recognized, this was a harder link to draw: "[Awards] attracted better people, which has led to better work, which has led to more business. I can't draw the exact line to the ROI [return on investment], but I really believe it. I actually believe it." This finding may explain why some research on awards' economic outcomes is equivocal (see Polonsky and Waller 1995); to the best of our knowledge, such research failed to distinguish between established and small upstart agencies.

24. We note that the relationship between the consecration of individuals and of organizational actors wasn't necessarily a smooth one. While managers talked about how awards helped them recruit and retain talent, awards often also propelled individuals to leave their agency for a better job—to move diagonally across agencies rather than sticking with their initial agency. Interestingly, managers did not talk about such an effect, although it was clearly visible in creatives' and planners' work trajectories, as well as in their narratives. It is possible that this potential drawback was less visible because of a high turnover rate. The implication is that awards were probably more effective for recruiting than for retaining talent. Although it is beyond the scope of this work, such dynamics open up more general questions about tensions between organizational and individual actors' trajectories that we should anticipate in the analysis of fields.

25. It is interesting to compare this dynamic to fashion design and modeling. Ashley Mears (2011) found that editorial and commercial modeling have quite different dynamics. The relationship between these two types is complex; editorial work pays less yet is creatively bold and high status, which may be then converted into salaries later on.

26. We draw here on Abend's (2014) notion of the moral background.

27. Here, there is a Kantian deontological (Kant [1785] 2012) understanding of morality lurking in the background that sees the moral as divorced from questions of the effects of action. In our context, action is deemed amoral if it is merely a means to an end and moral if the good is acted upon as an end unto itself.

28. In metaethical philosophical terms, this is an actor-centered argument.

29. More theoretically, we expect that awards in such fields give the semblance of a shared and agreed upon definition of the good. This has parallels to how uncertainty gives rise to mimetic isomorphism in organizations, where different organizations copy each other since they don't know what works. See DiMaggio and Powell 1983.

CHAPTER 5

1. For stigma management and goods in the advertising world, see Cohen and Dromi 2018. See also chapter 3.

2. See Waller 2010; Waller and Lanis 2009.

3. The language of passion itself is extremely important in this context. We return to this question in chapter 6.

4. See Duggan 2015.

5. Schimel 2018.

6. Lukes 1974. This is, for Lukes, the "second face" of power.

CHAPTER 6

1. Eliasoph, Lo, and Glaser 2019. For a discussion of logics and grammars of worth, see the introduction to this book.

2. Goffman 1963.

3. For an influential paper on stigma deflection in mental health patients, see Thoits 2011. For stigma deflection among failed entrepreneurs, see Walsh 2017. For a classic treatment of boundaries in sociology, see Lamont and Molnár 2002.

4. Unprompted, a third of interviewees ($n = 26$) used some form of stigma deflection. Interestingly, this often happened at the end of the interview. As the cases in this chapter show, we have reason to believe that such deflections are not an artifact of the interview situation. Interviewees often had specific agencies, or cases, ready at hand. Moreover, they sometimes referenced conversations they had about such agencies and projects with other advertising professionals.

5. Alexander 2018.

6. Butter 2016.

7. Oster 2016.

8. Bullock 2016.

9. Coffee 2016.

10. The notion of passion appeared in 40 of 73 interviews (55 percent). In two additional interviews, interviewees used the term after it was first evoked by Shelly, who unwittingly used the word herself after so many mentions of "passion"—an extremely telling slip of the interview guide.

11. Hirschman 1977, 15.

12. We note, in that regard, that there is a second Weberian argument moving parallel to the depiction of the iron cage. The notion of the vocation can be seen as a secularized extension of the Protestant "calling," another important element in the emergence of the Spirit of Capitalism.

13. See also Illouz's (2007) notion of emotional capitalism.

14. Bolles 2019, 245.

15. See De Keere (2014, forthcoming). For a Bourdieu-inspired analysis of the language of passion, see Cech (2021).

16. Boltanski and Chiapello 2005; Rose 1990.

17. Haggerty 2013.

18. There are a number of theoretical traditions that have focused on ambiguity. An increasingly common, and generative, way to depict such ambiguity is the notion of boundary objects—depicting how different actors can productively misunderstand each other to construct shared lines of action. See Star and Griesemer 1989. However, given that the object in question is a narrative device, we find the literature on polysemy (e.g., Tavory and Swidler 2009) and discursive "contaminations" (Wagner-Pacifici 1994) more apt, even as the language of "contamination" is antithetical to the thrust of the book.

CHAPTER 7

1. Barman 2016, 222.

2. See, e.g., WARC n.d.

3. Burns 2016.

4. For a discussion of "virality" as a cultural phenomenon, see Nahon and Hemsley 2013.

5. Weber 1978.

6. For Foucault-inspired studies of governmentality and the study of numbers and accountability, see Power 1997. See also Porter 1995; Desrosières 1998.

7. Hacking 1990; Desrosières 1998.

8. E.g., Lupton 2016.

9. See Espeland and Stevens 2008; Mennicken and Espeland 2019.

10. This is also the case in the nonprofit sector. See Barman 2016; Krause 2014.

11. Simmel (1900) 2004.

12. Petre 2015. See also Christin 2018; Schüll 2014.

13. This attempt to get at the local phenomenology of measurement in pro bono work is indebted to Jack Katz's work. See Katz 1988, 1999.

14. See Lefebvre 2004.

15. See, e.g., Nixon 2003.

16. Ronen n.d.

CHAPTER 8

1. Silverstein says this in a video in which he is sitting beside his cofounder Jeff Goodby. The two are giving advice about advertising in a promotional video for their MasterClass on the industry.

2. Barman 2016.

3. We note that while we are indebted to Friedland, our approach differs significantly. In constructing his "religious institutionalism" Friedland (2014, 2016, 2021) takes polytheism in a more mystical direction. That is, Friedland attempts to uncover different "substances" underlying different goods and how those substances act as Aristotelian "final causes" that beckon actors in different directions. As we outline throughout this book, our approach is a lot less committed: the actors we describe are not the religious virtuosi Friedland seems to be writing of—for whom the world is full of passionate choices and irrepressible draws. While people have committed moments, they are, usually, ordinary polytheists bumbling through life.

4. Weber (1919) 1946, 149. See also Freund 1986.

5. Perhaps, in this context, we need to be reminded of Weber's famous note about how "religiously unmusical" he was.

6. See Schutz 1970; Schutz and Luckmann 1973.

7. Tavory 2018.

8. Healy 2017; Steiner (1956) 1999.

9. Gibson 1979.

10. For an analysis of the "moodiness of the situation," see Silver 2011. Much as situations "have moods" that they evoke, situations evoke potential grammars.

11. Fine 2012.

12. Thinking in terms of multiple relevance structures with their nexus in the situation is both a theoretical provocation and a methodological one. Of course, what we have done here, in that regard, is far from perfect. As we return to in the methodological appendix, we have reasons to be confident that the general contours of the patterns hold. Still, one of the things we haven't been able to trace, because we relied on interviews, is how small shifts in practical situations shift relevance structures. That is, how different levels of analysis, always there *in potentia*, become practically organized. Which configuration of relevance structures is evoked when. There is much work to be done to trace how small situational shifts reorganize the configuration of relevance structures, something that would be best done ethnographically. We hope that such work will be taken up in the future.

13. Adut 2018. In this regard, Adut echoes the crucial insight of Guy Debord (1967) about the spectacular nature of the public sphere in late capitalism.

14. Noy 2017, 39.

15. Alexander 2018.
16. Cohen and Dromi 2018.
17. For a good overview of pro bono work in law, see Cummings 2004.
18. Court of Appeals, State of New York, n.d.
19. American Bar Association 2013.
20. Advisory Committee on New York State Pro Bono Bar Admission Requirements, 2012.
21. Granfield 2007.
22. Cummings and Rhode 2009, 2421.
23. Granfield 2007, 133–34.
24. Cummings and Sandefur 2013, 98.
25. Cummings and Rhode 2009.
26. Dinovitzer and Garth 2009; Boutcher 2017.
27. See den Hond, de Bakker, and Neergaard 2007; Haack et al. 2012; Windell 2007.
28. Wright 2016.
29. Tolve 2011.

APPENDIX

1. See, e.g., Ho 2009; Neff 2012.
2. Grow and Deng 2015.
3. See, e.g., Dávila 2012.
4. Jerolmack and Khan 2014.
5. For an analysis of symbolic contexts of talk, and the correlation between the situations we ask about and such talk, see LaPiere 1934; Tavory 2020. We note that Iddo's (Tavory 2020) article on inference from interviews was written specifically to think through the different kinds of inferences warranted within the current study.
6. See Gerson and Damaske 2020; Spradley 1979; Tavory 2020; Weiss 1995.
7. Tavory and Timmermans 2014; Timmermans and Tavory 2012, 2022.

References

Abbott, Andrew. 1988. *The System of Professions: An Essay on the Division of Expert Labor*. Chicago: University of Chicago Press.

Abend, Gabriel. 2014. *The Moral Background: An Inquiry into the History of Business Ethics*. Princeton, NJ: Princeton University Press.

———. 2020. "Making Things Possible." *Sociological Methods & Research*: https://doi.org/0049124120926204.

Adut, Ari. 2018. *Reign of Appearances: The Misery and Splendor of the Public Sphere*. Cambridge: Cambridge University Press.

Advisory Committee on New York State Pro Bono Bar Admission Requirements. 2012. *Report to the Chief Judge of the State of New York and the Presiding Justices of the Four Appellate Division Departments*, September.

Alexander, Jeffrey C. 2018. "The Societalization of Social Problems: Church Pedophilia, Phone Hacking, and the Financial Crisis." *American Sociological Review* 83 (6): 1049–78.

American Bar Association. 2013. "New York's 5-Hour Preadmission Pro Bono Rule: Weighing the Potential Pros and Cons." White paper presented by the American Bar Association's Standing Committee on Pro Bono and Public Service, October.

Anand, Narasimhan, and Brittany C. Jones. 2008. "Tournament Rituals, Category Dynamics, and Field Configuration: The Case of the Booker Prize." *Journal of Management Studies* 45 (6): 1036–60.

Art Directors Club. n.d. "Art Directors Club History." http://adcglobal.org/about/history/.

Barman, Emily. 2016. *Caring Capitalism*. Cambridge: Cambridge University Press.

Basu, Kunal, and Guido Palazzo. 2008. "Corporate Social Responsibility: A Process Model of Sensemaking." *Academy of Management Review* 33 (1): 122–36.

Battilana, Julie, and Silvia Dorado. 2010. "Building Sustainable Hybrid Organizations: The Case of Commercial Microfinance Organizations." *Academy of Management Journal* 53 (6): 1419–40.

Besharov, Marya L., and Wendy K. Smith. 2014. "Multiple Institutional Logics in Organizations: Explaining their Varied Nature and Implications." *Academy of Management Review* 39 (3): 364–81.

Binder, Amy. 2007. "For Love and Money: Organizations' Creative Responses to Multiple Environmental Logics." *Theory and Society* 36 (6): 547–71.

BipiZ. 2016. "Publicis Groupe Has Created More Than 300 Pro Bono Campaigns for Social Causes in 2013." https://www.bipiz.org/en/csr-best-practices/publicis-groupe-has-created-more-than-300-pro-bono-campaigns-for-social-causes-in-2007.html.

Bithel, Laura. n.d. "A History of Advertising" *Advertising Week* 360. https://www
.advertisingweek360.com/a-history-of-new-york-advertising/.

Bolles, Richard Nelson. 2019. *What Color Is Your Parachute? A Practical Manual for Job-Hunters
and Career-Changers.* New York: Random House.

Boltanski, Luc, and Eve Chiapello. 2005. *The New Spirit of Capitalism.* London: Verso.

Boltanski, Luc, and Laurent Thévenot. 2006. *On Justification: Economies of Worth.* Princeton,
NJ: Princeton University Press.

Bourdieu, Pierre. 1977. *Outline of a Theory of Practice.* Cambridge: Cambridge University
Press.

———. 1985. "The Social Space and the Genesis of Groups." *Theory and Society* 14 (6):
723–44.

———. 1993. *The Field of Cultural Production: Essays on Art and Literature.* New York: Columbia
University Press.

Bourdieu, Pierre, and Alain Darbel. 1991. *The Love of Art.* Cambridge, UK: Polity.

Boutcher, Steven A. 2017. "Private Law Firms in the Public Interest: The Organizational
and Institutional Determinants of Pro Bono Participation, 1994–2005." *Law & Social
Inquiry* 42 (2): 543–564.

Brammer, Stephen, Gregory Jackson, and Dirk Matten. 2012. "Corporate Social Responsibility and Institutional Theory: New Perspectives on Private Governance." *Socio-Economic
Review* 10 (1): 3–28.

Bullock, Ali. 2016. "An Open Letter to Grey Singapore: Why I Will Never Hire Grey as an
Agency in My Lifetime #Cannes." *Social Samosa Blog.* http://www.socialsamosa.com/
2016/07/open-letter-grey-singapore-cannes/.

Burke, Kenneth. 1945. *A Grammar of Motives.* New York: Prentice Hall.

Burke, Peter. 2014. *The Italian Renaissance: Culture and Society in Italy.* Princeton, NJ: Princeton University Press.

Burns, Will. 2016. "The Making of Donate Life's 'The World's Biggest A—hole." *Forbes,* September 8. https://www.forbes.com/sites/willburns/2016/09/08/the-making-of-donate
-lifes-the-worlds-biggest-a-hole/#4f8583709b18.

Butter, Susannah. 2016. "I Sea: The App Helping to Discover and Rescue Refugees in the
Mediterranean." *The Standard,* June 17. https://www.standard.co.uk /stayingin/tech
-gaming/i-sea-the-app-helping-to-discover-and-rescue-refugees-in-the-mediterranean
-a3273841.html.

Calkins, Ernest E., and Ralph Holden. 1905. *Modern Advertising.* New York: D. Appleton-
Century Co.

Campbell John L. 2007. "Why Would Corporations Behave in Socially Responsible Ways?
An Institutional Theory of Corporate Social Responsibility." *Academy of Management Review* 32 (3): 946–67.

Cannes Lions. n.d. "Cannes Lions 2019 Jury Presidents Announced." https://www
.canneslions.com/about/news/cannes-lions-jury-presidents-announced.

Cannes Lions. n.d. "What's New for the 2019 Cannes Lions Awards." https://www
.canneslions.com/about/news/awards-whats-new.

Carroll, Archie B. 1999. "Corporate Social Responsibility: Evolution of a Definitional Construct." *Business & Society* 38 (3): 268–95.

Cech, Erin A. 2021. *The Trouble with Passion: How Searching for Fulfillment at Work Fosters
Inequality.* Berkeley: University of California Press.

Christin, Angèle. 2018. "Counting Clicks: Quantification and Variation in Web Journalism
in the United States and France." *American Journal of Sociology* 123 (5): 1382–1415.

Clio Awards. n.d. "Clio Resources: Learn More about Our Awards Program and How to Enter." https://clios.com/how-to-enter/judging-process.

Coffee, Patrick. 2016. "Grey Officially Returns 'I SEA' App Lion, Clearly Isn't Happy about It." *Adweek*, July 6. https://www.adweek.com/agencyspy/grey-officially-returns-i-sea -app-lion-clearly-isnt-happy-about-it/112382/.

Cohen, Andrew C., and Shai M. Dromi. 2018. "Advertising Morality: Maintaining Moral Worth in a Stigmatized Profession." *Theory and Society* 47 (2): 175–206.

Court of Appeals, State of New York. n.d. "Part 520. Rules of the Court of Appeals for the Admission of Attorneys and Counselors at Law." https://www.nycourts.gov/ctapps/ 520rules10.htm#B16.

Cummings, Scott L. 2004. "The Politics of Pro Bono." *UCLA Law Review* 52: 1–149.

Cummings, Scott L., and Deborah L. Rhode. 2009. "Managing Pro Bono: Doing Well by Doing Better." *Fordham Law Review* 78: 2357–2442.

Cummings Scott L., and Rebecca L. Sandefur. 2013. "Beyond the Numbers: What We Know—And Should Know—About American Pro Bono." *Harvard Law & Policy Review* 7 (I): 83–112.

Darr, Asaf. 2003. "Gifting Practices and Interorganizational Relations: Constructing Obliga- tion Networks in the Electronics Sector." *Sociological Forum* 18 (I): 31–51.

Dávila, Arlene. 2012. *Latinos, Inc.: The Marketing and Making of a People*. Berkeley: University of California Press.

Debord, Guy. 1970. *The Society of the Spectacle*. Detroit: Black and Red.

De Keere, Kobe. 2014. "From a Self-Made to an Already-Made Man: A Historical Content Analysis of Professional Advice Literature." *Acta Sociologica* 57 (4): 311–24.

———. Forthcoming. "The Confessional Job-Seeker: Moralizing Occupational Gatekeeping."

den Hond, Frank, Frank G. A. De Bakker, and Peter Neergaard, eds. 2007. *Managing Corpo- rate Social Responsibility in Action: Talking, Doing and Measuring*. Burlington, VT: Ashgate.

Desrosières, Alain. 1998. *The Politics of Large Numbers: A History of Statistical Reasoning*. Cambridge, MA: Harvard University Press.

DiMaggio, Paul J., and Walter W. Powell. 1983. "The Iron Cage Revisited: Institutional Isomorphism and Collective Rationality in Organizational Fields." *American Sociological Review* 48 (2): 147–60.

Dinovitzer, Ronit, and Bryant Garth. 2009. "Pro Bono as an Elite Strategy in Early Law- yer Careers." In *Private Lawyers and the Public Interest: The Evolving Role of Pro Bono in the Legal Profession*, ed. Robert Granfield and Lynn Mather, 115–34. New York: Oxford University Press.

Duggan, Bill. 2015. "The Five Biggest Trends on the State of Ad Agencies Now from the Digiday Agency Summit." *American Association of National Advertisers* (blog). https://www .ana.net/blogs/show/id/37368.

Elder-Vass, Dave. 2015. "Free Gifts and Positional Gifts: Beyond Exchangism." *European Journal of Social Theory* 18 (4): 451–68.

Eliasoph, Nina. 2013. *Making Volunteers: Civic Life after Welfare's End*. Princeton, NJ: Prince- ton University Press.

Eliasoph, Nina, Jade Lo, and Vern L. Glaser. 2019. "'Navigation Techniques': How Ordi- nary Participants Orient Themselves in Scrambled Institutions." In *Microfoundations of Institutions*, ed. P. Haack, J. Sieweke, and L. Wessel, 143–68 (Research in the Sociology of Organizations 65B). New York: Emerald Publishing.

Emirbayer, Mustafa, and Ann Mische. 1998. "What Is Agency?" *American Journal of Sociol- ogy* 103 (4): 962–1023.

English, James F. 2002. "Winning the Culture Game: Prizes, Awards, and the Rules of Art." *New Literary History* 33 (1): 109–35.

———. 2005. *The Economy of Prestige: Prizes, Awards, and the Circulation of Cultural Value*. Boston: Harvard University Press.

Espeland, Wendy Nelson, and Mitchell L. Stevens. 2008. "A Sociology of Quantification." *European Journal of Sociology/Archives Européennes de Sociologie* 49 (3): 401–36.

Fine, Gary Alan. 2012. *Tiny Publics: A Theory of Group Action and Culture*. New York: Russell Sage Foundation.

Fine, Gary Alan, and Iddo Tavory. 2019. "Interactionism in the Twenty-First Century: On Being-in-a-Meaningful-World." *Symbolic Interaction* 42 (3): 457–67.

Fox, Stephen R. 1984. *The Mirror Makers: A History of American Advertising and Its Creators*. Champaign: University of Illinois Press.

Freund, Julien. 1986. "Le polythéisme chez Max Weber." *Archives de Sciences Sociales des Religions* 61 (1): 51–61.

Friedland, Roger. 2014. "Divine Institution: Max Weber's Value Spheres and Institutional Theory." *Research in the Sociology of Organizations* 41: 217–58.

———. 2016. "Counting on the Gods: Value and Divine Operations in Institutional Life." Paper presented at the Sociology of Culture Workshop, New York University, New York, October.

———. 2021. "Toward a Religious Institutionalism: Ontologies, Teleologies, and the God-ding of Institutions." In *Research in the Sociology of Organizations*, ed. Michael Lounsbury, Deborah A. Anderson, and Paul Spee, 70:29–118. New York: Emerald Publishing.

Friedland, Roger, and Robert R. Alford. 1991. "Bringing Society Back In: Symbols, Practices and Institutional Contradictions." In *The New Institutionalism in Organizational Analysis*, ed. Walter W. Powell and Paul DiMaggio, 232–63. Chicago: University of Chicago Press.

Galaskiewicz, Joseph, and Sondra N. Barringer. 2012. "Social Enterprises and Social Cat-egories." In *Social Enterprises: An Organizational Perspective*, edited by Benjamin Gidron and Yeheskel Hasenfeld, 47–70. Basingstoke, UK: Palgrave.

Gerber, Alison. 2017. *The Work of Art*. Stanford, CA: Stanford University Press.

Gerson, Kathleen, and Sarah Damaske. 2020. *The Science and Art of Interviewing*. Oxford: Oxford University Press.

Gibson, James J. 1979. *The Ecological Approach to Visual Perception*. Boston: Houghton Mif-flin Harcourt.

Gjølberg, Maria. 2009. "Measuring the Immeasurable?: Constructing an Index of CSR Practices and CSR Performance in 20 Countries." *Scandinavian Journal of Management* 25 (1): 10–22.

Godbout, Jacques T., and Alain C. Caillé. 1998. *The World of the Gift*. Montreal: McGill-Queen's University Press.

Goffman, Erving. 1963. *Stigma: Notes on the Management of Spoiled Identity*. New York: Simon and Schuster.

Goodby, Jeff, and Rich Silverstein. 2020. "Masterclass: Jeff Goodby and Rich Silverstein Teach Advertising and Creativity." https://www.youtube.com/watch?v=BiM6MjfBpzw&ab_channel=MasterClass.

Graeber, David. 2011. *Debt: The First Five Thousand Years*. New York: Melville House.

Granfield, Robert. 2007. "The Meaning of Pro Bono: Institutional Variations in Professional Obligations among Lawyers." *Law & Society Review* 41 (1): 113–46.

Grow, Jean M., and Tao Deng. 2015. "Tokens in a Man's World: Women in Creative Adver-

tising Departments." *Media Report to Women*. https://www.questia.com/magazine/1P3
-3616706491/tokens-in-a-man-s-world-women-in-advertising-creative.

Guttmann, Agnieszka. 2019a. "Advertising Industry Revenue in the United States 2004–
2018." *Statista*. https://www.statista.com/statistics/183932/estimated-revenue-in
-advertising-and-related-services-since-2000/.

———. 2019b. "Media Advertising Spending in the United States from 2015 to 2022." *Statista*.
https://www.statista.com/statistics/272314/advertising-spending-in-the-us/.

Haack, Patrick, Dennis Schoeneborn, and Christopher Wickert. 2012. "Talking the Talk,
Moral Entrapment, Creeping Commitment? Exploring Narrative Dynamics in Corporate
Responsibility Standardization." *Organization Studies* 33 (5–6): 815–45.

Hacking, Ian. 1990. *The Taming of Chance*. Cambridge: Cambridge University Press.

Haggerty, Angela. 2013. "How to Get a Job in Advertising: It's All about Passion—Otherwise
Forget It, Says MD at OgilvyOne, Jo Coombs." *The Drum*, April 22. https://www.thedrum
.com/news/2013/04/22/how-get-job-advertising-its-all-about-passion-otherwise-forget
-it-says-md-ogilvyone.

Hallett, Tim, and Amelia Hawbaker. 2020. "The Case for an Inhabited Institutionalism in
Organizational Research: Interaction, Coupling, and Change Reconsidered." *Theory and
Society*. https://doi.org/10.1007/s11186-020-09412-2.

Hallett, Tim, and Marc J. Ventresca. 2006. "Inhabited Institutions: Social Interactions and
Organizational Forms in Gouldner's Patterns of Industrial Bureaucracy." *Theory and
Society* 35 (2): 213–36.

Hauptman, Robert. 2019. "Advertising and Its Discontents." *Journal of Information Ethics*
28 (1): 3.

Haveman, Heather A., and Gillian Gualtieri. 2017. "Institutional Logics." In *Oxford Research
Encyclopedia of Business and Management*. http://oxfordre.com/business/view/10.1093/
acrefore/9780190224851.001.0001/acrefore-9780190224851-e-137.

Healy, Kieran. 2017. "Fuck Nuance." *Sociological Theory* 35 (2): 118–27.

Heimer, Carol A. 1999. "Competing Institutions: Law, Medicine, and Family in Neonatal
Intensive Care." *Law & Society Review* 33 (1): 17–66.

Heinich, Nathalie. 1999. *L'épreuve de la grandeur: Prix littéraires et reconnaissance*. Paris: La
Découverte.

Helgesen, Thorolf. 1994. "Advertising Awards and Advertising Agency Performance Criteria." *Journal of Advertising Research* 34 (4): 43–54.

Hemingway, Christine A. 2005. "Personal Values as a Catalyst for Corporate Social Entrepreneurship." *Journal of Business Ethics* 60 (3): 233–49.

Hester, Joe Bob. 1988. "The Organizational Impact of Advertising Awards." PhD diss., Texas
Tech University.

Hirschman, Albert O. 1977. *The Passions and the Interests: Political Arguments for Capitalism
before Its Triumph*. Princeton, NJ: Princeton University Press.

Hitlin, Steven, and Glen H. Elder Jr. 2007. "Time, Self, and the Curiously Abstract Concept
of Agency." *Sociological Theory* 25 (2): 170–91.

Ho, Karen. 2009. *Liquidated: An Ethnography of Wall Street*. Durham, NC: Duke University
Press.

Hochschild, Arlie Russell. 1983. *The Managed Heart: Commercialization of Human Feeling*.
Berkeley: University of California Press.

Homans, George C. 1958. "Social Behavior as Exchange." *American Journal of Sociology* 63
(6): 597–606.

Hyperakt. n.d. "About Our Agency." https://www.hyperakt.com/about.

Illouz, Eva. 2007. *Cold Intimacies: The Making of Emotional Capitalism*. Cambridge: Polity Press.

Interpublic Group. 2014. "IPG Launches Magazine Titled STRONGER." Press release. https://investors.interpublic.com/news-releases/news-release-details/ipg-launches -magazine-titled-stronger.

———. 2019. "Interpublic Announces Third Quarter and First Nine Months 2019 Results." Press release. https://investors.interpublic.com/news-releases/news-release-details/ interpublic-announces-third-quarter-and-first-nine-months-2019.

Jansen, Robert S. 2008. "Jurassic Technology? Sustaining Presumptions of Intersubjectivity in a Disruptive Environment." *Theory and Society* 37 (2): 127–59.

Jerolmack, Colin, and Shamus Khan. 2014. "Talk Is Cheap: Ethnography and the Attitudinal Fallacy." *Sociological Methods & Research* 43 (2): 178–209.

Jones, Bryn, and Peter Nisbet. 2011. "Shareholder Value versus Stakeholder Values: CSR and Financialization in Global Food Firms." *Socio-Economic Review* 9 (2): 287–314.

Kant, Emmanuel. (1785) 2012. *Groundwork of the Metaphysics of Morals*. Cambridge: Cambridge University Press.

Kaplan, Rami, and Daniel Kinderman. 2019. "The Business-Class Case for Corporate Social Responsibility: Mobilization, Diffusion, and Institutionally Transformative Strategy in Venezuela and Britain." *Theory and Society* 48 (1): 131–66.

Katz, Jack. 1988. *Seduction of Crime: The Moral and Sensual Attractions in Doing Evil*. New York: Basic Books.

———. 1999. *How Emotions Work*. Chicago: University of Chicago Press.

Kennedy, Robert F. 1968. "Remarks at the University of Kansas, March 18, 1968." JFK Library. https://www.jfklibrary.org/learn/about-jfk/the-kennedy-family/robert-f -kennedy/robert-f-kennedy-speeches/remarks-at-the-university-of-kansas-march-18 -1968.

Kinderman, Daniel. 2012. "'Free Us Up So We Can Be Responsible!' The Co-Evolution of Corporate Social Responsibility and Neo-Liberalism in the UK, 1977–2010." *Socio-Economic Review* 10 (1): 29–57.

Koos, Sebastian. 2011. "The Institutional Embeddedness of Social Responsibility: A Multilevel Analysis of Smaller Firms' Civic Engagement in Western Europe." *Socio-Economic Review* 10 (1): 135–62.

Krause, Monika. 2014. *The Good Project: Humanitarian Relief NGOs and the Fragmentation of Reason*. Chicago: University of Chicago Press.

Kuhn, Timothy, Annis G. Golden, Jane Jorgenson, Patrice M. Buzzanell, Brenda L. Berkelaar, Lorraine G. Kisselburgh, Sharon Kleinman, and Disraelly Cruz. 2008. "Cultural Discourses and Discursive Resources for Meaning/ful Work: Constructing and Disrupting Identities in Contemporary Capitalism." *Management Communication Quarterly* 22 (1): 162–71.

Lainer-Vos, Dan. 2013. "The Practical Organization of Moral Transactions Gift Giving, Market Exchange, Credit, and the Making of Diaspora Bonds." *Sociological Theory* 31 (2): 145–67.

Lamont, Michèle. 1992. *Money, Morals and Manners: The Culture of the French and American Upper-Middle Class*. Chicago: University of Chicago Press.

Lamont, Michèle, and Virag Molnar. 2002. "The Study of Boundaries in the Social Sciences." *Annual Review of Sociology* 28: 167–95.

Lamont, Michèle, and Ann Swidler. 2014. "Methodological Pluralism and the Possibilities and Limits of Interviewing." *Qualitative Sociology* 37 (2): 153–71.

LaPiere, Richard. 1934. "Attitudes vs. Actions." *Social Forces* 13: 230–37.

Latour, Bruno. 2013. *An Inquiry into Modes of Existence.* Cambridge, MA: Harvard University Press.

Lefebvre, Henri. 2004. *Rhythmanalysis: Space, Time and Everyday Life.* London: A&C Black.

Lichterman, Paul, and Nina Eliasoph. 2014. "Civic Action." *American Journal of Sociology* 120 (3): 798–863.

Lim, Alwyn, and Kiyoteru Tsutsui. 2012. "Globalization and Commitment in Corporate Social Responsibility: Cross-National Analyses of Institutional and Political-Economy Effects." *American Sociological Review* 77 (1): 69–98.

Lukes, Steven. 1974. *Power: A Radical View.* London: Macmillan.

———. 2008. *Moral Relativism.* London: Picador.

Lupton, Deborah. 2016. *The Quantified Self.* London: John Wiley & Sons.

Lytton, Charlotte. 2013. "Top 10: Climate Change Campaigns." *The Guardian,* November 15. https://www.theguardian.com/global-development-professionals-network/2013/nov/15/top-10-climate-change-campaigns.

Malefyt, Timothy De Waal, and Robert J. Morais. 2012. *Advertising and Anthropology: Ethnographic Practice and Cultural Perspectives.* Oxford, UK: Berg.

March, James G., and Johan P. Olsen. 1976. *Ambiguity and Choice in Organizations.* Bergen, Norway: Universitetsforlaget.

Marx, Karl. 2000. *Karl Marx: Selected Writings.* Edited by David McLellan. Oxford: Oxford University Press.

Matten, Dirk, and Jeremy Moon. 2008. "'Implicit' and 'Explicit' CSR: A Conceptual Framework for a Comparative Understanding of Corporate Social Responsibility." *Academy of Management Review* 33 (2): 404–24.

Mauss, Marcel. (1923–1924) 1990. *The Gift: The Form and Reason for Exchange in Archaic Societies.* London: Routledge.

McPherson, Chad Michael, and Michael Sauder. 2013. "Logics in Action: Managing Institutional Complexity in a Drug Court." *Administrative Science Quarterly* 58 (2):165–96.

Mears, Ashley. 2011. *Pricing Beauty: The Making of a Fashion Model.* Berkeley: University of California Press.

Mennicken, Andrea, and Wendy Nelson Espeland. 2019. "What's New with Numbers? Sociological Approaches to the Study of Quantification." *Annual Review of Sociology* 45: 223–45.

Mills, C. Wright. 1940. "Situated Actions and Vocabularies of Motive." *American Sociological Review* 5 (6): 940–53.

Moeran, Brian. 1996. *A Japanese Advertising Agency: An Anthropology of Media and Markets.* Honolulu: University of Hawaiʻi Press.

Muniesa, Fabian. 2011. "A Flank Movement in the Understanding of Valuation." *Sociological Review* 59: 24–38.

Nahon, Karine, and Jeff Hemsley. 2013. *Going Viral.* London: Polity.

Navon, Daniel. 2017. "Truth in Advertising: Rationalizing Ads and Knowing Consumers in the Early Twentieth-Century United States." *Theory and Society* 46 (2): 143–76.

Neff, Gina. 2012. *Venture Labor: Work and the Burden of Risk in Innovative Industries.* Cambridge, MA: MIT Press.

Neff, Jack, and E. J. Schultz. 2017. "Does Cannes Matter? Agencies Debate Spendy Festival in Lean Times." *Ad Age,* June 12. https://adage.com/article/print-edition/cannes-festival-creativity-matter/309354.

New York City Comptroller's Office. 2019. "The Creative Economy: Art Culture and Creativity in NYC." Report for New York City Controller Scott M. Stringer, October. https://comptroller.nyc.gov/reports/the-creative-economy/#ProfileAdvertising.

New York Times. 1921. "Advertising Art." March 20.

Nixon, Sean. 2003. *Advertising Cultures: Gender, Commerce, Creativity*. Thousand Oaks, CA: Sage.

Noy, Chaim. 2017. "Moral Discourse and Argumentation in the Public Sphere: Museums and their Visitors." *Discourse, Context & Media* 16: 39–47.

Omnicom Group. 2016. *Omnicom Group 2016 Corporate Social Responsibility Report*. https://csr.omnicomgroup.com/wp-content/uploads/2017/06/Omnicom -Group-2016-Corporate-Responsibility-Report.pdf.

———. n.d. "About Omnicom." https://www.omnicomgroup.com/about/.

Oster, Erik. 2016. "Cannes Lions Reviewing 'I Sea' App's Eligibility." *Adweek*, June 23. https://www.adweek.com/agencyspy/cannes-lions-reviewing-i-sea-apps-eligibility/111709/.

Pache, Anne-Claire, and Filipe Santos. 2010. "Worlds Collide: The Internal Dynamics of Organizational Responses to Conflicting Institutional Demands." *Academy of Management Review* 35 (3): 455–76.

———. 2015. "Embedded in Hybrid Contexts: How Individuals in Organizations Respond to Competing Institutional Logics." In *Institutional Logics in Action*, B:3–35. https://doi.org/10.1108/S0733-558X(2013)0039AB014.

Packard, Vance. 1957. *The Hidden Persuaders*. New York: McKay.

Petre, Caitlin. 2015. "Managing Metrics: The Containment, Disclosure, and Sanctioning of Audience Data at the New York Times." *The Tow Center For Digital Journalism* 1–35.

Polonsky, Michael Jay, and David S. Waller. 1995. "Does Winning Advertising Awards Pay? The Australian Experience." *Journal of Advertising Research* 35 (1): 25–35.

Porter, Theodore M. 1995. *Trust in Numbers: The Pursuit of Objectivity in Science and Public Life*. Princeton, NJ: Princeton University Press.

Power Michael, 1997. *The Audit Society: Rituals of Verification*. Oxford: Oxford University Press.

Publicis Groupe. n.d. "About Publicis Groupe." https://www.publicisgroupe.com/en/the -groupe/about-publicis-groupe.

Rayman-Bacchus, Lez. 2004. "Assessing Trust in, and Legitimacy of, the Corporate." In *Perspectives on Corporate Social Responsibility*, edited by David Crowther and Lez Rayman-Baccus, 21–41. New York: Routledge.

Ronen, Shelly. n.d. "Polyvalent Moral Codes: The Case of Design Solutionism." Unpublished manuscript.

Rose, Nikolas. 1990. *Governing the Soul: The Shaping of the Private Self*. London: Routledge.

Schimel, Elliot. 2018. "Employees Crave Career Development, So Why Are Agencies Ignoring It?" *Adweek*, March 13. https://www.adweek.com/agencies/employees-crave-career -development-so-why-are-agencies-ignoring-it/.

Schudson, Michael. 1984. *Advertising, the Uneasy Persuasion: Its Dubious Impact on American Society*. New York: Basic Books.

Schüll, Natasha Dow. 2014. *Addiction by Design: Machine Gambling in Las Vegas*. Princeton, NJ: Princeton University Press.

Schutz, Alfred. 1970. *Reflections on the Problem of Relevance*. New Haven, CT: Yale University Press.

Schutz, Alfred, and Thomas Luckmann. 1973. *The Structures of the Life World, Vol. I*. Evanston, IL: Northwestern University Press.

Schwartz, Ariel. 2012. "New York's Dirtiest Water, Now Conveniently Drinkable." *Fast*

Company, March 22. https://www.fastcompany.com/1679552/new-yorks-dirtiest-water
-now-conveniently-drinkable.

Sennett, Richard, and Jonathan Cobb. 1972. *Hidden Injuries of Class*. New York: W.W. Norton
& Company.

Shaban, Hamza. 2019. "Digital Advertising to Surpass Print and TV for the First Time, Report Says." *Washington Post*, February 20. https://www.washingtonpost.com/technology/
2019/02/20/digital-advertising-surpass-print-tv-first-time-report-says/.

Shamir, Ronen. 2004. "The De-Radicalization of Corporate Social Responsibility." *Critical
Sociology* 30 (3): 669–89.

———. 2008. "The Age of Responsibilization: On Market-Embedded Morality." *Economy
and Society* 37 (1): 1–19.

Silber, Ilana F. 2009. "Bourdieu's Gift to Gift Theory: An Unacknowledged Trajectory."
Sociological Theory 27 (2): 173–90.

Silver, Daniel. 2011. "The Moodiness of Action." *Sociological Theory* 29 (2): 199–222.

Simmel, Georg. 2004. *The Philosophy of Money*. London: Routledge.

Sivulka, Juliann. 1997. *Soap, Sex, and Cigarettes: A Cultural History of American Advertising*.
Belmont, CA: Wadsworth.

Skelcher, Chris, and Steven R. Smith. 2015. "Theorizing Hybridity: Institutional Logics,
Complex Organizations, and Actor Identities: The Case of Nonprofits." *Public Administration* 93 (2): 433–48.

Smets, Michael, Angela Aristidou, and Richard Whittington. 2017. "Toward a Practice-
Driven Institutionalism." In *The SAGE Handbook of Institutionalism*, edited by Royston
Greenwood, Christine Oliver, Thomas B. Lawrence and Renate E. Meyer, 365–92. Thou-
sand Oaks, CA: Sage.

Smith, Adam. (1776) 1999. *The Wealth of Nations, Books I–III*. London: Penguin.

Spradley, James P. 1979. *The Ethnographic Interview*. New York: Holt, Rinehart, and Winston.

Soule, Sarah A. 2009. *Contention and Corporate Social Responsibility*. Cambridge: Cambridge
University Press.

Star, Susan Leigh, and James R. Griesemer. 1989. "Institutional Ecology, Translations, and
Boundary Objects: Amateurs and Professionals in Berkeley's Museum of Vertebrate Zool-
ogy, 1907–39." *Social Studies of Science* 19 (3): 387–420.

Stark, David. 2011. *The Sense of Dissonance: Accounts of Worth in Economic Life*. Princeton,
NJ: Princeton University Press.

Steel, Emily. 2015. "Changing Course On Madison Ave." *New York Times*, April 4. https://
www.nytimes.com/2015/04/04/business/media/mad-men-and-the-era-that-changed
-advertising.html.

Steimel, Sarah. 2018. "Skills-Based Volunteering as Both Work and Not Work: A Tension-
Centered Examination of Constructions of 'Volunteer.'" *VOLUNTAS: International Journal
of Voluntary and Nonprofit Organizations* 29 (1):133–43.

Steiner, Franz B. (1956) 1999. *Taboo, Truth and Religion*. New York: Berghahn Books.

Swidler, Ann. 1986. "Culture in Action: Symbols and Strategies." *American Sociological Review* 51 (2): 273–86.

———. 2001. *Talk of Love: How Culture Matters*. Chicago: University of Chicago Press.

Tavory, Iddo. 2018. "Between Situations: Anticipations, Rhythms and the Theory of Interaction." *Sociological Theory* 36 (2): 117–33.

———. 2020. "Interviews and Inference: Making Sense of Interview Data in Qualitative
Research." *Qualitative Sociology* 43 (4): 449–65.

———. n.d. "Kill Your Darlings: Advertising, Expertise and Commercially Elicited
Knowledge."

Tavory, Iddo, and Ann Swidler. 2009. "Condom Semiotics: Meaning and Condom Use in Rural Malawi." *American Sociological Review* 74 (2): 171–89.

Tavory, Iddo, and Stefan Timmermans. 2014. *Abductive Analysis: Theorizing Qualitative Research*. Chicago: University of Chicago Press.

Taylor, Charles. 1989. *Sources of the Self*. Cambridge, MA: Harvard University Press.

Thévenot, Laurent, and Roger Friedland. 2016. "Terms of Engagement: Playing with Differences between Institutional Logics and Conventions of Worth." Paper presented at the Sociology of Culture Workshop, New York University, New York, May.

Thoits, Peggy A. 2011. "Resisting the Stigma of Mental Illness." *Social Psychology Quarterly* 74 (1): 6–28.

Thornton, Patricia H., William Ocasio, and Michael Lounsbury. 2012. *The Institutional Logics Perspective: A New Approach to Culture, Structure and Process*. Oxford: Oxford University Press.

Timmermans, Stefan, and Iddo Tavory. 2012. "Theory Construction in Qualitative Research: From Grounded Theory to Abductive Analysis." *Sociological Theory* 30 (3): 167–86.

———. 2022. *Data Analysis in Qualitative Research: Theorizing with Abductive Analysis*. Chicago: University of Chicago Press.

Tolve, Andrew. 2011. "Pharma and CSR: Why Good Deeds Are Good Business." *Reuters*, March 14. https://www.reutersevents.com/pharma/commercial/pharma-and-csr-why -good-deeds-are-good-business.

Velthuis, Olav. 2013. *Talking Prices: Symbolic Meanings of Prices on the Market for Contemporary Art*. Princeton, NJ: Princeton University Press.

Wagner-Pacifici, Robin. 1994. *Discourse and Destruction: The City of Philadelphia versus MOVE*. Chicago: University of Chicago Press.

Waller, David S. 2010. "Does Doing Good Do Good? How Pro Bono Work May Benefit Advertising Agencies." *Journal of Advertising Research* 50 (4): 440–49.

Waller, David S., and Roman Lanis. 2009. "Corporate Social Responsibility (CSR) Disclosure of Advertising Agencies: An Exploratory Analysis of Six Holding Companies' Annual Reports." *Journal of Advertising* 38 (1): 109–22.

Walsh, Grace S. 2017. "Re-entry Following Firm Failure: Nascent Technology Entrepreneurs' Tactics for Avoiding and Overcoming Stigma." In *Technology-Based Nascent Entrepreneurship*, edited by J. Cunningham and C. O'Kane, 95–117. London: Palgrave Macmillan.

WARC. n.d. "Effectiveness through Volatility." https://www.warc.com/content/paywall/ article/effies/donate-life-america-even-an-asshole-can-save-a-life/112229.

Weber, Max. 1994. Political Writings. Cambridge: Cambridge University Press.

Weiss, Robert S. 1995. *Learning from Strangers: The Art and Method of Qualitative Interview Studies*. New York: Simon and Schuster.

Windell, Karolina. 2007. "The Commercialization of CSR: Consultants Selling Responsibility." In *Managing Corporate Social Responsibility in Action: Talking, Doing and Measuring*, edited by Frank den Hond, Frank G. A. De Bakker, and Peter Neergaard, 33–53. Burlington, VT: Ashgate.

Witt, Michael A., and Gordon Redding. 2011. "The Spirits of Corporate Social Responsibility: Senior Executive Perceptions of the Role of the Firm in Society in Germany, Hong Kong, Japan, South Korea and the USA." *Socio-Economic Review* 10 (1): 109–34.

WPP. n.d. "About WPP." https://www.wpp.com/about.

Wright, Rob. 2016. "How Merck Approaches Corporate Social Responsibility." *Life Science Leader*, January 29. https://www.lifescienceleader.com/doc/how-merck-approaches -corporate-social-responsibility-0001.

Wu, Tim. 2017. *The Attention Merchants: The Epic Scramble to Get Inside our Heads*. New York: Vintage.

Zelizer, Viviana. 1997. *The Social Meaning of Money*. Princeton, NJ: Princeton University Press.

Zilber, Tammar B. 2002. "Institutionalization as an Interplay between Actions, Meanings, and Actors: The Case of a Rape Crisis Center in Israel." *Academy of Management Journal* 45 (1): 234–54.

Index

www.ingramcontent.com/pod-product-compliance
Lightning Source LLC
Chambersburg PA
CBHW032136020426
42334CB00016B/1185